Student Mathematics Handbook and Integral Table for

Calculus

Fourth Custom Edition

Karl Smith

Taken from:
Student Mathematics Handbook and Integral Table for Calculus, Third Edition
by Karl Smith

STUDENT MATHEMATICS HANDBOOK

AND

INTEGRAL TABLE

FOR

CALCULUS, 3rd Edition

Cover image: *Umedas1* by Barry Cronin

Taken from:

Student Mathematics Handbook and Integral Table for Calculus, Third Edition
by Karl Smith
Copyright © 2002 by Prentice-Hall, Inc.
A Pearson Education Company
Upper Saddle River, New Jersey 07458

This special edition published in cooperation with Pearson Custom Publishing.

Printed in the United States of America

10 9 8 7 6 5 4 3 2

ISBN 0-536-29461-5

2006360124

MC

Please visit our web site at *www.pearsoncustom.com*

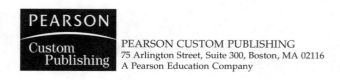

PEARSON CUSTOM PUBLISHING
75 Arlington Street, Suite 300, Boston, MA 02116
A Pearson Education Company

CONTENTS

vi   Contents

Contents   vii

PREFACE

Calculus is probably the first mathematics course you have taken that is not self-contained in the sense that the material from previous mathematics courses is expected *without* specifically mentioning it in the textbook. This supplement is a convenient reference book to be used along with your textbook, *Calculus*, to remind you of those formulas or topics that you may have forgotten.

This handbook is organized so that it can be used in two ways. The first use is as a reference manual providing a summary of terminology, formulas, and tables, not only of prerequisite mathematics, but also of the material covered in a standard calculus course. The second use is as a brief review of material assumed as a prerequisite for a course in calculus. This material is presented with examples, brief written exposition, and practice problems. The topics that are included with exposition and practice problems are sometimes missing from the backgrounds of many students who otherwise have the prerequisites for calculus. We remind the student that nearly everyone qualified to enroll in calculus has, for a variety of reasons, gaps in knowledge of prerequisite material, and the brief review in this handbook can help to bridge that gap. We provide this supplement to *Calculus* free of charge with the purchase of the textbook, in an attempt to help ensure your success in calculus. Use this book for reference, and as a handbook as you progress through the course.

There are many places in your textbook where you will see the [sᴹʜ] logo. You will find this same logo in this manual, and if you want extra help on these topics, you will see here some of the background information that is not usually included in a calculus textbook. As you use this handbook, remember that it was written to accompany the book *Calculus, Third Edition* by Strauss, Bradley, and Smith. When you see a reference in this manual to the text, that reference is to your textbook, not this handbook. Also, if the reference is to Problem Set 3.2, for example, that is the reference to the text, whereas a reference Problem Set 3 is to this handbook. That is, problem sets designated by counting numbers are in this handbook, and those with decimals are in the textbook.

In addition, new technology has changed the emphasis of many of the topics in a calculus course. One recent change is the acknowledgment of the role of calculators and computers to help not only with the mechanics of algebra, but also with the mechanics of differentiation and integration in calculus. Outside of the academic environment, engineers and physicists tells us that using available technology, as well as tables of integration, is by far more important than many of the esoteric topics they were taught in their calculus courses many years ago. For that reason, calculus books are evolving, and the emphasis is not on obscure esoteric topics, but rather practical knowledge that balances between application and theory. To capture this new emphasis, we see the need for you to have a more complete integration table, so one has been provided in this handbook.

CHAPTER 1
Review of Geometry

In this book, we use the following variables when stating formulas: A = area, P = perimeter, C = circumference, S = surface area, and V = volume. Also, r denotes radius, h altitude, l slant height, b base, B area of base, and θ central angle expressed in radians.

1.1   Polygons

CLASSIFICATION

Type	Number of sides
triangle	3
quadrilateral	4
pentagon	5
hexagon	6
heptagon	7
octagon	8
nonagon	9
decagon	10
undecagon	11
dodecagon	12

TRIANGLES

$A = \frac{1}{2}bh$ The sum of the measures of the angles of a triangle is 180°.

$P = a + b + c$

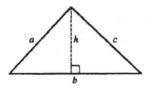

Pythagorean theorem: The sum of the squares of the lengths of the legs of a right triangle is equal to the square of the length of the hypotenuse.

45°–45°–90° triangle theorem: For any right triangle with acute angles measuring 45°, the legs are the same length, and the hypotenuse has a length equal to $\sqrt{2}$ times the length of one of those legs.

30°–60°–90° triangle theorem: For any right triangle with acute angles measuring 30° and 60°,

1. The hypotenuse is twice as long as the leg opposite the 30° angle (the shorter leg).
2. The leg opposite the 30° angle (the shorter leg) is $\frac{1}{2}$ as long as the hypotenuse.
3. The leg opposite the 60° angle (the longer leg) equals the length of the other (shorter) leg times $\sqrt{3}$.
4. The leg opposite the 30° angle equals the length of the other leg divided by $\sqrt{3}$.

Equilateral triangle: For any equilateral triangle:

$$\alpha = \beta = \gamma = 60° \qquad A = \tfrac{1}{4}b^2\sqrt{3} \qquad h = \tfrac{1}{2}b\sqrt{3}$$

QUADRILATERALS

Rectangle
$A = \ell w$
$P = 2\ell + 2w$
Diagonal $= \sqrt{\ell^2 + w^2}$

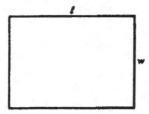

Square
$A = s^2$
$P = 4s$
Diagonal $= s\sqrt{2}$

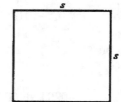

Parallelogram
$A = bh = ab\sin\theta$
$P = 2a + 2b$

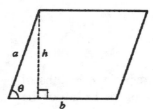

Trapezoid
$A = \tfrac{1}{2}h(a + b)$
$P = a + b$
    $+h(\csc\theta + \csc\phi)$

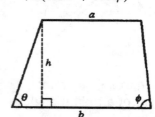

REGULAR POLYGON OF *n* SIDES

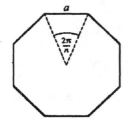

central angle: $\dfrac{2\pi}{n}$

$A = \frac{1}{4}na^2 \cot \dfrac{\pi}{n}$

$P = an$

1.2   Circles

TERMINOLOGY

Definition: In a plane, a **circle** is the set of all points a given distance, called the **radius**, from a given point, called the **center**.

Circumference: distance around a circle.

Chord: a line joining two points of a circle.

Diameter: a chord through the center: *AB* in Figure 1.1.

Arc: part of a circle: *BC*, *AC*, or *ACB* in Figure 1.1. The length *s* of an arc of a circle of radius *r* with central angle θ (measured in radians) is $s = r\theta$.

To *intercept an arc* is to cut off the arc; in Figure 1.1, $\angle COB$ intercepts *BC*.

A *tangent* of a circle is a line that intersects the circle at one and only one point.

A *secant* of a circle is a line that intersects the circle at exactly two points.

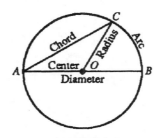

FIGURE 1.1

An *inscribed polygon* is a polygon, all of whose sides are chords of a circle. A regular inscribed polygon is a polygon, all of whose sides are the same length.

An *inscribed circle* is a circle to which all the sides of a polygon are tangents.

A *circumscribed polygon* is a polygon, all of whose sides are tangents to a circle.

A *circumscribed circle* is a circle passing through each vertex of a polygon.

BASIC FORMULAS

Circle

$A = \pi r^2$

$C = 2\pi r = \pi d$

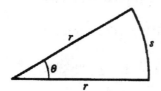

Sector

$A = \frac{1}{2} r^2 \theta$

$s = r\theta$

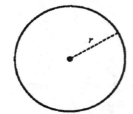

[SMH] *We first use this in the text in Section 2.2 proving a very important limit property.*

Segment

$A = \frac{1}{2} r^2 (\theta - \sin \theta)$

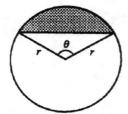

1.3   Solid Geometry

Rectangular parallelepiped (box)

$V = abc$

$\text{Diagonal} = \sqrt{a^2 + b^2 + c^2}.$

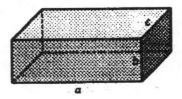

Prism

$V = Bh$

B is area of the base

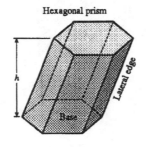

Pyramid

$V = \frac{1}{3}Bh$

B is area of the base

[sMH] *This formula is derived in Example 2, Section 6.2, of the text.*

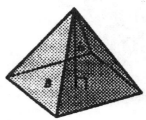

Tetrahedron
(a pyramid with a triangular base)
$V = \frac{1}{3}h\sqrt{s(s-a)(s-b)(s-c)}$
where $s = \frac{1}{2}(a+b+c)$

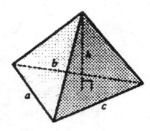

Right circular cylinder
$V = \pi r^2 h$
Lateral surface $= 2\pi rh$
$S = 2\pi rh + 2\pi r^2$

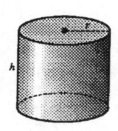

Right circular cone
$V = \frac{1}{3}\pi r^2 h$
Lateral surface $= \pi rl$
$S = \pi rl + \pi r^2$
[sMH] *The formula for the lateral surface is derived in Section 6.4 of the text.*

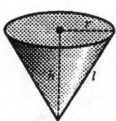

Frustum of a right circular cone
$V = \frac{1}{3}\pi h(r^2 + rR + R^2)$ or
$V = \frac{1}{3}h(B_1 + \sqrt{B_1 B_2} + B_2)$
Note: $h = h_1 - h_2$
[sMH] *This formula is derived in Problem 66 of Problem Set 6.2.*

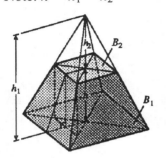

Frustum of a pyramid

$V = \frac{1}{3}h(B_1 + \sqrt{B_1 B_2} + B_2)$

Note: $h = h_1 - h_2$

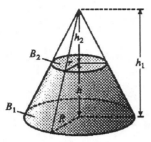

Torus

$S = 4\pi^2 Rr$

[sMH] *This formula is derived in Problem 55 of Problem Set 12.6.*

$V = 2\pi^2 Rr^2$

[sMH] *This formula is derived in Example 7 of Section 6.5.*

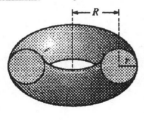
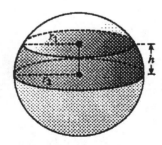

Spherical segment

$S = 2\pi rh$, with radius r

$V = \frac{1}{6}\pi h(3r_1{}^2 + 3r_2{}^2 + h^2)$, with cross sections of radii r_1 and r_2

For the "cap,"

$S = 2\pi r(r - h)$, with radius r

$V = \frac{\pi}{3}(2r^2 - 3r^2 h + h^3)$, with cross sections of radii r_1 and r_2

[sMH] *This volume for the cap is Problem 65 of Problem Set 6.2.*

Cylinder with a cross-sectional area A

$V = Ah; \; S = p\ell + 2A$

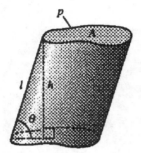

Prismatoid, pontoon, wedge

$V = \frac{1}{6}h(B_0 + 4B_1 + B_2)$

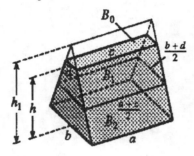

Quadric Surfaces

Sphere

$x^2 + y^2 + z^2 = r^2$

$V = \frac{4}{3}\pi r^3$

$S = 4\pi r^2$

[SMH]

We derive the formula for the volume of a sphere in Example 3 of Section 12.3 and again in Example 5 of Section 12.7.

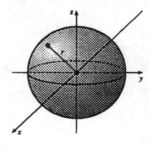

Ellipsoid

$$\frac{x^2}{a^2} + \frac{y^2}{b^2} + \frac{z^2}{c^2} = 1$$

$$V = \frac{4}{3}\pi abc$$

[SMH]

A special case of this formula is derived in Problem 46 of the supplementary problems for Chapter 6, where $r = 0$ and $c = b$.

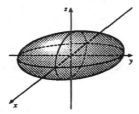

Elliptic Paraboloid

$$\frac{x^2}{a^2} + \frac{y^2}{b^2} = z$$

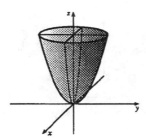

Hyperboloid of One Sheet

$$\frac{x^2}{a^2} + \frac{y^2}{b^2} - \frac{z^2}{c^2} = 1$$

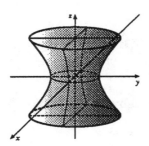

Hyperboloid of Two Sheets

$$\frac{x^2}{a^2} + \frac{y^2}{b^2} - \frac{z^2}{c^2} = -1$$

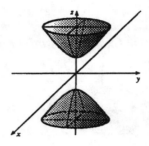

Hyperbolic paraboloid

$$\frac{y^2}{a^2} - \frac{x^2}{b^2} = z$$

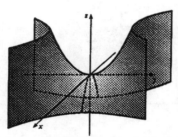

An **oblate spheroid** is formed by the rotation of the ellipse $\frac{x^2}{a^2} + \frac{y^2}{b^2} = 1$ about its minor axis, b. Let ϵ be the eccentricity.

$$V = \frac{4}{3}\pi a^2 b$$

$$S = 2\pi a^2 + \pi \frac{b^2}{\epsilon} \ln\left(\frac{1+\epsilon}{1-\epsilon}\right)$$

A **prolate spheroid** is formed by the rotation of the ellipse $\frac{x^2}{a^2} + \frac{y^2}{b^2} = 1$ about its minor axis, a. Let ϵ be the eccentricity.

$$V = \frac{4}{3}\pi a b^2$$

$$S = 2\pi b^2 + \pi \frac{ab}{\epsilon} \sin^{-1}\epsilon$$

1.4   Congruent Triangles

We say that two figures are **congruent** if they have the same size and shape. For **congruent triangles** ABC and DEF, denoted by $\triangle ABC \simeq \triangle DEF$, we may conclude that all six **corresponding parts** (three angles and three sides) are congruent.

EXAMPLE 1.1   Corresponding parts of a triangle

Name the corresponding parts of the given triangles.
a. $\triangle ABC \simeq \triangle A'B'C'$ **b.** $\triangle RST \simeq \triangle UST$

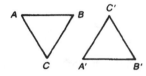 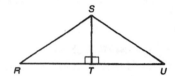

Solution

a. $\overline{AB}$ corresponds to $\overline{A'B'}$ **b.** $\overline{RS}$ corresponds to $\overline{US}$
$\overline{AC}$ corresponds to $\overline{A'C'}$ $\overline{RT}$ corresponds to $\overline{UT}$
$\overline{BC}$ corresponds to $\overline{B'C'}$ $\overline{ST}$ corresponds to $\overline{ST}$
$\angle A$ corresponds to $\angle A'$ $\angle R$ corresponds to $\angle U$
$\angle B$ corresponds to $\angle B'$ $\angle RTS$ corresponds to $\angle UTS$
$\angle C$ corresponds to $\angle C'$ $\angle RST$ corresponds to $\angle UST$

$\square$

Two angles are equal if they have the same measure. For the triangles in Example 1.1, we see that $\angle A$ corresponds to $\angle A'$. This means that these angles are the same size, or have the same **measure**. We write $m\angle A = m\angle A'$ to mean that the angles have the same measure, or in other words, the same size and shape.

Line segments, angles, triangles, or other geometric figures are *congruent* if they have the same size and shape. In Example 1.1, since $m\angle A = m\angle A'$, we say that angles A and A' are congruent, and we write $\angle A \simeq \angle A'$.

In this section, we focus on triangles.

CONGRUENT TRIANGLES

> Two triangles are **congruent** if their corresponding sides have the same length and their corresponding angles have the same measure.

To prove that two triangles are congruent, you must show that they have the same size and shape. It is not necessary to show that all six parts (three sides and three angles) are congruent; if certain of these six parts are congruent, it necessarily follows that the other parts are congruent. Three important properties are used to show congruence of triangles:

CONGRUENT-TRIANGLE PROPERTIES

> **SIDE–SIDE–SIDE (SSS)**
> If three sides of one triangle are congruent to three sides of another triangle, then the two triangles are congruent.
>
> **SIDE–ANGLE–SIDE (SAS)**
> If two sides of one triangle and the angle between those sides are congruent to the corresponding sides and angle of another triangle, then the two triangles are congruent.
>
> **ANGLE–SIDE–ANGLE (ASA)**
> If two angles and the side that connects them on one triangle are congruent to the corresponding angles and side of another triangle, then the two triangles are congruent.

EXAMPLE 1.2   Finding congruent triangles

Determine whether each pair of triangles is congruent. If so, cite one of the congruent-triangle properties.

Solution

a.

Congruent; SAS

b.

Not congruent

c.
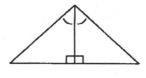

d.
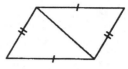

Congruent; ASA   Congruent; SSS

A side that is in common to two triangles obviously is equal in length to itself and does not need to be marked.   □

In geometry, the main use of congruent triangles is when we want to know whether an angle from one triangle is congruent to an angle from a different triangle or when we want to know whether a side from one triangle is the same length as the side from another triangle. In order to do this, we often prove that one triangle is congruent to the other (using one of the three congruent-triangle properties) and then use the following property:

CONGRUENT-TRIANGLE PROPERTY

Corresponding parts of congruent triangles are congruent.

1.5   Similar Triangles

[sMh]   *See Sections 3.7 and 4.6 of the text for examples in which we use these ideas in calculus.*

It is possible for two figures to have the same shape, but not necessarily the same size. These figures are called **similar** figures. We will now focus on **similar triangles**. If $\triangle ABC$ is similar to $\triangle DEF$, we write

$$\triangle ABC \sim \triangle DEF$$

Similar triangles are shown in Figure 1.2.

You should note that congruent triangles must be similar, but similar triangles are not necessarily congruent. Since similar figures have the same shape, we talk about **corresponding angles** and **corresponding sides**. The corresponding angles of similar triangles are the angles that have the same measure. It is customary to label the vertices of triangles with capital letters and the sides opposite the angles at those

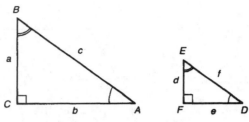

Figure 1.2   Similar triangles

vertices with corresponding lowercase letters. It is easy to see that, if the triangles are similar, the corresponding sides are the sides opposite equal angles. In Figure 1.2, we see that

$\angle A$ and $\angle D$ are corresponding angles;
$\angle B$ and $\angle E$ are corresponding angles; and
$\angle C$ and $\angle F$ are corresponding angles.

Side a ($\overline{BC}$) is opposite $\angle A$, and d ($\overline{EF}$) is opposite $\angle D$, so we say that
a corresponds to d;
b corresponds to e; and
c corresponds to f.

Even though corresponding angles are the same size, corresponding sides do not need to be the same length. If they are the same length, then the triangles are congruent. However, when they are not the same length, we can say they are *proportional*. As Figure 1.2 illustrates, when we say the sides are proportional, we mean that

$$\frac{a}{b} = \frac{d}{e} \qquad \frac{a}{c} = \frac{d}{f} \qquad \frac{b}{c} = \frac{e}{f}$$
$$\frac{b}{a} = \frac{e}{d} \qquad \frac{c}{a} = \frac{f}{d} \qquad \frac{c}{b} = \frac{f}{e}$$

SIMILAR TRIANGLES

Two triangles are **similar** if two angles of one triangle have the same measure as two angles of the other triangle. If the triangles are similar, then their corresponding sides are proportional.

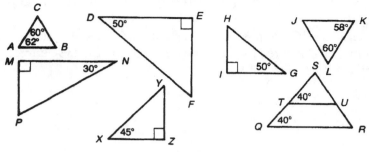

FIGURE 1.3

EXAMPLE 1.3   Similar triangles

Identify pairs of triangles that are similar in Figure 1.3.

Solution $\triangle ABC \sim \triangle JKL$; $\triangle DEF \sim \triangle GIH$; $\triangle SQR \sim \triangle STU$. $\square$

EXAMPLE 1.4   Finding unknown lengths in similar triangles

Given the following similar triangles, find the unknown lengths marked b' and c':

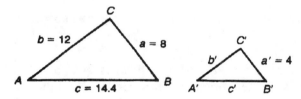

Solution   Since corresponding sides are proportional (other proportions are possible), we have

$$\frac{a'}{a} = \frac{b'}{b} \qquad\qquad \frac{a}{c} = \frac{a'}{c'}$$

$$\frac{4}{8} = \frac{b'}{12} \qquad\qquad \frac{8}{14.4} = \frac{4}{c'}$$

$$b' = \frac{4(12)}{8} \qquad\qquad c' = \frac{14.4(4)}{8}$$

$$= 6 \qquad\qquad\qquad = 7.2$$

$\square$

EXAMPLE 1.5   Finding a perimeter by using similar triangles

In equilateral $\triangle ABC$, suppose $DE = 2$ and is parallel to $\overline{AB}$, as shown at the right. If $\overline{AB}$ is three times as long as $\overline{DE}$, what is the perimeter of quadrilateral $ABED$?

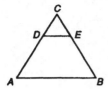

Solution $\triangle ABC \sim \triangle DEC$, so $\triangle DEC$ is equilateral. This means that $\overline{CE}$ and $\overline{DC}$ both are of length 2; thus, $\overline{EB}$ and $\overline{AD}$ both are of length 4. The perimeter of the quadrilateral is

$$|\overline{AB}| + |\overline{BE}| + |\overline{DE}| + |\overline{AD}| = 6 + 4 + 2 + 4 = 16 \qquad \square$$

Finding similar triangles is simplified even further if we know that the triangles are right triangles, because then the triangles are similar if one of the acute angles has the same measure as an acute angle of the other triangle.

EXAMPLE 1.6   Using similar triangles to find an unknown length

Suppose that a tree and a yardstick are casting shadows as shown in Figure 1.4. If the shadow of the yardstick is 3 yards long and the shadow of the tree is 12 yards long, use similar triangles to estimate the height of the tree if you know that angles S and S' are the same size.

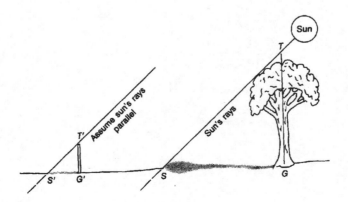

FIGURE 1.4

Solution   Since $\angle G$ and $\angle G'$ are right angles, and since S and S' are the same size, we see that $\triangle SGT \sim \triangle S'G'T'$. Therefore, corresponding sides are proportional. Hence,

$$\frac{1}{3} = \frac{h}{12}$$

$$h = \frac{1(12)}{3}$$

$$= 4$$

The tree is 4 yards tall.   □

EXAMPLE 1.7   Similar triangles in a pyramid

[sMH]   *This example is adapted from Example 2 of Section 6.2*

A regular pyramid has a square base of side L, and its apex is located H units above the center of its base. The pyramid is shown in Figure 1.5.

Suppose a cut is made h units from the bottom, thus forming two triangles, as shown at the right in Figure 1.5. Use similar triangles to find the length ℓ of the cut.

Solution   Let ℓ be the length of the cut. We recognize two triangles: $\triangle ABC$ and $\triangle DEC$, and we want to show that these triangles are similar. Obviously, $m\angle C = m\angle C$ in both triangles. Since the line segment $\overline{AB}$ is parallel to the line segment $\overline{DE}$, and we can consider the line passing through A and D to be a transversal, we conclude that $m\angle A = m\angle D$ because $\angle A$ and $\angle D$ are corresponding angles. Since two angles of one triangle have the same measure as the corresponding angles in the other triangle, we conclude that $\triangle ABC \sim \triangle DEC$. It follows that if the triangles are similar, then their corresponding sides

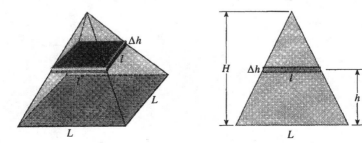

Figure 1.5   Pyramid with a square base

are proportional.

$$\frac{\ell}{L} = \frac{H - h}{H} \quad \text{Note that the height of } \triangle DEC \text{ is } H - h$$

$$\ell = \left(1 - \frac{h}{H}\right) L \quad \text{Multiply both sides by } L. \qquad \square$$

1.6   PROBLEM SET 1

1. In $\triangle TRI$ and $\triangle ANG$ shown at right, $\angle R \simeq \angle N$ and $|\overline{TR}| = |\overline{AN}|$. Name other pairs you would need to know in order to show that the triangles are congruent by
    a. SSS   **b.** SAS   **c.** ASA

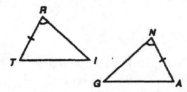

2. In $\triangle ABC$ and $\triangle DEF$ shown at right, $\angle A \simeq \angle D$ and $|\overline{AC}| = |\overline{DF}|$. Name other pairs you would need to know in order to show that the triangles are congruent by
    a. SSS   **b.** SAS   **c.** ASA

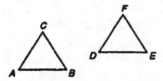

Name the corresponding parts of the triangles in Problems 3–6.

3.   4.

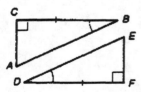   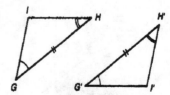

5.

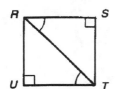

6.

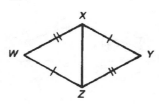

In Problems 7–10, determine whether each pair of triangles is congruent. If so, cite one of the congruent-triangle properties.

7.

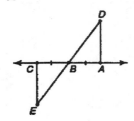

8.

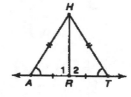

9.

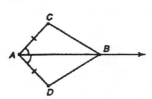

10.

In Problems 11–16, tell whether it is possible to conclude that the pairs of triangles are similar.

11.

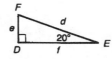

12.

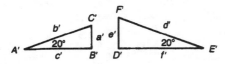

13.

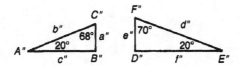

14.

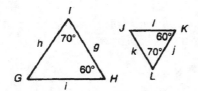

15.

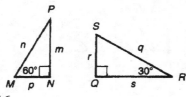

16.

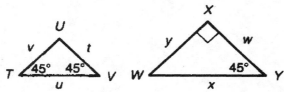

Given the two similar triangles shown, find the unknown lengths in Problems 17–22.

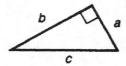

17. $a = 4, b = 8, a' = 2$; find b'.
18. $b = 5, c = 15, b' = 2$; find c'.
19. $c = 6, a = 4, c' = 8$; find a'.
20. $a' = 7, b' = 8, a = 5$; find b.
21. $b' = 8, c' = 12, c = 4$; find b.
22. $c' = 9, a' = 2, c = 5$; find a.
23. How far from the base of a building must a 26-ft ladder be placed so that it reaches 10 ft up the wall?
24. How high up a wall does a 26-ft ladder reach if the bottom of the ladder is placed 6 ft from the building?

25. A carpenter wants to be sure that the corner of a building is square and measures 6 ft and 8 ft along the sides. How long should the diagonal be?

26. What is the exact length of the hypotenuse if the legs of a right triangle are 2 in. each?

27. What is the exact length of one leg of an isosceles right triangle if the hypotenuse is 3 ft?

28. An empty rectangular lot is 40 ft by 65 ft. How many feet would you save by walking diagonally across the lot instead of walking the length and width? Round your answer to the nearest foot.

29. A television antenna is to be erected and held by guy wires. If the guy wires are 15 ft from the base of the antenna and the antenna is 10 ft high, what is the exact length of each guy wire? What is the length of each guy wire, rounded to the nearest foot? If three guy wires are attached, how many feet of wire should be purchased if it cannot be bought in fractions of a foot?

30. In equilateral $\triangle ABC$, shown below, D is the midpoint of segment $\overline{AB}$. What is the length of $\overline{CD}$?

31. In the figure shown below, AB and DE are parallel. What is the length of AB?

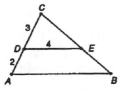

32. Ben walked diagonally across a rectangular field that measures 100 ft by 240 ft. How far did Ben walk?

33. Use similar triangles and a proportion to find the length of the lake shown in the following figure:

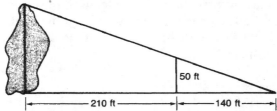

34. Use similar triangles and a proportion to find the height of the house shown in the following figure:

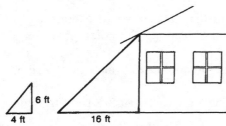

35. If a tree casts a shadow of 12 ft at the same time a 6-ft person casts a shadow of $2\frac{1}{2}$ ft, find the height of the tree to the nearest foot.

36. If an inverted circular cone (vertex at the bottom) of height 10 cm and a radius of 4 cm contains liquid with height measuring 3.8 cm, what is the volume of the liquid?

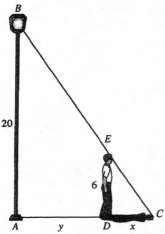

37. A person 6 ft tall is walking away from a streetlight 20 ft high at the rate of 7 ft/s. How long (to the nearest ft) is the person's shadow at the instant when the person is 10 ft from the base of the lamppost?

【sᴹн】   *Example 2, Section 3.7*

38. A bag is tied to the top of a 5-m ladder resting against a vertical wall. Suppose the ladder begins sliding down the wall in such a way that the foot of the ladder is moving away from the wall. How high is the bag at the instant when the base of the ladder is 4 m from the base of the wall?

【sᴹн】   *Example 3, Section 3.7*

39. A tank filled with water is in the shape of an inverted cone 20 ft high with a circular base (on top) whose radius is 5 ft. How much water does the tank hold when the water level is 8 ft deep?

[sMH]   *See Example 5 of Section 3.7 of the text.*

CHAPTER 2

Review of Algebra

2.1 Real Numbers

⟨sᴹн⟩ *The text assumes that you know these sets of numbers. You are asked to characterize each set in Problem 1 of Chapter 1 review.*

Name	Symbol	Set	Examples
Counting numbers or natural numbers	$\mathbb{N}$	$\{1, 2, 3, 4, \cdots\}$	$72; 2{,}345, 950; \sqrt{25}; \sqrt{1}$
Whole numbers	$\mathbb{W}$	$\{0, 1, 2, 3, \cdots\}$	$0; 72; \dfrac{10}{2}; \dfrac{16,425}{25}$
Integers	$\mathbb{Z}$	$\{\cdots, -2, -1, 0, 1, 2, \cdots\}$	$-5; 0; \dfrac{-10}{2}; 9{,}562; -82$
Rational numbers	$\mathbb{Q}$	Numbers that can be written in the form $\frac{p}{q}$, where p and q are integers with $q \neq 0$	$\dfrac{1}{3}; \dfrac{4}{17}; .863214; .8666\cdots;$ $5; 0; \dfrac{-11}{3}; -15; \sqrt{\dfrac{1}{4}};$ $3.1416; 8.\overline{6}$
Irrational numbers	$\mathbb{Q}'$	Numbers whose decimal representations do not terminate and do not repeat	$5.123456789101112\cdots;$ $\sqrt{2}; \sqrt{3};$ $4.31331333133331\cdots; \pi;$ $\dfrac{\pi}{2}$
Real numbers	$\mathbb{R}$	The collection of all rational and irrational numbers	All examples listed on this page are real numbers. Not all numbers are real numbers, however. There is another set of numbers (not considered in this handbook) called *complex numbers*, which includes the real numbers as a subset.

2.2 Algebraic Processes

In order to review the basic algebraic processes with which you need to be familiar in calculus, we begin with a review of some terminology.

TERM	DEFINITION	EXAMPLES
Numerical expression	A number or several numbers connected by defined mathematical operations.	$6; 5 + 2; 5\pi - \sqrt{2}$
Algebraic expression	A numerical expression with at least one variable.	$6x; x + y; 2x^2 - 3x + 4$
Term	A number, a variable, or a product of numbers and variables.	$6; x; 6x; 2x^2; \dfrac{1}{2}y^3$
Polynomial	A term or a sum of terms. (Note: Since $x - y = x + (-y)$, differences are included.)	$6; x + y; 4x^3 - 3x + 1$
Rational expression	A polynomial divided by a nonzero polynomial. (Note: Includes polynomials, because if P is a polynomial, it can be written as $P = \dfrac{P}{1}$.)	$\dfrac{x + y}{x - y}; \dfrac{1}{x} + \dfrac{1}{y}$
Radical expression	An algebraic expression with a variable expression as a radicand (the expression under a radical sign).	$\sqrt{x}; \sqrt[3]{y}; \dfrac{\sqrt{x^2 + y^2}}{2}$

Many of the processes in algebra are based on an agreement, called the **order-of-operations agreement**, that tells us how to deal with expressions with more than one operation:

First, carry out those operations enclosed in parentheses.
Second, carry out all multiplications and divisions as they occur, left to right.

Third, carry out all additions and subtractions as they occur, left to right.

If there are exponents, use what is sometimes called the **extended order-of-operations agreement** which instructs us to do the operations involving exponents just before those involving multiplications and divisions.

There are four principal processes used in algebra:

Factor To *factor* an expression means to write the expression as a product. An expression is called *completely factored* if all fractions are eliminated by common factoring and if no further factoring is possible over the set of integers.

Simplify To *simplify a numerical expression* means to carry out all the operations, according to their order, and write your answer as a single number.

To *simplify a polynomial* means to carry out all the operations, according to their order, combine similar terms, and write your answer by arranging the terms in decreasing degree. If there are different terms of the same degree, then they are arranged alphabetically.

To *simplify a rational expression* means to carry out all the operations, according to their order, factor the numerator and denominator, and make sure that there is no common factor (other than 1 or -1). If there is a negative, then the expression is written in the form $\dfrac{p}{q}$ or $\dfrac{-p}{q}$ for positive p and q.

To *simplify a radical expression* means to carry out all the operations, according to their order, and to make sure that the following conditions are satisfied:

1. When the radicand is written in completely factored form, there is no factor raised to a power greater than or equal to the index of the radical.
2. No radical appears in a denominator.
3. No fraction (or negative exponent) appears within a radical.
4. There is no common factor (other than 1) between the power of the radicand and the index of the radical.

Sometimes the word **expand** is used instead of simplify. For example, to expand the expression $(x + y)^2$ means to simplify it; that is, write

$$(x + y)^2 = x^2 + 2xy + y^2$$

Evaluate To *evaluate* an algebraic expression means to replace the variable or variables with a given number and then simplify the expression. In calculus, we often evaluate a function at two values and then we subtract those values. For example, if the function $f(x) = x^2 + x + 1$ is evaluated at $x = 2$, we have $f(2) = 2^2 + 2 + 1 = 7$, and if f is evaluated at $x = 1$, we have $f(1) = 1^2 + 1 + 1 = 3$. Finally, if we subtract these evaluations, we get $f(2) - f(1) = 7 - 3 = 4$. Since this is a frequent calculation, a compact notation is sometimes used:

$$f(x)|_1^2 = f(2) - f(1)$$

For example,

$$[x^2 + x + 1]|_1^2 = [2^2 + 2 + 1] - [1^2 + 1 + 1]$$

$$= 7 - 3$$

$$= 4$$

2.3 Powers and roots

EXPONENTS

Definition of Exponent:

In the expression x^n, the number n is called the **exponent**, the number b is called the **base**, and x^n is called a **power**. If n is a positive integer, then $x^n = \underbrace{x \cdot x \cdot x \cdots x}_{n \text{ factors}}$, and $x^0 = 1$; $x^{-n} = \dfrac{1}{x^n}$

If m and n are integers, then

$$x^{\frac{1}{n}} = \sqrt[n]{x} \text{ whenever } \sqrt[n]{x} \text{ is defined}$$

and

$$x^{\frac{m}{n}} = (x^{\frac{1}{n}})^m = (\sqrt[n]{x})^m \text{ whenever } \sqrt[n]{x} \text{ is defined}$$

Factorial numbers:
$n! = n(n - 1)(n - 2) \cdots 3 \cdot 2 \cdot 1 \qquad 0! = 1 \quad$ for n a nonnegative integer

ROOTS

Recall that for any positive *even* integer n (called the *index* of the radical) and any positive number x (called the *radicand*),

$$y = \sqrt[n]{x} \text{ if and only if } y > 0 \text{ and } y^n = x$$

We call y *the positive nth root of x*. For example, the positive fourth root of 16 is denoted by $\sqrt[4]{16}$; we write $\sqrt[4]{16} = 2$, since $2^4 = 16$.

For any positive *odd* integer n and any number x (positive or negative),

$$y = \sqrt[n]{x} \text{ and only if } y^n = x$$

and y is called the *nth root* of x. For example, $\sqrt[3]{-8} = -2$, since $(-2)^3 = -8$.

Note that $\sqrt{x^2} = |x|$ for any number x.

LAWS OF EXPONENTS

If r and s are real numbers, then

$$x^r \cdot x^s = x^{r+s}$$

$$(x^r)^s = x^{rs} \text{ whenever } x^r \text{ is meaningful}$$

$$(xy)^r = x^r y^r \text{ whenever } x^r \text{ and } y^r \text{ are meaningful}$$

$$\left(\frac{x}{y}\right)^r = \frac{x^r}{y^r} \text{ whenever } x^r \text{ and } y^r \text{ are meaningful and } y^r \neq 0$$

$$\frac{x^r}{x^s} = x^{r-s} \text{ whenever } x^r \text{ and } x^s \text{ are meaningful and } x^s \neq 0$$

FACTORS AND EXPANSIONS

Difference of squares: $a^2 - b^2 = (a-b)(a+b)$
Perfect square: $(a+b)^2 = a^2 + 2ab + b^2$
Difference of cubes: $a^3 - b^3 = (a-b)(a^2 + ab + b^2)$
Sum of cubes: $a^3 + b^3 = (a+b)(a^2 - ab + b^2)$
Perfect cube: $(a+b)^3 = a^3 + 3a^2b + 3ab^2 + b^3$

Binomial theorem:
$$(a+b)^n = \binom{n}{0} a^n b^0 + \binom{n}{1} a^{n-1} b +$$
$$\binom{n}{2} a^{n-2} b^2 + \cdots + \binom{n}{n} a^0 b^n$$

where

$$\binom{n}{0} = 1, \binom{n}{1} = \frac{n}{1}, \binom{n}{2} = \frac{n(n-1)}{1 \cdot 2}, \cdots,$$

$$\binom{n}{r} = \frac{n!}{r!(n-r)!}, \cdots, \binom{n}{n} = 1$$

The following factoring procedure will work for most of the factoring problems you encounter in calculus:

To factor an expression: First, look for the greatest common factor.
Next, check to see if the expression is a special type:

Difference of squares: $x^2 - y^2 = (x - y)(x + y)$
Difference of cubes: $x^3 - y^3 = (x - y)(x^2 + xy + y^2)$
Sum of cubes: $x^3 + y^3 = (x + y)(x^2 - xy + y^2)$
Perfect square: $x^2 + 2xy + y^2 = (x + y)^2$
$x^2 - 2xy + y^2 = (x - y)^2$

Finally, if the expression is a trinomial, factor it into two binomials. Sometimes, grouping the terms will help you to factor.

EXAMPLE 2.1   Common factoring

Factor the following expressions:

a.   Common monomial factors: $a^2b + 5a^3b^2 + 7a^2b^3$
b.   Common binomial factors: $5x(3a - 5b) + 9y(3a - 5b)$
c.   Common factoring to provide integral coefficients: $\frac{1}{36}x - y$
d.   Multiple common factoring:

$$(2x - 3)(3)(1 - x)(1 + x)(-1) - (1 + x)^3(-3)$$

Solution

a.   The common factor is a^2b:

$$a^2b + 5a^3b^2 + 7a^2b^3 = a^2b(1 + 5ab + 7b^2)$$

b.   The common factor is $(3a - 5b)$:

$$5x(3a - 5b) + 9y(3a - 5b) = (5x + 9y)(3a - 5b)$$

c. Treat the fraction as a common factor:

$$\frac{1}{36}x - y = \frac{1}{36}x - \frac{36}{36}y$$

$$= \frac{1}{36}(x - 36y)$$

d. The common factor is $3(1 + x)$:

$$(2x - 3)(3)(1 - x)(1 + x)(-1) - (1 + x)^3(-3)$$

$$= 3(1 + x)[(2x - 3)(1 - x)(-1) - (1 + x)^2(-1)]$$

$$= 3(1 + x)[(2x - 2x^2 - 3 + 3x)(-1) + 1 + 2x + x^2]$$

$$= 3(1 + x)[3x^2 - 3x - 2] \qquad\qquad \square$$

EXAMPLE 2.2   Factoring special types

Factor the following expressions:

a. $3x^2 - 75$
b. $(x + 3y)^3 + 8$
c. $\dfrac{9a^2}{b^2} - (a + 3b)^2$
d. $x^6 - 1$

Solution

a. $3x^2 - 75 = 3(x^2 - 25)$ *Common factor first*

$$= 3(x - 5)(x + 5)\ \textit{Difference of squares}$$

b. Recognize this as a sum of cubes:

$$(x + 3y)^3 + 8 = [(x + 3y) + 2][(x + 3y)^2 - (x + 3y)(2) + (2)^2]$$

$$= (x + 3y + 2)(x^2 + 6xy + 9y^2 - 2x - 6y + 4)$$

c. Use common factoring to provide integral coefficients:

$$\frac{9a^2}{b^2} - (a + 3b)^2 = \frac{1}{b^2}[9a^2 - b^2(a + 3b)^2]\ \textit{Common factor}$$

$$= \frac{1}{b^2}[3a - b(a + 3b)][3a + b(a + 3b)]$$

$$\textit{Difference of squares}$$

$$= \frac{1}{b^2}(3a - ab - 3b^2)(3a + ab + 3b^2)$$

d. Treat this as a difference of squares.

$$x^6 - 1 = (x^3)^2 - (1^3)^2$$
$$= (x^3 - 1)(x^3 + 1)$$
$$= (x - 1)(x^2 + x + 1)(x + 1)(x^2 - x + 1) \qquad \square$$

EXAMPLE 2.3   Factoring trinomials

Factor the following expressions:
a. $x^2 - 8x + 15$ **b.** $6w^2 - 9w - 15$
c. $6(x + y)^2 - 9(x + y) - 15$ **d.** $4x^4 - 13x^2 y^2 + 9y^4$

Solution

a. $x^2 - 8x + 15 = (x - 5)(x - 3)$

b. $6w^2 - 9w - 15 = 3(2w^2 - 3w - 5)$ *Common factor first*
$$= 3(2w - 5)(w + 1)$$

c. $6(x + y)^2 - 9(x + y) - 15 = 3[2(x + y)^2 - 3(x + y) - 5]$
$$= 3[2(x + y) - 5][(x + y) + 1]$$
$$= 3(2x + 2y - 5)(x + y + 1)$$

d. $4x^4 - 13x^2 y^2 + 9y^4 = (x^2 - y^2)(4x^2 - 9y^2)$
$$= (x - y)(x + y)(2x - 3y)(2x + 3y) \qquad \square$$

EXAMPLE 2.4   Factoring using negative exponents

$$x^{-\frac{1}{2}} y^{\frac{1}{2}} - x^{\frac{1}{2}} y^{-\frac{1}{2}} = x^{-\frac{1}{2}} y^{-\frac{1}{2}}(y - x) = \frac{y - x}{\sqrt{xy}} \qquad \square$$

RADICALS

An algebraic expression containing radicals is **simplified** if all four of the following conditions are satisfied:

1. When the radicand is written in completely factored form, there is no factor raised to a power greater than or equal to the index of the radical.
2. No radical appears in a denominator.
3. No fraction (or negative exponent) appears within a radical.
4. There is no common factor (other than 1) between the exponent of the radicand and the index of the radical.

LOGARITHMS

In $y = \log_b x$, y is called a **logarithm** and b is called the **base**. The logarithm (y) is defined as the exponent on a base b that equals the number x.

Properties of logarithms

$\log(MN) = \log M + \log N$

$\log(M/N) = \log M - \log N$

$\log M^n = n \log M$

$\log \sqrt[n]{M} = \dfrac{1}{n} \log M$

$\log_b b = 1$

$\log_n 1 = 0$

Special bases:

$\log x = \log_{10} x$; this is called a common logarithm

$\ln x = \log_e x$, where $e \approx 2.71828182845905$; is called the natural logarithm

EXAMPLE 2.5   Using laws of exponents

a. $(2x^2 y^3)^4 \quad = 2^4 x^{2 \cdot 4} y^{3 \cdot 4} = 16 x^8 y^{12}$

b. $(2x^2 + y^3)^4 = (2x^2)^4 + 4(2x^2)^3(y^3) + 6(2x^2)^2(y^3)^2$

$$+ 4(2x^2)(y^3)^3 + (y^3)^4$$

$$= 16x^8 + 32x^6 y^3 + 24x^4 y^6 + 8x^2 y^9 + y^{12} \qquad \square$$

EXAMPLE 2.6   Simplifying radical expressions

$$\sqrt[3]{\frac{x^6 y^7}{z^9}} = \left(\frac{x^6 y^7}{z^9}\right)^{1/3} = \frac{x^{6(1/3)} y^{7(1/3)}}{z^{9(1/3)}} = \frac{x^2 y^{7/3}}{z^3} = \frac{x^2 y^2 (\sqrt[3]{y})}{z^3} \qquad \square$$

Note that $y^{7/3} = y^{(6/3 + 1/3)} = y^{2 + 1/3} = y^2 y^{1/3} = y^2(\sqrt[3]{y})$

EXAMPLE 2.7   Simplifying expressions with negative exponents

a. $(x^{-1} + y^{-1})^{-1} = \left(\dfrac{1}{x} + \dfrac{1}{y}\right)^{-1} = \left(\dfrac{x + y}{xy}\right)^{-1} = \dfrac{xy}{x + y}$

b. $(x^{-1}y^{-1})^{-1} = xy$ $\qquad\qquad\qquad\qquad\qquad\qquad$ $\square$

EXAMPLE 2.8   Expanding an expression by using the binomial theorem

Expand $(2x - 3y)^5$.

Solution   In the binomial theorem, replace a by $2x$ and b by $(-3y)$. With $n = 5$, we have

$$(2x - 3y)^5 = (1)(2x)^5(-3y)^0 + 5(2x)^4(-3y)^1 + \frac{5 \cdot 4}{2}(2x)^3(-3y)^2$$

$$+ \frac{5 \cdot 4 \cdot 3}{2 \cdot 3}(2x)^2(-3y)^3 + \frac{5 \cdot 4 \cdot 3 \cdot 2}{2 \cdot 3 \cdot 4}(2x)^1(-3y)^4$$

$$+ (1)(2x)^0(-3y)^5$$

$$= 32x^5 - 240x^4y + 720x^3y^2 - 1080x^2y^3$$

$$+ 810xy^4 - 243y^5 \qquad\qquad \square$$

2.4   Sequences and Series

SMH   *This material is required in Chapter 8 of the text. A sequence is a list, as in $\{s_0, s_1, s_2, \cdots, s_n\}$; a series is a sum: $s_0 + s_1 + s_2 + \cdots + a_n$.*

Arithmetic sequence   If a_n denotes the nth term, d the common difference, and n the number of terms, then

$$a_n = a_1 + (n - 1)d$$

Arithmetic series   If A_n denotes the nth partial sum of an arithmetic sequence, then

$$A_n = \frac{n}{2}(a_1 + a_n) \text{ or } A_n = \frac{n}{2}[2a_1 + (n - 1)d]$$

Geometric sequence   If g_n denotes the nth term, r the common ratio, and n the number of terms, then

$$g_n = g_1r^{n-1} \text{ for } n \geq 1$$

Geometric series   If G_n denotes the nth partial sum of a geometric sequence, then

$$G_n = \frac{g_1(1 - r^n)}{1 - r}, r \neq 1$$

Infinite geometric series If G is the sum of an infinite geometric series, then

$$G = \frac{g_1}{1 - r}, \text{ for } |r| < 1$$

SUMS OF POWERS OF THE FIRST n INTEGERS

[sMH]   *You can use these formulas to help find Riemann sums in Chapter 5 of the text.*

$$\sum_{k=1}^{n} 1 = n$$

$$\sum_{k=1}^{n} k = 1 + 2 + 3 + \cdots + n = \frac{n(n + 1)}{2}$$

$$\sum_{k=1}^{n} k^2 = 1^2 + 2^2 + 3^2 + \cdots + n^2 = \frac{n(n + 1)(2n + 1)}{6}$$

$$\sum_{k=1}^{n} k^3 = 1^3 + 2^3 + 3^3 + \cdots + n^3 = \frac{n^2(n + 1)^2}{4}$$

$$\sum_{k=1}^{n} k^4 = 1^4 + 2^4 + 3^4 + \cdots + n^4 = \frac{n(n + 1)(2n + 1)(3n^2 + 3n - 1)}{30}$$

2.5 SOLVING EQUATIONS

Even though there are many aspects of algebra that are important to the scientist and mathematician, the ability to solve simple equations is important to the layperson and can be used in a variety of everyday applications.

Pay attention to the difference between an expression and an equation. Also, note that "to solve" is not the same as "to simplify." An **equation** is a statement of equality. There are three types of equations: *true, false,* and *open.* An *open equation* is an equation with a variable.

A *true equation* is an equation that lacks variables and that is true, such as

$$2 + 3 = 5$$

A *false equation* is an equation that lacks variables and that is false, such as

$$2 + 3 = 15$$

Our focus is on *open equations* — those equations with a variable. The values that make an open equation true are said to **satisfy** the equation and are called the **solutions** or **roots** of the equation. To **solve** an open equation is to find all replacements for the variable(s) that make the equation true. There are three types of open equations. Those that are always true, such as

$$x + 3 = 3 + x$$

are called *identities*. Those that are always false, such as

$$x + 3 = 4 + x$$

are called *contradictions*. Most open equations, such as

$$2 + x = 15$$

are true for some replacements of the variable and false for other replacements. These are called *conditional equations*. Generally, when we speak of equations, we mean conditional equations. Our concern in solving equations is to find the numbers that satisfy a given equation, so we look for things to do to equations to make the solutions or roots more obvious. Two equations with the same solutions are called **equivalent equations**. An equivalent equation may be easier to solve than the original equation, so we try to get successively simpler equivalent equations until the solution is obvious. There are certain procedures you can use to create equivalent equations. In this section, we will discuss solving the two most common types of equations you will encounter: *linear* and *quadratic*.

Linear equations : $ax + b = 0$ $(a \neq 0)$

Quadratic equations : $ax^2 + bx + c = 0$ $(a \neq 0)$

Linear Equations

To solve the first-degree (or linear) equation, isolate the variable on one side. That is, the solution of $ax + b = 0$ is

$$x = -\frac{b}{a}, \text{ where } a \neq 0$$

To solve a linear equation, use the following steps:

Step 1:   Use the distributive property to clear the equation of parentheses. If the equation is a rational expression, multiply both sides by the appropriate expression to eliminate the denominator. Be sure to check the solutions obtained by "plugging" the values back into the original equation.

Step 2:   Add the same number to both sides of the equality to obtain an equation in which all of the terms involving the variable are on one side and all of the other terms are on the other side.

Step 3:   Multiply (or divide) both sides of the equation by the same nonzero number to isolate the variable on one side.

EXAMPLE 2.9   Solving a linear equation

Solve $4(x - 3) + 5x = 5(8 + x)$.

Solution

$$4(x - 3) + 5x = 5(8 + x)$$
$$4x - 12 + 5x = 40 + 5x$$
$$9x - 12 = 40 + 5x$$
$$4x - 12 = 40$$
$$4x = 52$$
$$x = 13$$

Check: $4(13 - 3) + 5(13) = 145$, and $5(8 + 13) = 145$.   □

EXAMPLE 2.10   Solving a rational equation

Solve $\dfrac{x + 1}{x - 2} = \dfrac{x + 2}{x - 2}$.

Solution

$$(x + 1)(x - 2) = (x + 2)(x - 2)$$
$$x^2 - 2x + x - 2 = x^2 - 4$$
$$-x - 2 = -4$$

$$-x = -2$$

$$x = 2$$

Notice that $x = 2$ causes division by 0, so the solution set is empty. □

EXAMPLE 2.11   Solving a literal equation

Solve $4x + 5xy + 3y^2 = 10$ for x.

Solution

$$4x + 5xy = 10 - 3y^2$$

$$(4 + 5y)x = 10 - 3y^2$$

$$x = \frac{10 - 3y^2}{4 + 5y}, \; y \neq -\frac{4}{5} \qquad \square$$

Quadratic Equations: To solve a second-degree (or quadratic) equation, first obtain a zero on one side. Next, try to factor the quadratic. If it is factorable, set each factor equal to zero and solve. If it is not factorable, use the quadratic formula:

HANDBOOK THEOREM 1   Quadratic Formula
The solution of $ax^2 + bx + c = 0$ is

$$x = \frac{-b \pm \sqrt{b^2 - 4ac}}{2a}, \quad \text{where} \quad a \neq 0 \qquad \blacksquare$$

sMH   *Examples 2.12–2.16 here are similar to Problems 7–18 in Problem Set 1.1.*

EXAMPLE 2.12   Solving a quadratic equation by factoring

Solve $2x^2 - x - 3 = 0$.

Solution   Factoring yeilds $(2x - 3)(x + 1) = 0$. If $2x - 3 = 0$, then $x = \frac{3}{2}$; if $x + 1 = 0$, then $x = -1$. The solution is $x = \frac{3}{2}, -1$.   □

EXAMPLE 2.13   Solving a quadratic equation by using the quadratic formula

Solve $5x^2 - 3x - 4 = 0$.

Solution $a = 5, b = -3$, and $c = -4$; thus (since the equation does not factor),

$$x = \frac{3 \pm \sqrt{9 - 4(5)(-4)}}{2(5)} = \frac{3 \pm \sqrt{89}}{10} \qquad \square$$

EXAMPLE 2.14   Solving a literal equation by using the quadratic formula

Solve $x^2 + 2xy + 3y^2 - 4 = 0$ for x.

Solution $a = 1, b = 2y, c = 3y^2 - 4$; thus,

$$x = \frac{-2y \pm \sqrt{4y^2 - 4(1)(3y^2 - 4)}}{2(1)}$$

$$= \frac{-2y \pm \sqrt{16 - 8y^2}}{2}$$

$$= -y \pm \sqrt{4 - 2y^2} \qquad \square$$

EXAMPLE 2.15   Solving an absolute-value equation

Solve $|5x + 2| = 12$.

Solution   Use Property 7 of Table 1.1 in the text to write the absolute-value equation as two equations:

$$
\begin{array}{ll}
5x + 2 = 12 & 5x + 2 = -12 \\
5x = 10 & 5x = -14 \\
x = 2 & x = \dfrac{-14}{5}
\end{array}
$$

The solution is $x = 2, -\dfrac{14}{5}$. $\qquad \square$

Exponential Equations: See Examples 4, 7, and 9 of Section 2.4 of the text.

Logarithmic Equations: See Examples 5 and 8 of Section 2.4 of the text.

Higher Degree Equations: See Examples 2.36, 2.37, and 2.38 on pp. 40–41.

Trigonometric Equations: See Section 4.7, pp. 71–74.

EXAMPLE 2.16   Solving absolute-value equations

a. Solve $|5x + 2| = 12$.   **b.** Solve $|5 - 3w| = -3$.

Solution
a.   Use property 7 of Table 1.1 in the text to write two equations:

$$5x + 2 = 12 \qquad\qquad 5x + 2 = -12$$
$$5x = 10 \qquad\qquad 5x = -14$$
$$x = 2 \qquad\qquad x = \frac{-14}{5}$$

The solution is $x = 2, \dfrac{-14}{5}$.

b.   Use property 1 of Table 1.1 of the text, $|a| \geq a$, to see that there are no real values for w that make this equation true.   □

2.6   Completing the Square

[SMH]   *In Section 1.1 of the text, this procedure of completing the square is used to find the equation of a circle.*

In algebra, the method of completing the square was first introduced as a technique for solving quadratic equations. The method leads to a proof of the quadratic formula. However, when we are working with conic sections, we need to complete the square whenever the conic is not centered at the origin. (See Chapters 6 and 7 of this *Handbook.*) Consider

$$Ax^2 + Bx + C = 0$$

We wish to put this into the form

$$(x+?)^2 = \text{some number}$$

To do this, we perform the following steps below:

Step 1:   Subtract C (the constant term) from both sides:

$$Ax^2 + Bx = -C$$

Step 2:   Divide both sides by A. ($A \neq 0$; if $A = 0$, the equation would not be quadratic.) That is, we want the coefficient of the squared term to be 1. The result of dividing by A is

$$x^2 + \frac{B}{A}x = -\frac{C}{A}$$

Step 3:   Add $\left(\dfrac{B}{2A}\right)^2$ to both sides. That is, take one-half of the coefficient of the first-degree term, square it, and add it to both sides:

$$x^2 + \frac{B}{A}x + \left(\frac{B}{2A}\right)^2 = \frac{B^2}{4A^2} - \frac{C}{A}$$

Step 4:   The expression on the left is now a perfect square and can be factored:

$$\left(x + \frac{B}{2A}\right)^2 = \frac{B^2}{4A^2} - \frac{C}{A}$$

EXAMPLE 2.17   Completing the square

Complete the square for $x^2 + 2x - 5 = 0$.

Solution

$$x^2 + 2x - 5 = 0$$
$$x^2 + 2x = 5$$
$$x^2 + 2x + 1 = 5 + 1$$
$$(x + 1)^2 = 6 \qquad\qquad \square$$

EXAMPLE 2.18   Completing the square when the expression involves fractions

Complete the square for $3x^2 + 5x - 4 = 0$.

Solution

$$3x^2 + 5x - 4 = 0$$
$$3x^2 + 5x = 4$$
$$x^2 + \frac{5}{3}x = \frac{4}{3}$$
$$x^2 + \frac{5}{3}x + \left(\frac{5}{6}\right)^2 = \frac{4}{3} + \frac{25}{36}$$
$$\left(x + \frac{5}{6}\right)^2 = \frac{73}{36} \qquad\qquad \square$$

EXAMPLE 2.19   Completing the square in two variables

Complete the square in both the x and the y terms:

$$x^2 + y^2 + 4x - 9y - 13 = 0$$

Solution   Associate the x and y terms:

$$(x^2 + 4x) + (y^2 - 9y) = 13$$

$$(x^2 + 4x + 4) + \left(y^2 - 9y + \frac{81}{4} \right) = 13 + 4 + \frac{81}{4}$$

$$(x + 2)^2 + \left(y - \frac{9}{2} \right)^2 = \frac{149}{4} \qquad \square$$

EXAMPLE 2.20   Completing the square in two variables

Complete the square in both the x and the y terms:

$$2x^2 - 3y^2 - 12x + 6y + 7 = 0$$

Solution   Associate the x and y terms:

$$(2x^2 - 12x) + (-3y^2 + 6y) = -7$$

In this example, we cannot divide by the coefficient of the squared terms, because we need to make *both* the x^2 and the y^2 coefficients equal to 1. Instead, we factor

$$2(x^2 - 6x) - 3(y^2 - 2y) = -7$$

Now we complete the square; be sure you add the *same number* to both sides.

$$\underbrace{2(x^2 - 6x + 9)}_{\text{add 18 to both sides}} - \underbrace{3(y^2 - 2y + 1)}_{\text{add } -3 \text{ to both sides}} = -7 + 18 - 3$$

$$2(x - 3)^2 - 3(y - 1)^2 = 8 \qquad \square$$

2.7   Solving Inequalities

Linear Inequalities

The first-degree inequality is solved following the steps outlined in the previous section for solving first-degree equations. The only difference is that, when we multiply or divide both sides of an inequality by a negative value, the order of the inequality is reversed. That is, if $a < b$, then

$$a + c < b + c \text{ for any number } c$$

$$a - c < b - c \text{ for any number } c$$

$$ac < bc \text{ for any positive number } c$$

$$ac > bc \text{ for any negative number } c$$

A similar result holds if we use $\leq$, $>$, or $\geq$.

   Answers to inequality problems are often intervals on a real-number line. We use the following notation for intervals:

> SMH   *Interval notation is first introduced in Section 1.1 of the text. Interval notation is used in stating the solutions to most inequalities. You might wish to review in this section how interval notation is used.*

closed interval (endpoints included) :

$$[a, b]$$

open interval (endpoints excluded) :

$$(a, b)$$

$$(a, \infty)$$

half-open (or half-closed) interval :

$$(a, b]$$

$$[a, b)$$

$$(-\infty, a]$$

   To denote two intervals that are not connected, we use the notation for the union of two sets:

$$[a, b) \cup (c, d]$$

$$[a, b) \cup (b, c]$$

EXAMPLE 2.21   Solving a linear inequality

Solve $5x + 3 < 3x - 15$.

Solution

$$2x + 3 < -15$$

$$2x < -18$$

$$x < -9$$

The solution is $(-\infty, -9)$.   □

EXAMPLE 2.22   Solving a linear inequality

Solve $(2x + 1)(x - 5) \leq (2x - 3)(x + 2)$

Solution

$$2x^2 - 9x - 5 \leq 2x^2 + x - 6$$

$$-9x - 5 \leq x - 6$$

$$-10x \leq -1$$

$$x \geq \frac{1}{10}$$

The solution set is $[0.1, \infty)$.   □

The word *between* is often used with a double inequality. We say that **x is between *a* and *b*** if $a < x < b$ and that **x is between *a* and *b*, inclusive** if $a \leq x \leq b$.

EXAMPLE 2.23   Solving a between relationship

Solve $-5 \leq x + 4 \leq 5$.

Solution

$$-5 \leq x + 4 \leq 5$$

$$-5 - 4 \leq x + 4 - 4 \leq 5 - 4$$

$$-9 \leq x \leq 1$$

The solution set is $[-9, 1]$. We say that x is between -9 and 1, inclusive.   □

Quadratic Inequalities

The method of solving quadratic inequalities is similar to the method of solving quadratic equations:

Step 1:   Obtain a zero on one side of the inequality.

Step 2:   Factor if possible. If the inequality is a rational expression, factor the numerator and the denominator separately.

Step 3:   Set each factor equal to zero. These values are not necessarily the solution of the inequality. If the inequality is not factorable, we treat the entire expression as a single factor and solve by the quadratic formula. Values for which the factors are zero are called the *critical values of x*. Plot these values on a number line. The points determine one or more intervals on the line.

Step 4:   Choose some value in each interval. It will make the inequality true or false in that interval; we accordingly include or exclude that interval from the solution set.

EXAMPLE 2.24   Solving a quadratic inequality by factoring

Solve $x^2 < 6 - x$.

Solution

$$x^2 + x - 6 < 0$$
$$\underbrace{(x - 2)(x + 3)}_{\text{Factors}} < 0$$

Product of factors < 0 means that the product of factors is negative; product of factors > 0 means that the product of factors is positive. For this example, we are seeking values of x that make the product of the factors negative.

Signs of factors:

Solve: $x - 2 = 0$

$x = 2$ This is a critical value.

$\downarrow$

$x - 2$: $x < 2 \mid x > 2$

$x - 2$ **is neg** $\leftarrow \mid \rightarrow x - 2$ **is pos**

Write: $-\quad -\;-\;-\;- \mid + + + + + +$

−3   2

$x + 3 = 0$

$x = -3$ This is a critical value.

$\downarrow$

$x + 3$: $x < -3 \mid x > -3$

$x + 3$ **is neg** $\leftarrow \mid \rightarrow x + 3$ **is pos**

Write: $-\;-\;- \mid + + + + + + +$

−3   2

We summarize these steps by writing

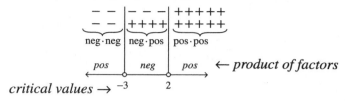

We see from the number line that the segment labeled negative is $(-3, 2)$; this is the solution (except for a consideration of the endpoints). In this example, the endpoints are not included, so the solution is an open interval. These steps are summarized as

$$
\begin{array}{ccc}
- \; - & - \; + & + \; + \qquad \leftarrow \textit{signs of factors}
\end{array}
$$

$$
\underset{pos \quad\;\; a \quad\; neg \quad\;\; b \quad\; pos}{\xleftrightarrow{\qquad\qquad\qquad\qquad}} \quad \leftarrow \textit{sign of product (negative because of} <)
$$

$\square$

EXAMPLE 2.25   Solving an inequality by examining the factors

Solve $(2 - x)(x + 3)(x - 1) \geq 0$.

Solution   Plotting critical values and checking the signs of the factors, we have

$$
\begin{array}{cccc}
+-- & ++- & +++ & -++
\end{array}
$$

$$
\underset{pos \quad\; neg \quad\; pos \quad\; neg}{\xleftrightarrow{\;\;\bullet\;\;\;\;\bullet\;\;\;\;\bullet\;\;}} \quad \textit{Endpoints included because of} \geq
$$

$$
\underset{-3 \qquad 1 \qquad 2}{}
$$

The solution is $(-\infty, -3] \cup [1, 2]$. $\square$

EXAMPLE 2.26   Solving a rational inequality

Solve $\dfrac{x + 3}{x - 2} < 0$.

Solution   Be careful not to multiply both sides by $(x - 2)$, since we do not know whether $(x - 2)$ is positive or negative. We could consider separate cases, but instead we solve the inequality as if it were quadratic. We set the numerator and denominator each equal to zero to obtain the critical values $x = -3$, $x = 2$. We then plot these values on a number line and check a value in each interval to determine the solution.

$$
\begin{array}{ccc}
-- & +- & ++
\end{array}
$$

$$
\underset{-3 \qquad 2}{\xleftrightarrow{\;\;\circ\;\;\;\;\circ\;\;}}
$$

The solution is $(-3, 2)$. $\square$

EXAMPLE 2.27   Solving a rational inequality

Solve $\dfrac{x-3}{x} > 1$.

Solution

$$\frac{x-3}{x} - 1 > 0$$

$$\frac{x-3-x}{x} > 0$$

$$\frac{-3}{x} > 0$$

Since $-3 < 0$ for $\dfrac{-3}{x}$, we have

$$
\begin{array}{c|c}
x < 0 & x > 0 \\
\text{neg} \div \text{neg} & \text{neg} \div \text{pos} \\
\underbrace{- \ -} & \underbrace{- \ +} \\
\end{array}
$$

The solution is $(-\infty, 0)$. $\square$

EXAMPLE 2.28   Solving a rational inequality

Solve $\dfrac{x+2}{2x} \geq 5$.

Solution

$$\frac{x+2}{2x} - 5 \geq 0$$

$$\frac{x+2-10x}{2x} \geq 0$$

$$\frac{2-9x}{2x} \geq 0$$

The solution is $(0, \frac{2}{9}]$. The endpoints are included when we have intervals with $\geq$ or $\leq$. However, values of the variable that cause division by zero are excluded. $\square$

EXAMPLE 2.29   Solving a quadratic inequality that does not factor

Solve $x^2 + 2x - 4 < 0$.

Solution   The left-hand expression is in simplified form and cannot be factored. Therefore, we proceed by considering $(x^2 + 2x - 4)$ as a single factor. To find the critical values, we find the values for which the factor is zero:

$$x^2 + 2x - 4 = 0$$

$$x = \frac{-2 \pm \sqrt{4 - 4(1)(-4)}}{2}$$

$$= -1 \pm \sqrt{5}$$

Next, we plot the critical values and check the sign of the expression in each of the intervals:

The solution is $(-1 - \sqrt{5}, -1 + \sqrt{5})$.   □

2.8   Determinants

| $\boxed{\text{sMh}}$ | *Determinants are used in calculus in several places. We first see them in Section 9.4 of the text, when they are used as memory devices of an operation called the cross product. In Sections 12.3 and 12.8, we use determinants to calculate what is called the Jacobian of a transformation. Finally, in Chapter 14, the Wronskian is defined in terms of an $n \times n$ determinant.* |

The following arrays of numbers are examples of *matrices*:

$$\begin{pmatrix} a_1 & b_1 \\ a_2 & b_2 \end{pmatrix} \begin{pmatrix} a_1 & b_1 \\ a_2 & b_2 \\ a_3 & b_3 \end{pmatrix} \begin{pmatrix} a_1 & b_1 & c_1 & d_1 \\ a_2 & b_2 & c_2 & d_2 \end{pmatrix}$$

The first of these matrices has two rows and two columns and is called a "two-by-two matrix" (written "2×2 matrix"), the second is a 3×2 matrix, since it has three rows and two columns, and the last one is a 2×4 matrix. The a's, b's, c's, etc., that appear are called the *entries* of the matrix. An $n \times n$ matrix (i.e., a matrix with n rows and n columns, and hence a matrix with the same number of rows and columns) is called a *square* matrix. Associated with each square matrix is a certain number called the *determinant* of the matrix. We shall show how to find the determinant of a 2×2 matrix and a 3×3 matrix.

DETERMINANT

If A is the 2×2 matrix $\begin{bmatrix} a & b \\ c & d \end{bmatrix}$, then the determinant of A is defined to be the number $ad - bc$.

Some notations for this determinant are det A, $\begin{vmatrix} a & b \\ c & d \end{vmatrix}$, and $|A|$. We will generally use $|A|$.

WARNING ➤ *Note that determinants always have the same number of rows and columns; that is, they are* **square**: $2 \times 2, 3 \times 3, 4 \times 4, \cdots$.

EXAMPLE 2.30   Evaluating determinants

a. $\begin{vmatrix} 4 & -2 \\ -1 & 3 \end{vmatrix} = 4 \cdot 3 - (-2)(-1) = 12 - 2 = 10$

b. $\begin{vmatrix} 2 & 2 \\ 2 & 2 \end{vmatrix} = 2 \cdot 2 - 2 \cdot 2 = 0$

c. $\begin{vmatrix} 1 & 0 \\ 0 & 1 \end{vmatrix} = 1 \cdot 1 - 0 \cdot 0 = 1$

d. $\begin{vmatrix} 1 & 2 \\ 2 & 4 \end{vmatrix} = 1 \cdot 4 - 2 \cdot 2 = 0$ ☐

We next define the determinant of a 3×3 matrix. We need a preliminary observation. If we delete the first row and first column of the matrix

$$A = \begin{bmatrix} a_1 & b_1 & c_1 \\ a_2 & b_2 & c_2 \\ a_3 & b_3 & c_3 \end{bmatrix}$$

We obtain the 2×2 matrix $\begin{bmatrix} b_2 & c_2 \\ b_3 & c_3 \end{bmatrix}$. This 2×2 matrix is referred to as the *minor* associated with the entry in the first row and first column. Similarly, the minor associated with b_1 is obtained by deleting the first row and *second* column of A, and hence this minor is $\begin{bmatrix} a_2 & c_2 \\ a_3 & c_3 \end{bmatrix}$. The minor associated with c_1 is $\begin{bmatrix} a_2 & b_2 \\ a_3 & b_3 \end{bmatrix}$. The determinant of the 3×3 matrix A is obtained by using these minors as follows:

$$|A| = a_1 \begin{vmatrix} b_2 & c_2 \\ b_3 & c_3 \end{vmatrix} - b_1 \begin{vmatrix} a_2 & c_2 \\ a_3 & c_3 \end{vmatrix} + c_1 \begin{vmatrix} a_2 & b_2 \\ a_3 & b_3 \end{vmatrix}$$

$$= a_1 \begin{pmatrix} \text{minor} \\ \text{associated} \\ \text{with } a_1 \end{pmatrix} - b_1 \begin{pmatrix} \text{minor} \\ \text{associated} \\ \text{with } b_1 \end{pmatrix} + c_1 \begin{pmatrix} \text{minor} \\ \text{associated} \\ \text{with } c_1 \end{pmatrix}$$

EXAMPLE 2.31   Evaluating a determinant

$$\begin{vmatrix} 1 & 4 & -1 \\ -2 & 0 & 2 \\ 3 & 1 & 2 \end{vmatrix} = 1 \begin{vmatrix} 0 & 2 \\ 1 & 2 \end{vmatrix} - 4 \begin{vmatrix} -2 & 2 \\ 3 & 2 \end{vmatrix} + (-1) \begin{vmatrix} -2 & 0 \\ 3 & 1 \end{vmatrix}$$

$$= -2 + 4(10) + 2 = 40 \qquad \square$$

It is not difficult to show that $\begin{vmatrix} a & 0 & 0 \\ 0 & b & 0 \\ 0 & 0 & c \end{vmatrix} = abc$.

We found the determinant for a 3×3 matrix by using the entries in the first row and their minors. In fact, it is possible to find the determinant using any row (or column); the formulas are similar and use the minors of the terms in the given row (or column), but adjustments must be made for the signs of the minors. The interested reader can find these results in any standard college algebra book. The following four properties of determinants are worth noting:

HANDBOOK THEOREM 2   Properties of determinants

Property 1   If B is the matrix obtained from A by multiplying a row (or column) of A by a real number k, then $|B| = k|A|$.

Property 2   If B is the matrix obtained from A by adding to a row (or column) of A a multiple of some other row (or column) of A, then $|B| = |A|$.

Property 3   If the matrix B is obtained from A by interchanging two rows (or columns), then $|B| = -|A|$.

Property 4   If two rows (or columns) of a matrix A are equal or proportional, then $|A| = 0$. ∎

EXAMPLE 2.32   Properties of determinants illustrated

a. Property 1: $\begin{vmatrix} ka_1 & kb_1 \\ a_2 & b_2 \end{vmatrix} = \begin{vmatrix} a_1 & b_1 \\ ka_2 & kb_2 \end{vmatrix} = k \begin{vmatrix} a_1 & b_1 \\ a_2 & b_2 \end{vmatrix}$

b. Property 2: Multiplying each entry in the first row of the matrix $\begin{pmatrix} 1 & 2 \\ 2 & 5 \end{pmatrix} = A$ by -2, and adding the result to the corresponding entry in the second row, we obtain the matrix $B = \begin{pmatrix} 1 & 2 \\ 0 & 1 \end{pmatrix}$, and property 2 asserts that $|A| = |B|$. (Check for yourself to see that this is correct.)

c. Property 3 (interchange the first and third rows):

$$\begin{vmatrix} 1 & 3 & -5 \\ 3 & -2 & 1 \\ 7 & 1 & 5 \end{vmatrix} = - \begin{vmatrix} 7 & 1 & 5 \\ 3 & -2 & 1 \\ 1 & 3 & -5 \end{vmatrix}$$

d. $\begin{vmatrix} 1 & 2 \\ 2 & 4 \end{vmatrix} = 0$

Note that 2 times an entry in row 1 is equal to the corresponding entry in row 2. $\square$

EXAMPLE 2.33   Multiplicative property of determinants

Verify that 2×2 determinants have the following multiplicative property:

$$\begin{vmatrix} a_1 & b_1 \\ c_1 & d_1 \end{vmatrix} \begin{vmatrix} a_2 & b_2 \\ c_2 & d_2 \end{vmatrix} = \begin{vmatrix} a_1a_2 + b_1c_2 & a_1b_2 + b_1d_2 \\ c_1a_2 + d_1c_2 & c_1b_2 + d_1d_2 \end{vmatrix}$$

Solution

$$\begin{vmatrix} a_1 & b_1 \\ c_1 & d_1 \end{vmatrix} \begin{vmatrix} a_2 & b_2 \\ c_2 & d_2 \end{vmatrix} = (a_1d_1 - b_1c_1)(a_2d_2 - b_2c_2)$$

$$= a_1a_2d_1d_2 - b_1c_1a_2d_2 - a_1d_1b_2c_2 + b_1b_2c_1c_2$$

$$= (a_1a_2 + b_1c_2)(c_1b_2 + d_1d_2) - (a_1b_2 + b_1d_2)(c_1a_2 + d_1c_2)$$

$$= \begin{vmatrix} a_1a_2 + b_1c_2 & a_1b_2 + b_1d_2 \\ c_1a_2 + d_1c_2 & c_1b_2 + d_1d_2 \end{vmatrix} \qquad \square$$

2.9   Functions

Definition: A function f is a rule that assigns, to each element x of a set X, a unique element y of a set Y. (See Section 1.3 of the text.)

In this handbook, we will simply list and categorize some of the more common types of functions you will encounter in calculus.

ALGEBRAIC FUNCTIONS:

Definition: An algebraic function is a function that satisfies an equation of the form

$$a_n(x)y^n + a_{n-1}(x)y^{n-1} + \cdots + a_0(x) = 0$$

where the coefficient functions $a_k(x)$ are polynomials in x.

Polynomial Functions

Definition: $f(x) = a_nx^n + a_{n-1}x^{n-1} + a_{n-2}x^{n-2} + \cdots + a_2x^2 + a_1x + a_0, a_n \neq 0$

Constant function: $f(x) = a$

Linear function: $f(x) = ax + b$

Standard form: $Ax + By + C = 0$

Point-slope form: $y - k = m(x - h)$

Slope-intercept form: $y = mx + b$

Two-point form: $y - y_1 = \left(\dfrac{y_2 - y_1}{x_2 - x_1} \right)(x - x_1)$ or

$$\begin{vmatrix} x & y & 1 \\ x_1 & y_1 & 1 \\ x_2 & y_2 & 1 \end{vmatrix} = 0$$

Intercept form: $\dfrac{x}{a} + \dfrac{y}{b} = 1$

Horizontal line: $y = k$

Vertical line: $x = h$

Quadratic function: $f(x) = ax^2 + bx + c, a \neq 0$
Cubic function: $f(x) = ax^3 + bx^2 + cx + d, a \neq 0$

Miscellaneous Algebraic Functions

Absolute value function: $f(x) = |x| = \begin{cases} x & \text{if } x \geq 0 \\ -x & \text{if } x < 0 \end{cases}$

Greatest integer function: $f(x) = [[x]]$ This is the unique integer $[[x]]$ satisfying $[[x]] \leq x < [[x]] + 1$; this means that $[[x]]$ is the largest integer not exceeding x. For example, $[[2.3]] = 2, [[-2.3]] = -3$, and $[[2]] = 2$.

Power function: $f(x) = x^r$ for any real number r.

Rational function: $f(x) = \dfrac{P(x)}{D(x)}$, where $P(x)$ and $D(x)$ are two polynomial functions, with $D(x) \neq 0$.

TRANSCENDENTAL FUNCTIONS:
Definition: Functions that are not algebraic are called transcendental.

Exponential function: $f(x) = b^x$ $(b > 0, b \neq 1)$

Logarithmic function: $f(x) = \log_b x (b > 0, b \neq 1)$
  If $b = 10$, then f is a common logarithm: $f(x) = \log x$
  If $b = e$, then f is a natural logarithm: $f(x) = \ln x$

Trigonometric functions: Let θ be any angle in standard position, and let $P(x, y)$ be any point on the terminal side of the angle a distance of r from the origin $(r \neq 0)$. Then $\cos\theta = \dfrac{x}{r}$, $\sin\theta = \dfrac{y}{r}$, $\tan\theta = \dfrac{y}{x}$, $\sec\theta = \dfrac{r}{x}$, $\csc\theta = \dfrac{r}{y}$, and $\cot\theta = \dfrac{x}{y}$.

2.10   Polynomials

THEOREMS   Let $P(x)$ and $Q(x)$ be polynomial functions.

Zero factor theorem: If $P(x)Q(x) = 0$, then either $P(x) = 0$ or $Q(x) = 0$ (or both).

Remainder theorem: If $P(x)$ is divided by $x - r$ until a constant is obtained, then the remainder is equal to $P(r)$.

Intermediate-value theorem for a polynomial function: If $P(x)$ is a polynomial function on $[a, b]$ such that $P(a) \neq P(b)$, then P takes on every value between $P(a)$ and $P(b)$ over the interval $[a, b]$.

Factor theorem: If r is a root of the polynomial equation $P(x) = 0$, then $x - r$ is a factor of $P(x)$. Also, if $x - r$ is a factor of $P(x)$, then r is a root of the polynomial equation $P(x) = 0$.

Root limitation theorem: A polynomial function of degree n has, at most, n distinct roots.

Location theorem: If P is a polynomial function such that $P(a)$ and $P(b)$ are opposite in sign, then there is at least one real root on the interval $[a, b]$.

Rational root theorem: If $P(x)$ has integer coefficients and has a rational root p/q (where p/q is reduced), then p is a factor of the constant term, a_0, and q is a factor of the leading coefficient, a_n.

Upper and lower bound theorem: If $a > 0$ and, in the synthetic division of $P(x)$ by $x - a$, all the numbers in the last row are either positive or negative, then a is an upper bound for the roots of $P(x) = 0$. If $b < 0$ and, in the synthetic division of $P(x)$ by $x - b$, the numbers in the last row alternate in sign, then b is a lower bound for the roots of $P(x) = 0$.

Descartes's rule of signs: Let $P(x)$ be written in descending powers of x. Then

1. The number of positive real zeros is equal to the number of sign changes or is equal to that number decreased by an even integer.

2. The number of negative real zeros is equal to the number of sign changes in $P(-x)$ or is equal to that number decreased by an even integer.

Fundamental theorem of algebra: If $P(x)$ is a polynomial of degree $n \geq 1$ with complex coefficients, then $P(x) = 0$ has at least one complex root.

Number-of-roots theorem: If $P(x)$ is a polynomial of degree $n \geq 1$ with complex coefficients, then $P(x) = 0$ has exactly n roots (if roots are counted according to their multiplicity).

EXAMPLE 2.34   Synthetic division

Divide $x^4 + 3x^3 - 12x^2 + 5x - 2$ by $x - 2$.

Solution   To do synthetic division, the divisor must be of the form $x - b$.

This is the number b.

```
↓     1    3   −12    5    −2   ← Coefficients of
2|         2*   10   −4     2     given polynomial
     ─────────────────────────
      1    5   −2    1     0
      ↑    ↑
      └────┴── Add              ↑
                            Remainder
Bring down leading coefficient
```

*The numbers in this row are found as follows:

$$2 \cdot 1 = 2; \ 2 \cdot 5 = 10; \ 2 \cdot (-2) = -4; \ 2 \cdot 1 = 2$$

The degree of the result is one less than the degree of the given polynomial and has coefficients given by the last row (1, 5, −2, and 1 for this example; the last entry is the remainder). Thus,

$$\frac{x^4 + 3x^3 - 12x^2 + 5x - 2}{x - 2} = x^3 + 5x^2 - 2x + 1 \qquad \Box$$

EXAMPLE 2.35   Synthetic division with zero coefficients and a remainder

Divide $x^5 - 3x^2 + 1$ by $x - 2$.

Solution   Note: $x^5 - 3x^2 + 1 = x^5 + 0x^4 + 0x^3 - 3x^2 + 0x + 1.$

$$
\begin{array}{r|rrrrrr}
 & 1 & 0 & 0 & -3 & 0 & 1 \\
2| & & 2 & 4 & 8 & 10 & 20 \\
\hline
 & 1 & 2 & 4 & 5 & 10 & 21 \quad \leftarrow (R)
\end{array}
$$

$$\frac{x^5 - 3x^2 + 1}{x - 2} = x^4 + 2x^3 + 4x^2 + 5x + 10 + \frac{21}{x - 2}$$

$\square$

EXAMPLE 2.36   Solving a polynomial equation

Solve $12x^3 - 6x^2 - 24x + 18 = 0$.

Solution   Using the rational root theorem, $p = \pm1, \pm2, \pm3, \pm6, \pm9, \pm18$ and $q = 1, 2, 3, 4, 6, 12$. There are many possible rational roots of the form $\dfrac{p}{q}$. We try these values using synthetic division, until we find a root that, in turn, allows us to write a factorization of polynomials of a degree lower than that of the original polynomial. We obtain

$$
\begin{array}{r|rrrr}
 & 12 & -6 & -24 & 18 \\
\hline
1 \,| & 12 & 6 & -18 & 0
\end{array}
$$

The root is 1 (zero remainder), so $(x - 1)$ and $(12x^2 + 6x - 18)$ are factors. Solving thus yields

$$12x^3 - 6x^2 - 24x + 18 = 0$$
$$(x - 1)(12x^2 + 6x - 18) = 0$$
$$6(x - 1)(2x^2 + x - 3) = 0$$
$$6(x - 1)(2x + 3)(x - 1) = 0$$

The roots are $-\frac{3}{2}$, 1, where 1 has multiplicity 2. $\square$

EXAMPLE 2.37   Solving a polynomial equation with repeated roots

Solve $r^4 - 5r^3 + 6r^2 + 4r - 8 = 0$.

Solution   The possible rational roots are ±1, ±2, ±4, and ±8.

$$
\begin{array}{r|rrrrl}
 & 1 & -5 & 6 & 4 & -8 \quad \leftarrow \text{Coefficients of} \\
-1| & & -1 & 6 & -12 & 8 \quad \text{given polynomial} \\
\hline
 & 1 & -6 & 12 & -8 & 0 \\
2| & & & 2 & -8 & 8 \\
\hline
 & 1 & -4 & 4 & 0
\end{array}
$$

Solving the remaining quadratic:

$$x^2 - 4x + 4 = 0$$

$$(x - 2)^2 = 0$$

$$x = 2$$

The roots are -1 and 2. *Note*: The root 2 has multiplicity 3.   □

EXAMPLE 2.38   Solving a polynomial equation that has no rational roots

Solve $x^4 - 3x^2 - 6x - 2 = 0$.

Solution p: ±1, ±2 and q: 1, so $\dfrac{p}{q}$: ±1, ±2. We try these values, using synthetic division:

	1	0	-3	-6	-2	
1	1	1	-2	-8	-10	
2	1	2	1	-4	-10	
-1	1	-1	-2	-4	2	
-2	1	-2	1	-8	14	← Lower bound

There are no rational roots. (We have tried all the numbers on our list.) Next, we verify the type of roots by using Descartes's rule of signs. First,

$$f(x) = x^4 - 3x^2 - 6x - 2$$

There is one sign change, so there is one positive root. Next,

$$f(-x) = x^4 - 3x^2 + 6x - 2$$

There are three sign changes, so we have three negative roots or one negative root.

Using synthetic division to find some additional points yields

$(0, -2)$ for the y-intercept;

$(1.5, -12.6875)$;

$(3, 34)$; there are no roots larger than 3

Using the intermediate-value theorem and synthetic division, we can find the roots to any desired degree of accuracy. We find the following:

56   Chapter 2

	1	0	−3	−6	−2
−0.5	1	−0.5	−2.75	−4.625	0.3125
−0.4	1	−0.4	−2.84	−4.864	−0.0544
−0.41	1	−0.41	−2.8319	−4.8389	−0.0161
−0.42	1	−0.42	−2.8236	−4.8141	0.0219

Remember that there is a root between −0.41 and −0.42, since the remainder is positive for −0.42 and negative for −0.41. We continue in this fashion to approximate the root to any degree of accuracy desired. This is a good problem for a calculator or a computer. We repeat the procedure for the other roots to find (correct to the nearest tenth) −0.4, 2.4. The graph can be used to verify that these are the only real roots.   □

You may need to consult a precalculus textbook for a review of how to solve polynomial equations.

2.11   PROBLEM SET 2

Perform the indicated operations in Problems 1–12.

1. $2^5 \cdot 2^7$ **2.** $5^2 \cdot 5^8$ **3.** $(5^2)^3$ **4.** $(8^2)^4$

5. $\dfrac{3^8}{3^5}$ **6.** $\dfrac{3^5}{3^8}$ **7.** $2^{-5} \cdot 2^8$ **8.** $\dfrac{2^{-5}}{2^8}$

9. $\dfrac{2^{-3}}{2^{-4}}$ **10.** $8^{2/3} \cdot 4^{1/2}$ **11.** $16^{3/4} \cdot 8^{-1/3}$ **12.** $\dfrac{8^{2/3}}{4^{1/2}}$

Perform the indicated operations Problems 13–22.   Assume that a, b, and c are positive real numbers.

13. $(a^2b^3c^5) \cdot (a^3b^5c^2)$ **14.** $(a^2b^3c^5) \cdot (a^{-2}b^{-4}c^{-2})$

15. $(ab^2c^3)^4$ **16.** $\left(\dfrac{a^2b^3}{c^2}\right)^5$

17. $\left(\dfrac{a^{-2}b^2}{c^2}\right)^{-1}$ **18.** $\left(\dfrac{a^{-2}b^{-2}}{c^2}\right)^{-1}$

19. $\left(\dfrac{a^{-2}b^{-2}}{c^{-2}}\right)^{-2}$ **20.** $x^{-2} + y^{-2}$

21. $(x^{-2} + y^{-2})^{-2}$ **22.** $(a^{1/2}b^{2/3}c^{1/5})^{15}$

Factor the expressions in Problems 23–32.

23. $2a^{1/2}b^{-1/2} + 3a^{-1/2}b^{1/2}$ **24.** $-3a^{-1/2}b + 4a^{1/2}$
25. $a^{1/2}b + a^{-1/2}b^2$ **26.** $a^{1/2}b^{-1/3} + a^{-1/2}b^{1/3}$
27. $(x - 12)^4 - 2(x - 12)$
    (*Adapted from Problem 20, Section 4.3, of text.*)

28. $12u^3 - 6u^2 - 24u$
(*Adapted from Problem 22, Section 4.3, of text.*)
29. $2x(2x + 3)^2 + 2x^2(2x + 3)(2)$
(*Adapted from Problem 42, Section 3.5, of text.*)
30. $[2x](4x + 5)^3 + x^2[3(4x + 5)^2(4)]$
(*From Example 9, Section 3.5, of text.*)
31. $(x + 1)^3(2)(2x + 3)(2) + (2x + 3)^2(3)(x + 1)^2(1)$
32. $4(2x^2 + 1)^3(4x)(x^2 - 2)^5 + 5(2x^2 + 1)^4(2x)(x^2 - 2)^4$

In Problems 33–58, solve each equation or inequality for x.

33. $3x - 9 \geq 12$ **34.** $-x > -36$
35. $3(2 - 4x) \leq 0$ **36.** $5(3 - x) > 3x - 1$
37. $-5 \leq 5x \leq 25$ **38.** $3 \leq -x < 8$
39. $-5 < 3x + 2 \leq 5$ **40.** $-5 \leq 3 - 2x < 18$
41. $x^2 + 5x - 6 = 0$ **42.** $x^2 + 5x + 6 = 0$
43. $3x^2 = 7x$ **44.** $7x^2 = 2$
45. $5x = 3 - 4x^2$ **46.** $4x^2 = 12x - 9$
47. $2x^2 + x - w = 0$ **48.** $2x^2 + wx + 5 = 0$
49. $4x^2 - 4x + (1 - t^2) = 0$ **50.** $y = 2x^2 + x + 6$
51. $4x^2 - (3t + 10)x + (6t + 4) = 0, t > 2$
52. $(x - 3)^2 + (y - 2)^2 = 4$
53. $(x + 1)(2x + 5)(7 - 3x) > 0$
54. $(x - 2)(3x + 2)(3 - 2x) < 0$
55. $\dfrac{x(2x - 1)}{5 - x} > 0$ **56.** $\dfrac{x}{(2x + 3)(x - 2)} < 0$
57. $2x^2 + 4x + 5 \geq 0$ **58.** $x^2 - 2x - 6 \leq 0$

In Problems 59–70, find the value of the given determinant.

59. $\begin{vmatrix} 3 & 0 & 0 \\ -5 & 2 & 0 \\ \frac{5}{2} & \frac{1}{5} & -1 \end{vmatrix}$ **60.** $\begin{vmatrix} 0 & 1 & 0 \\ -1 & 32 & 1 \\ 2 & 48 & -1 \end{vmatrix}$

61. $\begin{vmatrix} 2 & 0 & 1 \\ 1 & 3 & -2 \\ 2 & -3 & 2 \end{vmatrix}$ **62.** $\begin{vmatrix} 0 & -1 & -1 \\ 1 & 3 & 2 \\ 1 & -4 & 2 \end{vmatrix}$

63. $\begin{vmatrix} -1 & 1 & 2 \\ 0 & 1 & 3 \\ 1 & 0 & -1 \end{vmatrix}$ **64.** $\begin{vmatrix} 2 & -1 & 1 \\ 1 & 0 & 0 \\ 0 & -1 & 2 \end{vmatrix}$

65. $\begin{vmatrix} 1 & -2 & 3 \\ -4 & 7 & -11 \\ 5 & 9 & -1 \end{vmatrix}$ **66.** $\begin{vmatrix} \mathbf{i} & \mathbf{j} & \mathbf{k} \\ 2 & -1 & 3 \\ 0 & 7 & -4 \end{vmatrix}$

[sMH] (*From Example 5, Section 9.4, of text.*)   *For variables $\mathbf{i}, \mathbf{j}$, and $\mathbf{k}$.* (*From Example 1, Section 9.4, of text.*)

67. $\begin{vmatrix} 1 & 2 & 3 \\ 0 & 0 & 1 \\ 0 & 1 & 0 \end{vmatrix}$ **68.** $\begin{vmatrix} 2 & 3 & 4 \\ 2 & 0 & 0 \\ 0 & 1 & 1 \end{vmatrix}$

69. $\begin{vmatrix} 1 & 2 & 3 & 4 \\ 8 & -1 & 5 & 7 \\ 2 & 4 & 6 & 8 \\ -1 & 5 & 3 & 7 \end{vmatrix}$ **70.** $\begin{vmatrix} 8 & 1 & -7 & 5 \\ -1 & 2 & 2 & 3 \\ -7 & 8 & 15 & 4 \\ -3 & 6 & 6 & 9 \end{vmatrix}$

In Problems 71–76, expand the given quantity.

71. $(a+b)^4$ **72.** $(a+2b)^3$ **73.** $(3x+2y)^3$

74. $(-x+2y)^5$ **75.** $(\frac{1}{x}+y)^4$ **76.** $(\sqrt{a}+2b)^5$

Solve the polynomial equations in Problems 77–90.

77. $x^3 - x^2 - 4x + 4 = 0$
78. $2x^3 - x^2 - 18x + 9 = 0$
79. $x^3 - 2x^2 - 9x + 18 = 0$
80. $x^3 + 2x^2 - 5x - 6 = 0$
81. $x^3 + 3x^2 - 4x - 12 = 0$
82. $2x^3 + x^2 - 13x + 6 = 0$
83. $2x^3 - 3x^2 - 32x - 15 = 0$
84. $x^4 - 12x^3 + 54x^2 - 108x + 81 = 0$
85. $x^4 + 3x^3 - 19x^2 - 3x + 18 = 0$
86. $x^4 - 13x^2 + 36 = 0$
87. $x^3 + 15x^2 + 71x + 105 = 0$
88. $x^5 + 6x^4 + x^3 - 48x^2 - 92x - 48 = 0$
89. $x^6 - 3x^4 + 3x^2 - 1 = 0$
90. $x^7 + 3x^6 - 4x^5 - 16x^4 - 13x^3 - 3x^2 = 0$
91.   Evaluate the determinant

$$\begin{vmatrix} \sin\phi\cos\theta & -\rho\sin\phi\sin\theta & \rho\cos\phi\cos\theta \\ \sin\phi\sin\theta & \rho\sin\phi\cos\theta & \rho\cos\phi\sin\theta \\ \cos\phi & 0 & -\rho\sin\phi \end{vmatrix}$$

$\boxed{\text{sMH}}$ *This problem is from Example 6 of Section 12.8*

CHAPTER 3
Systems of Equations

3.1 Elementary Methods

Two or more equations that are to be solved at the same time make up a **system of equations**. The **simultaneous solution** of a system of equations is the intersection of the solution sets of the individual equations. We use a brace to show that we are looking for a simultaneous solution. If all the equations in a system are linear, the system is called a **linear system**.

GRAPHING METHOD

The graph of each equation in a system of linear equations in two variables is a line; in the Cartesian plane, two lines must be related to each other in one of three ways:

1. The graphs intersect at a single point.
2. The graphs are parallel lines. In this case, the solution set is empty, and the system is called *inconsistent*. In general, any system that has an empty solution set is referred to as an **inconsistent system**.
3. The graphs are the same line. In this case, there are infinitely many points in the solution set, and any solution of one equation is also a solution of the other. Such a system is called a **dependent system**.

In other words, we graph the equations and check for the intersection point. If the graphs do not intersect, then the equations represent an inconsistent system. If the graphs coincide, then the equations represent a dependent system. When we solve a system by graphing the equations and then looking for points of intersection, we call the technique the **graphing method**.

EXAMPLE 3.1   Graphing method

Solve the given systems by graphing:

a. $\begin{cases} 2x - 3y = -8 \\ x + y = 6 \end{cases}$ **b.** $\begin{cases} 2x - 3y = -8 \\ 4x - 6y = 0 \end{cases}$ **c.** $\begin{cases} 2x - 3y = -8 \\ y = \frac{2}{3}x + \frac{8}{3} \end{cases}$

Solution

a. Graph the line $2x - 3y = -8$:

$$3y = 2x + 8$$

$$y = \tfrac{2}{3}x + \tfrac{8}{3}$$

Graph the line $x + y = 6$:

$$y = -x + 6$$

Look at the point(s) of intersection, as shown in Figure 3.1. The solution appears to be (2, 4), which can be verified by direct substitution into both the given equations.

b. The graphs of the given lines are shown in Figure 3.2.

Notice that these lines are parallel; you can show this analytically by noting that the slopes of the lines are the same. Since the lines are distinct and parallel, there is no point of intersection. This is an *inconsistent system*.

c. The graphs of the given lines are shown in Figure 3.3.

The equations represent the same line. This is a *dependent system*.

□

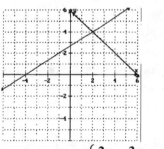

Figure 3.1   Graph of $\begin{cases} 2x - 3y = -8 \\ x + y = 6 \end{cases}$

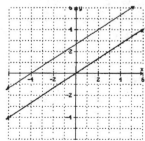

Figure 3.2   Graph of $\begin{cases} 2x - 3y = -8 \\ 4x - 6y = 0 \end{cases}$

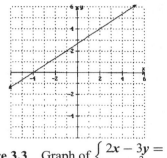

Figure 3.3   Graph of $\begin{cases} 2x - 3y = -8 \\ y = \frac{2}{3}x + \frac{8}{3} \end{cases}$

SUBSTITUTION METHOD

The graphing method can give solutions as accurate as the graphs you can draw; consequently, it is adequate for many applications. However, there is often a need for more exact methods.

In general, given a system, the procedure for solving is to write a simpler equivalent system. Two systems are said to be **equivalent** if they have the same solution set. In this book, we limit ourselves to finding only real roots. There are several ways to go about writing equivalent systems. The first nongraphical method we consider comes from the substitution property of real numbers and leads to a **substitution method** for solving systems.

SUBSTITUTION METHOD FOR SOLVING SYSTEMS OF EQUATIONS WITH TWO EQUATIONS AND TWO UNKNOWNS

1. *Solve* one of the equations for one of the variables.
2. *Substitute* the expression that you obtain into the other equation.
3. *Solve* the resulting equation.
4. *Substitute* that solution into either of the original equations to find the value of the other variable.
5. *State* the solution.

EXAMPLE 3.2   Substitution method

Solve: $\begin{cases} 2p + 3q = 5 \\ q = -2p + 7 \end{cases}$.

Solution   Since $q = -2p + 7$, substitute $-2p + 7$ for q in the other equation:

$$2p + 3q = 5$$
$$2p + 3(-2p + 7) = 5$$
$$2p - 6p + 21 = 5$$
$$-4p = -16$$
$$p = 4$$

Now, substitute 4 for p in either of the given equations:

$$q = -2p + 7$$
$$= -2(4) + 7$$
$$= -1$$

The solution is $(p, q) = (4, -1)$. If the variables are not x and y, then you must also show the variables along with the ordered pair. This establishes which variable is associated with which number — here, $p = 4$ and $q = -1$.   □

LINEAR COMBINATION (ADDITION) METHOD

A third method for solving systems is termed the **linear combination method** (or, as it is often called, the **addition method**). The method involves substitution and the idea that if equal quantities are added to equal quantities, the resulting equation is equivalent to the original system. In general, addition will not simplify the system unless the numerical coefficients of one or more terms are opposites. However, you can often force them to be opposites by multiplying one or both of the given equations by nonzero constants.

LINEAR COMBINATION METHOD FOR SOLVING SYSTEMS
OF EQUATIONS

1. *Multiply* one or both of the equations by a constant or constants so that the coefficients of one of the variables become opposites.
2. *Add* corresponding members of the equations to obtain a new equation in a single variable.
3. *Solve* the derived equation for that variable.
4. *Substitute* the value found into either of the original equations, and solve for the second variable.
5. *State* the solution.

EXAMPLE 3.3   Linear combination method

Solve the following system by the linear combination method:

$$\begin{cases} 3x + 5y = -2 \\ 2x + 3y = 0 \end{cases}$$

Solution   Multiply **both sides** of the first equation by 2 and **both sides** of the second equation by -3. This procedure forces the coefficients of x to be opposites:

$$\begin{array}{c} 2 \\ -3 \end{array} \begin{cases} 3x + 5y = -2 \\ 2x + 3y = 0 \end{cases}$$

This means you should add the equations.

$$\begin{array}{c} \downarrow \\ + \end{array} \begin{cases} 6x + 10y = -4 \\ -6x - 9y = 0 \end{cases}$$
$$\overline{\qquad\qquad y = -4} \qquad \textit{Add the equations.}$$

If $y = -4$, then $2x + 3y = 0$ means that $2x + 3(-4) = 0$, which implies that $x = 6$. The solution is $(6, -4)$.   □

EXAMPLE 3.4   Method of substitution followed by addition

Solve the system

[SMH]   *This is from Example 1 of Section 11.8.*

$$\begin{cases} -2x = \lambda(1) \\ -2y = \lambda(1) \\ x + y = 1 \end{cases}.$$

Solution   We use substitution. Since the first and second equations are both equal to λ, they must be equal to each other, giving the system

$$\begin{cases} -2x = -2y \\ x + y = 1 \end{cases}$$

We write this system in standard form as

$$\begin{cases} 2x - 2y = 0 \\ x + y = 1 \end{cases}$$

or

$$+\begin{cases} x - y = 0 \\ x + y = 1 \end{cases}$$

We add the equations to obtain

$$2x = 1$$

$$x = \tfrac{1}{2}$$

By substitution, $\tfrac{1}{2} - y = 0$, or $y = \tfrac{1}{2}$. Finally, if $x = \tfrac{1}{2}$ and $y = \tfrac{1}{2}$, then that $\lambda = -2(\tfrac{1}{2}) = -1$. The solution is $x = \tfrac{1}{2}$, $y = \tfrac{1}{2}$, $\lambda = -1$. $\square$

3.2   Matrix Methods

One of the most common types of problems to which we can apply mathematics in a variety of different disciplines is the solution of systems of equations. In fact, common real-world problems require the simultaneous solution of systems involving 3, 4, 5, or even 20 or 100 unknowns. The methods of the previous section will not suffice, and, in practice, techniques that allow a computer or a calculator to help in solving systems are common. In this section, we introduce a general way of solving large systems of equations so that we can handle the solution of a system of m equations with n unknowns.

DEFINITION OF A MATRIX

Consider a system with unknowns x_1 and x_2. We use **subscripts** 1 and 2 to denote the unknowns, instead of using variables x and y, because we want to be able to handle n unknowns, which we can easily denote as $x_1, x_2, x_3, \cdots, x_n$; if we continued by using $x, y, z, \cdots$ for systems in general, we would soon run out of letters. Here is the way we will write a general system of two equations with two unknowns.

$$\begin{cases} a_{11}x_1 + a_{12}x_2 = b_1 \\ a_{21}x_1 + a_{22}x_2 = b_2 \end{cases}$$

The coefficients of the unknowns use **double subscripts** to denote their position in the system; a_{11} is used to denote the numerical coefficient of the first variable in the first row, a_{12} denotes the numerical coefficient of the second variable in the first row, and so on. The constants are denoted by b_1 and b_2.

We now separate the parts of this system of equations into *rectangular arrays* of numbers. An **array** of numbers is called a **matrix**. A matrix is denoted by enclosing the array in large brackets.

Let [A] be the matrix (array) of coefficients: $\begin{bmatrix} a_{11} & a_{12} \\ a_{21} & a_{22} \end{bmatrix}$.

Let [X] be the matrix of unknowns: $\begin{bmatrix} x_1 \\ x_2 \end{bmatrix}$.

Let [B] be the matrix of constants: $\begin{bmatrix} b_1 \\ b_2 \end{bmatrix}$.

We will write the system of equations as a **matrix equation**, [A][X] = [B], but before we do this, we need to do some preliminary work with matrices.

Matrices are classified by the number of (horizontal) **rows** and (vertical) **columns**. The numbers of rows and columns of a matrix need not be the same, but if they are, the matrix is called a **square matrix**.

The **order** or **dimension** of a matrix is given by an expression *m* × *n* (pronounced ''*m* by *n*''), where *m* is the number of rows and *n* is the number of columns. For example, the preceding matric [A] is a matrix of order 2×2, and matrices (plural for matrix) [X] and [B] have order 2×1.

MATRIX FORM OF A SYSTEM OF EQUATIONS

We write a system of equations in the form of an **augmented matrix**. The matrix refers to the matrix of coefficients, and we *augment* (add to, or affix) this matrix by writing the constant terms at the right of the matrix (separated by a dashed line):

$$\begin{cases} a_{11}x_1 + a_{12}x_2 = b_1 \\ a_{21}x_1 + a_{22}x_2 = b_2 \end{cases} \text{ in matrix form is } \left[\begin{array}{cc|c} a_{11} & a_{12} & b_1 \\ a_{21} & a_{22} & b_2 \end{array}\right]$$

GAUSS–JORDAN ELIMINATION

Gauss–Jordan elimination is a general method for solving all these types of systems. We write the system in augmented matrix form and then carry out a process that transforms the matrix until the solution is obvious.

ELEMENTARY ROW OPERATIONS AND PIVOTING

What process will allow us to transform a matrix into diagonal form? We begin with some steps called **elementary row operations**. Elementary row operations change the *form* of a matrix, but the new form represents an equivalent system. Matrices that represent equivalent systems are called **equivalent matrices**; we now introduce the elementary row operations, which allow us to write equivalent matrices. Let us work with a system consisting of three equations and three unknowns (any size will work the same way), for example,

$$\text{\textit{System format}} \qquad\qquad \text{\textit{Matrix format}}$$

$$\begin{cases} 2x - 2y + 4z = 14 \\ x - y - 2z = -9 \\ 3x + 2y + z = 16 \end{cases} \quad [A] = \begin{bmatrix} 2 & -2 & 4 & | & 14 \\ 1 & -1 & -2 & | & -9 \\ 3 & 2 & 1 & | & 16 \end{bmatrix}$$

For the discussion that follows, we call this matrix A and denote it by $[A]$.

Elementary Row Operation 1: RowSwap

Interchanging two equations is equivalent to interchanging two rows in the matrix format, and certainly, if we do this, the solution to the system will be the same:

$$\text{\textit{System format}} \qquad\qquad \text{\textit{Matrix format}}$$

$$\begin{cases} x - y - 2z = -9 \\ 2x - 2y + 4z = 14 \\ 3x + 2y + z = 16 \end{cases} \quad \begin{bmatrix} 1 & -1 & -2 & | & -9 \\ 2 & -2 & 4 & | & 14 \\ 3 & 2 & 1 & | & 16 \end{bmatrix}$$

In this example, we interchanged the first and the second rows of the matrix. If we denote the original matrix as $[A]$, then we indicate the operation of interchanging the first and second rows of matrix A by RowSwap($[A]$, 1, 2).

Elementary Row Operation 2: Row+

Since adding the entries of one equation to the corresponding entries (similar terms) of another equation will not change the solution of a system of equations, the second elementary row operation is called *row addition*. (The same step is called *linear combination* in the previous section.) In terms of matrices, we see that this operation corresponds to adding one row to another:

System format   *Matrix format*

$$\begin{cases} 2x - 2y + 4z = 14 \\ x - y - 2z = -9 \\ 3x + 2y + z = 16 \end{cases} \quad [A] = \begin{bmatrix} 2 & -2 & 4 & | & 14 \\ 1 & -1 & -2 & | & -9 \\ 3 & 2 & 1 & | & 16 \end{bmatrix}$$

Add row 1 to row 3:

System format   *Matrix format*

$$\begin{cases} 2x - 2y + 4z = 14 \\ x - y - 2z = -9 \\ 5x + 5z = 30 \end{cases} \quad \begin{bmatrix} 2 & -2 & 4 & | & 14 \\ 1 & -1 & -2 & | & -9 \\ 5 & 0 & 5 & | & 30 \end{bmatrix}$$

Notice that only row 3 changes; we call the row being added to (i.e., the row that is being changed) the **target row**. We indicate this operation by Row + ([A], 1, 3).

targetrow

Elementary Row Operation 3: *Row

Multiplying or dividing both sides of an equation by any nonzero number does not change the simultaneous solution; then, in matrix format, the solution will not be changed if any row is multiplied or divided by a nonzero constant. In this context, we call the constant a **scalar**. For example, we can multiply both sides of the first equation of the original system by $\frac{1}{2}$. (Note that dividing both sides of an equation by 2 can be considered as multiplying both sides by $\frac{1}{2}$.) The original system is

System format   *Matrix format*

$$\begin{cases} 2x - 2y + 4z = 14 \\ x - y - 2z = -9 \\ 3x + 2y + z = 16 \end{cases} \quad [A] = \begin{bmatrix} 2 & -2 & 4 & | & 14 \\ 1 & -1 & -2 & | & -9 \\ 3 & 2 & 1 & | & 16 \end{bmatrix}$$

Multiply the first row by $\frac{1}{2}$ to obtain

$$\begin{array}{cc} \textit{System format} & \textit{Matrix format} \\ \left\{\begin{array}{l} x - y + 2z = 7 \\ x - y - 2z = -9 \\ 3x + 2y + z = 16 \end{array}\right. & \left[\begin{array}{ccc|c} 1 & -1 & 2 & 7 \\ 1 & -1 & -2 & -9 \\ 3 & 2 & 1 & 16 \end{array}\right] \end{array}$$

We indicate this operation by *Row+($\frac{1}{2}$,[A], 1).

where the scalar is $\frac{1}{2}$ and the target row is 1.

Elementary Row Operation 4: *Row+

In solving systems, more often than not we need to multiply both sides of an equation by a scalar before adding to make the coefficients opposites. Elementary row operation 4 combines row operations 2 and 3 so that the two can be accomplished in one step. Let us return to the original system:

$$\begin{array}{cc} \textit{System format} & \textit{Matrix format} \\ \left\{\begin{array}{l} 2x - 2y + 4z = 14 \\ x - y - 2z = -9 \\ 3x + 2y + z = 16 \end{array}\right. \quad [A] = & \left[\begin{array}{ccc|c} 2 & -2 & 4 & 14 \\ 1 & -1 & -2 & -9 \\ 3 & 2 & 1 & 16 \end{array}\right] \end{array}$$

We can change this system by multiplying the second equation by -2 and adding the result to the first equation. In matrix terminology, we say that we multiply the second row by -2 and add it to the first row. We denote this by

$$*\text{Row} + (-2, [A], 2, 1)$$

where the scalar is -2 and the target row is 1.

$$\begin{array}{cc} \textit{System format} & \textit{Matrix format} \\ \left\{\begin{array}{l} 8z = 32 \\ x - y - 2z = -9 \\ 3x + 2y + z = 16 \end{array}\right. & \left[\begin{array}{ccc|c} 0 & 0 & 8 & 32 \\ 1 & -1 & -2 & -9 \\ 3 & 2 & 1 & 16 \end{array}\right] \end{array}$$

Once again, multiply the second row, this time by -3, and add it to the third row. Wait! Why -3? Where did that come from? The idea is the same one we used in the linear combination method: We use a number that will give a zero coefficient to the x in the third equation:

$$\begin{array}{cc} \textit{System format} & \textit{Matrix format} \\ \left\{\begin{array}{l} 8z = 32 \\ x - y - 2z = -9 \\ 5y + 7z = 43 \end{array}\right. & \left[\begin{array}{ccc|c} 0 & 0 & 8 & 32 \\ 1 & -1 & -2 & -9 \\ 0 & 5 & 7 & 43 \end{array}\right] \end{array}$$

Note that the multiplied row is not changed; instead, the changed row is the one to which the multiplied row is added. We call the original row the **pivot row**. Note also that we worked, not with the original matrix [A], but rather with the previous answer, so we indicate this by

$$*\text{Row} + (-\underset{\underset{\text{scalar}}{\uparrow}}{3}, [\text{Ans}], \underset{\underset{\text{target row}}{\uparrow}}{\overset{\overset{\text{pivot row}}{\downarrow}}{2}}, 3)$$

There you have it! You can carry out these four elementary operations until you have a system for which the solution is obvious, as illustrated by the next example.

EXAMPLE 3.5   Comparing system and matrix formats

Solve, using both system format and matrix format: $\begin{cases} 2x - 5y = 5 \\ x - 2y = 1 \end{cases}$.

Solution

System format	*Matrix format*	*Operation performed*
$\begin{cases} 2x - 5y = 5 \\ x - 2y = 1 \end{cases}$	$[A] = \begin{bmatrix} 2 & -5 & \mid & 5 \\ 1 & -2 & \mid & 1 \end{bmatrix}$	RowSwap([A], 1, 2)
$\begin{cases} x - 2y = 1 \\ 2x - 5y = 5 \end{cases}$	$\begin{bmatrix} 1 & -2 & \mid & 1 \\ 2 & -5 & \mid & 5 \end{bmatrix}$	This matrix is called [Ans] because it is the result of the previous operation. *Row + (−2, [Ans], 1, 2)
$\begin{cases} x - 2y = 1 \\ -y = 3 \end{cases}$	$\begin{bmatrix} 1 & -2 & \mid & 1 \\ 0 & -1 & \mid & 3 \end{bmatrix}$	This matrix is now referred to as [Ans]. *Row(−1,[Ans],2)
$\begin{cases} x - 2y = 1 \\ y = -3 \end{cases}$	$\begin{bmatrix} 1 & -2 & \mid & 1 \\ 0 & 1 & \mid & -3 \end{bmatrix}$	*Row+(2,[Ans],2,1)
$\begin{cases} x = -5 \\ y = -3 \end{cases}$	$\begin{bmatrix} 1 & 0 & \mid & -5 \\ 0 & 1 & \mid & -3 \end{bmatrix}$	

The solution $(-5, -3)$ is now obvious.   □

As you study Example 3.5, first look at how the elementary row operations led to a system equivalent to the first — but one for which the solution is obvious. The steps chosen in that example illustrate a very efficient method of using the elementary row operations to determine a system whose solution is obvious. Let us restate the elementary row operations and the operation called *pivoting*.

PIVOTING

There are four *elementary row operations* for producing equivalent matrices:

1. **RowSwap**   Interchange any two rows.
2. **Row+**   Row addition: Add a row to any other row.
3. ***Row**   Scalar multiplication: Multiply (or divide) all the elements of a row by the same nonzero real number.
4. ***Row+**   Multiply all the entries of a row (the **pivot row**) by a nonzero real number, and add each resulting product to the corresponding entry of another specified row (the **target row**).

This operation changes only the target row.

These elementary row operations are used together in a process called **pivoting**, in which we

1. divide all entries in the row in which the pivot appears (called the **pivot row**) by the nonzero pivot element so that the pivot entry becomes a 1. This procedure uses elementary row operation 3.
2. obtain zeros above and below the pivot element by using elementary row operation 4.

You are now ready to see the method worked out by Gauss and Jordan, known as **Gauss–Jordan elimination**. It efficiently uses the elementary row operations to diagonalize the matrix. That is, the first pivot is the first entry in the first row, first column; the second is the entry in the second row, second column; and so on, until the solution is obvious. A **pivot** element is an element that is used to eliminate elements above and below it in a given column by using elementary row operations.

GAUSS-JORDAN ELIMINATION

> *Step 1.* Select as the first pivot the element in the first row, first column, and pivot.
>
> *Step 2.* The next pivot is the element in the second row, second column; pivot.
>
> *Step 3.* Repeat the process until you arrive at the last row or until the pivot element is a zero. If it is a zero and you can interchange that row with a row below it, so that the pivot element is no longer a zero, do so and continue. If the pivot element is zero and you cannot interchange rows so that it is not a zero, continue with the next row. The final matrix is called the **row-reduced form**.

EXAMPLE 3.6   Gauss–Jordan method

Solve $\begin{cases} x + 2y - z = 0 \\ 2x + 3y - 2z = 3 \\ -x - 4y + 3z = -2 \end{cases}$.

Solution   We solve this system by choosing the steps according to the Gauss–Jordan method:

$$[A] = \begin{bmatrix} 1 & 2 & -1 & | & 0 \\ 2 & 3 & -2 & | & 3 \\ -1 & -4 & 3 & | & -2 \end{bmatrix} \quad \textbf{First pivot (row 1, col. 1)}$$

$$\rightarrow \begin{bmatrix} 1 & 2 & -1 & | & 0 \\ 0 & -1 & 0 & | & 3 \\ 0 & -2 & 2 & | & -2 \end{bmatrix} \quad \begin{array}{l} *\text{Row} + (-2, [A], 1, 2) \\ *\text{Row} + (1, [\text{Ans}], 1, 3) \end{array}$$

$$\rightarrow \begin{bmatrix} 1 & 2 & -1 & | & 0 \\ 0 & 1 & 0 & | & -3 \\ 0 & -2 & 2 & | & -2 \end{bmatrix} \quad *\text{Row}(-1, [\text{Ans}], 2)$$

Second pivot (row 2, col. 2)

$$\rightarrow \begin{bmatrix} 1 & 0 & -1 & | & 6 \\ 0 & 1 & 0 & | & -3 \\ 0 & 0 & 2 & | & -8 \end{bmatrix} \quad \begin{array}{l} *\text{Row} + (-2, [\text{Ans}], 2, 1) \\ *\text{Row} + (2, [\text{Ans}], 2, 3) \end{array}$$

$$\rightarrow \begin{bmatrix} 1 & 0 & -1 & | & 6 \\ 0 & 1 & 0 & | & -3 \\ 0 & 0 & 1 & | & -4 \end{bmatrix} \quad * \text{Row}(0.5, [\text{Ans}], 3)$$

Third pivot (row 3, col. 3)

$$\rightarrow \begin{bmatrix} 1 & 0 & 0 & | & 2 \\ 0 & 1 & 0 & | & -3 \\ 0 & 0 & 1 & | & -4 \end{bmatrix} \quad * \text{Row} + (1, [\text{Ans}], 3, 1)$$

The solution $(2, -3, -4)$ is found by inspection, since the last matrix represents the system

$$\begin{cases} 1x + 0y + 0z = 2 \\ 0x + 1y + 0z = -3 \\ 0x + 0y + 1z = -4 \end{cases} \qquad \Box$$

INVERSE MATRICES

The availability of computer software and calculators that can carry out matrix operations has considerably increased the importance of a matrix solution of systems of equations, which involves the inverse of a matrix. If [A] is a square matrix and if there exists a matrix $[A]^{-1}$ such that

$$[A]^{-1}[A] = [A][A]^{-1} = [I]$$

where [I] is the identity matrix for multiplication, then $[A]^{-1}$ is called the **inverse** of [A] for multiplication.

If we let [A] be the matrix of coefficients of a system of equations, [X] the matrix of unknowns, and [B] the matrix of constants, we can then represent the system of equations by the **matrix equation**

$$[A][X] = [B]$$

Note that $[A]^{-1}$ does not mean $\frac{1}{[A]}$, but rather means the inverse of matrix [A].

If we can define an inverse matrix, denoted by $[A]^{-1}$, we should be able to solve the *system* by finding

$$[X] = [A]^{-1}[B]$$

To understand this simple process, you need to understand what it means for matrices to be inverses and develop a basic algebra for matrices. This is done in other courses, but for this course we assume that you use a calculator or computer program to carry out basic matrix operations defined in the next box.

MATRIX OPERATIONS

Equality:
[M] = [N] if and only if matrices [M] and [N] are the same order and their corresponding entries are the same.

Addition:
[M] + [N] = [S] if and only if [M] and [N] are the same order and the entries of [S] are found by adding the corresponding entries of [M] and [N].

Multiplication by a scalar:
c[M] = [M]c is the matrix in which each entry of [M] is multiplied by the scalar (real number) c.

Subtraction:
[M] − [N] = [D] if and only if [M] and [N] are the same order and the entries of [D] are found by subtracting the entries of [N] from the corresponding entries of [M].

Multiplication:
Let [M] be an $m \times r$ matrix and [N] an $r \times n$ matrix. Then the product matrix [M][N] = [P] is an $m \times n$ matrix. The entry in the ith row and jth column of [M][N] is *the sum of the products formed by multiplying each entry of the ith row of* [M] *by the corresponding element in the jth column of* [N].

If an addition or multiplication cannot be performed because of the order of the given matrices, the matrices are said to be **nonconformable**.

EXAMPLE 3.7   Matrix operations

Let $[A] = [\begin{matrix} 5 & 2 & 1 \end{matrix}]$, $[B] = [\begin{matrix} 4 & 8 & -5 \end{matrix}]$, $[C] = \begin{bmatrix} 7 & 3 & 2 \\ 5 & -4 & -3 \end{bmatrix}$,

$[D] = \begin{bmatrix} 0 & 1 & 2 \\ 2 & -1 & 1 \\ -1 & 1 & 0 \end{bmatrix}$, and $E] = \begin{bmatrix} 3 & 4 & -1 \\ 2 & 0 & 5 \\ -4 & 2 & 3 \end{bmatrix}$. Find

a. [A] + [B]   **b.** [A] + [C]

c. [D] + [E]   **d.** (−5)[C]

e. 2[A] − 3[B]   **f.** [D][E]

g. [E][D]   **h.** $[D]^{-1}$

Solution

a. $[A] + [B] = [5\ 2\ 1] + [4\ 8\ -5]$

$$= [5+4 \quad 2+8 \quad 1+(-5)]$$

$$= [9 \quad 10 \quad -4]$$

b. [A] + [C] is not defined, because [A] and [C] are nonconformable.

c. $[D] + [E] = \begin{bmatrix} 0 & 1 & 2 \\ 2 & -1 & 1 \\ -1 & 1 & 0 \end{bmatrix} + \begin{bmatrix} 3 & 4 & -1 \\ 2 & 0 & 5 \\ -4 & 2 & 3 \end{bmatrix}$

$$= \begin{bmatrix} 3 & 5 & 1 \\ 4 & -1 & 6 \\ -5 & 3 & 3 \end{bmatrix}$$

Add, entry by entry.

d. $(-5)[C] = (-5) \begin{bmatrix} 7 & 3 & 2 \\ 5 & -4 & -3 \end{bmatrix}$

$$= \begin{bmatrix} -35 & -15 & -10 \\ -25 & 20 & 15 \end{bmatrix}$$

Multiply each entry by −5.

e. $2[A] - 3[B] = 2[5 \quad 2 \quad 1] + (-3)[4 \quad 8 \quad -5]$

$$= [10 \quad 4 \quad 2] + [-12 \quad -24 \quad 15]$$

$$= [-2 \quad -20 \quad 17]$$

f. $[D][E] = \begin{bmatrix} 0 & 1 & 2 \\ 2 & -1 & 1 \\ -1 & 1 & 0 \end{bmatrix} \begin{bmatrix} 3 & 4 & -1 \\ 2 & 0 & 5 \\ -4 & 2 & 3 \end{bmatrix}$

$$= \begin{bmatrix} 0+2-8 & 0+0+4 & 0+5+6 \\ 6-2-4 & 8+0+2 & -2+5+0 \\ -3+2+0 & -4+0+0 & 1+5+0 \end{bmatrix}$$

$$= \begin{bmatrix} -6 & 4 & 11 \\ 0 & 10 & 3 \\ -1 & -4 & 6 \end{bmatrix}$$

g. $[E][D] = \begin{bmatrix} 3 & 4 & -1 \\ 2 & 0 & 5 \\ -4 & 2 & 3 \end{bmatrix} \begin{bmatrix} 0 & 1 & 2 \\ 2 & -1 & 1 \\ -1 & 1 & 0 \end{bmatrix}$

$$= \begin{bmatrix} 0+8+1 & 3-4-1 & 6+4+0 \\ 0+0-5 & 2+0+5 & 4+0+0 \\ 0+4-3 & -4-2+3 & -8+2+0 \end{bmatrix}$$

$$= \begin{bmatrix} 9 & -2 & 10 \\ -5 & 7 & 4 \\ 1 & -3 & -6 \end{bmatrix}$$

Note: From parts **f** and **g**, we see that matrix multiplication is not commutative; that is, $[D][E] \neq [E][D]$.

h.   Using a calculator or a computer program, we find that

$$[D]^{-1} = \begin{bmatrix} -1 & 2 & 3 \\ -1 & 2 & 4 \\ 1 & -1 & -2 \end{bmatrix}$$

If a given matrix has an inverse, we say that the matrix is **nonsingular**.   □

INVERSE MATRIX METHOD

We can now see how to solve a system of linear equations by using the inverse. Consider a system of n linear equations with n unknowns whose matrix of coefficients $[A]$ has an inverse $[A]^{-1}$:

$$[A][X] = [B] \quad \textit{Given system}$$

$$[A]^{-1}[A][X] = [A]^{-1}[B] \quad \textit{Multiply both sides by } [A]^{-1}.$$

$$([A]^{-1}[A])[X] = [A]^{-1}[B] \quad \textit{Associative property}$$

$$[I][X] = [A]^{-1}[B] \quad \textit{Inverse property}$$

$$[X] = [A]^{-1}[B] \quad \textit{Identity property}$$

What this says: To solve a system of equations, look to see whether the number of equations is the same as the number of unknowns. If so, find the inverse of the matrix of the coefficients (if it exists), and multiply it (on the right) by the matrix of the constants.

EXAMPLE 3.8   Inverse matrix method

Solve $\begin{cases} y + 2z = 0 \\ 2x - y + z = -1 \\ y - x = 1 \end{cases}$.

Solution   Write the system in matrix form:

$$[A] = \begin{bmatrix} 0 & 1 & 2 \\ 2 & -1 & 1 \\ -1 & 1 & 0 \end{bmatrix}, \quad [X] = \begin{bmatrix} x \\ y \\ z \end{bmatrix}, \quad [B] = \begin{bmatrix} 0 \\ -1 \\ 1 \end{bmatrix}.$$

By calculator, $[A]^{-1} = \begin{bmatrix} -1 & 2 & 3 \\ -1 & 2 & 4 \\ 1 & -1 & -2 \end{bmatrix}$. Thus,

$$[X] = [A]^{-1}[B] = \begin{bmatrix} -1 & 2 & 3 \\ -1 & 2 & 4 \\ 1 & -1 & -2 \end{bmatrix} \begin{bmatrix} 0 \\ -1 \\ 1 \end{bmatrix} = \begin{bmatrix} 1 \\ 2 \\ -1 \end{bmatrix}$$

Therefore, the solution to the system is $(x, y, z) = (1, 2, -1)$.   □

3.3   Equality-of-Coefficients Method

In equating functions of some variable, say, x, a system of equations is sometimes used to find the values of several unknowns. For example, if

$$3x^4 + 5x^3 - 2x^2 + 1 = Ax^4 + Bx^3 + Cx^2 + Dx + E$$

then it follows that

$$A = 3, B = 5, C = -2, D = 0, \text{ and } E = 1$$

$\boxed{\text{s}^{\text{M}}\text{H}}$

Examples 1 and 2 in Section 7.4 of the text illustrate this procedure. The next example fills in the details for Example 3 in that section of the text.

EXAMPLE 3.9   Method of equal coefficients

Find the values for $A_1, A_2, B_1,$ and B_2, where

$$-3x^3 - x = (A_1x + B_1)(x^2 + 1) + (A_2x + B_2)$$

Solution

$$-3x^3 - x = A_1x^3 + A_1x + B_1x^2 + B_1 + A_2x + B_2$$
$$= A_1x^3 + B_1x^2 + (A_1 + A_2)x + (B_1 + B_2)$$

We equate the coefficients:

$$\begin{cases} -3 = A_1 \\ 0 = B_1 \\ -1 = A_1 + A_2 \\ 0 = B_1 + B_2 \end{cases}$$

We substitute the values from the first two equations into the second two equations to obtain

$$\begin{cases} -1 = -3 + A_2 & \text{or} \quad A_2 = 1 \\ 0 = 0 + B_2 & \text{or} \quad B_2 = 0 \end{cases}$$

Thus, $A_1 = -3, A_2 = 2, B_1 = 0,$ and $B_2 = 0$.   □

SMH   *There is an example of solving a nonlinear system in Example 4 of Section 11.8 of the text.*

3.4   PROBLEM SET 3

Solve the systems in Problems 1–30 for all real solutions, using any suitable method.

1. $\begin{cases} x + y = 7 \\ x - y = -1 \end{cases}$ 2. $\begin{cases} x - y = 8 \\ x + y = 2 \end{cases}$

3. $\begin{cases} -x + 2y = 2 \\ 4x - 7y = -5 \end{cases}$ 4. $\begin{cases} x - 6y = -3 \\ 2x + 3y = 9 \end{cases}$

5. $\begin{cases} y = 3x + 1 \\ x - 2y = 8 \end{cases}$ 6. $\begin{cases} 2x + 3y = 9 \\ x = 5y - 2 \end{cases}$

7. $\begin{cases} x + y = 4 \\ 2x + 3y = 9 \end{cases}$ 8. $\begin{cases} 3x + 4y = 8 \\ x + 2y = 2 \end{cases}$

9. $\begin{cases} 2x - y = 6 \\ 4x + y = 3 \end{cases}$ 10. $\begin{cases} 6x + 9y = -4 \\ 9x + 3y = 1 \end{cases}$

11. $\begin{cases} 5x - 2y = -1 \\ 3x + y = 17 \end{cases}$ 12. $\begin{cases} 5x + 4y = 9 \\ 9x + 3y = 12 \end{cases}$

13. $\begin{cases} 100x - y = 0 \\ 50x + y = 300 \end{cases}$ **14.** $\begin{cases} x = \frac{3}{4}y - 2 \\ 3y - 4x = 5 \end{cases}$

15. $\begin{cases} q + d = 147 \\ 0.25q + 0.10d = 24.15 \end{cases}$ **16.** $\begin{cases} x + y = 10 \\ 0.4x + 0.9y = 0.5(10) \end{cases}$

17. $\begin{cases} 12x - 5y = -39 \\ y = 2x + 9 \end{cases}$ **18.** $\begin{cases} y = 2x - 1 \\ y = -3x - 9 \end{cases}$

19. $\begin{cases} x - y = 1 \\ x + z = 1 \\ y - z = 1 \end{cases}$ **20.** $\begin{cases} x + y = 2 \\ x - z = 1 \\ -y + z = 1 \end{cases}$

21. $\begin{cases} x + 5z = 9 \\ y + 2z = 2 \\ 2x + 3z = 4 \end{cases}$ **22.** $\begin{cases} x + 2z = 13 \\ 2x + y = 8 \\ -2y + 9z = 41 \end{cases}$

23. $\begin{cases} 4x + y = -2 \\ 3x + 2z = -9 \\ 2y + 3z = -5 \end{cases}$ **24.** $\begin{cases} 5x + z = 9 \\ x - 5z = 7 \\ x + y - z = 0 \end{cases}$

25. $\begin{cases} x + y = -2 \\ y + z = 2 \\ x - y - z = -1 \end{cases}$ **26.** $\begin{cases} x + y = -1 \\ y + z = -1 \\ x + y + z = 1 \end{cases}$

27. $\begin{cases} x + 2z = 9 \\ 2x + y = 13 \\ 2y + z = 8 \end{cases}$ **28.** $\begin{cases} x + 2z = 0 \\ 3x - y + 2z = 0 \\ 4x + y = 6 \end{cases}$

29. $\begin{cases} -4x = \lambda \\ -2y = \lambda \\ -2z = \lambda \\ x + y + z = 1 \end{cases}$ **30.** $\begin{cases} -2A_1 = 2 \\ 2A_1 - 2A_2 = -4 \\ 2A_1 + A_2 - 2A_3 = 0 \end{cases}$

SMH   *From Example 2, Section 11.8.*   *From Example 1, Section 14.3.*

Solve the systems in Problems 31–35 by solving the corresponding matrix equation with an inverse if possible.

31. a. $\begin{cases} 4x - 7y = -2 \\ -x + 2y = 1 \end{cases}$ **b.** $\begin{cases} 4x - 7y = -65 \\ -x + 2y = 18 \end{cases}$

c. $\begin{cases} 4x - 7y = 48 \\ -x + 2y = -13 \end{cases}$ **d.** $\begin{cases} 4x - 7y = 2 \\ -x + 2y = 3 \end{cases}$

32. a. $\begin{cases} 8x + 6y = 12 \\ -2x + 4y = -14 \end{cases}$ **b.** $\begin{cases} 8x + 6y = 16 \\ -2x + 4y = 18 \end{cases}$

c. $\begin{cases} 8x + 6y = -6 \\ -2x + 4y = -26 \end{cases}$ d. $\begin{cases} 8x + 6y = -28 \\ -2x + 4y = 18 \end{cases}$

33. a. $\begin{cases} 2x + 3y = 9 \\ x - 6y = -3 \end{cases}$ b. $\begin{cases} 2x + 3y = 2 \\ x - 6y = 16 \end{cases}$

c. $\begin{cases} 2x + 3y = 2 \\ x - 6y = -14 \end{cases}$ d. $\begin{cases} 2x + 3y = 9 \\ x - 6y = 42 \end{cases}$

34. a. $\begin{cases} x + 2z = 7 \\ 2x + y = 16 \\ -2y + 9z = -3 \end{cases}$ b. $\begin{cases} x + 2z = 4 \\ 2x + y = 0 \\ -2y + 9z = 19 \end{cases}$

c. $\begin{cases} x + 2z = 4 \\ 2x + y = 0 \\ -2y + 9z = 31 \end{cases}$ d. $\begin{cases} x + 2z = 7 \\ 2x + y = 1 \\ -2y + 9z = 28 \end{cases}$

35. a. $\begin{cases} 6x + y + 20z = 27 \\ x - y = 0 \\ y + 3z = 4 \end{cases}$ b. $\begin{cases} 6x + y + 20z = 14 \\ x - y = 1 \\ y + 3z = 1 \end{cases}$

c. $\begin{cases} 6x + y + 20z = -12 \\ x - y = 6 \\ y + 3z = -7 \end{cases}$ d. $\begin{cases} 6x + y + 20z = 57 \\ x - y = 1 \\ y + 3z = 5 \end{cases}$

36. To control a certain type of crop disease, it is necessary to use 23 gal of chemical A and 34 gal of chemical B. The dealer can order commercial spray I, each container of which holds 5 gal of chemical A and 2 gal of chemical B, and commercial spray II, each container of which holds 2 gal of chemical A and 7 gal of chemical B. How many containers of each type of commercial spray should be used to obtain exactly the right proportion of chemicals needed?

37. A candy maker mixes chocolate, milk, and mint extract to produce three kinds of candy (I, II, and III) with the following proportions:

I: 7 lb chocolate, 5 gal milk, 1 oz mint extract
II: 3 lb chocolate, 2 gal milk, 2 oz mint extract
III: 4 lb chocolate, 3 gal milk, 3 oz mint extract

If 67 lb of chocolate, 48 gal of milk, and 32 oz of mint extract are available, how much of each kind of candy can be produced?

38. Using the data from Problem 37, how much of each type of candy can be produced with 62 lb of chocolate, 44 gal of milk, and 32 oz of mint extract?

CHAPTER 4
Review of Trigonometry

One of the prerequisites for calculus is trigonometry. You are reminded of this fact in Section 1.1 of your textbook. In this chapter, we provide a brief summary and review of ideas from trigonometry that are needed as you progress through your calculus course.

4.1 Trigonometric Functions

The geometric definition of an angle as two rays with an common endpoint (called the **vertex**) is sometimes referred to as a **geometric angle**. In higher mathematics, an **angle** is defined as the amount of rotation of a ray from one position, called its **initial side**, to another position, called its **terminal side**. If the rotation is in a counterclockwise direction, the angle is called a **positive angle**, and if the rotation is in a clockwise direction, the angle is called a **negative angle**. If a coordinate system is drawn so that the origin of the system is at the vertex of the angle and the positive x-axis coincides with the initial side, then the angle is said to be in **standard position**.

Let θ be any angle in standard position, and let $P(x, y)$ be any point on the terminal side of the angle a distance r from the origin ($r \neq 0$). Then

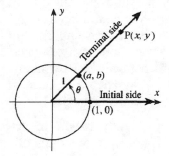

Standard position angle

$$\cos\theta = \frac{x}{r} \qquad \sin\theta = \frac{y}{r} \qquad \tan\theta = \frac{y}{x}$$

$$\sec\theta = \frac{r}{x} \qquad \csc\theta = \frac{r}{y} \qquad \cot\theta = \frac{x}{y}$$

RADIANS AND DEGREES

$360° = 2\pi$ radians $= 1$ revolution

$$1 \text{ radian} = \left(\frac{180}{\pi}\right)^{\circ} \approx 57.2957\cdots \text{ degrees}$$

$$1 \text{ degree} = \left(\frac{\pi}{180}\right) \approx 0.0174532\cdots \text{ radian}$$

Angle measures, unless stated otherwise, are in radian measure. For example, an angle of 6 means that the angle has a measure of 6 **radians**, whereas if you want to denote an angle with measure of six degrees, then the word **degrees** or the degree symbol, as in 6°, must be stated.

In calculus, it is often necessary to determine when a given function is not defined. For example, in Problem 22 of Problem Set 1.1 in the textbook, we need to know when

$$f(x) = (3 \tan x + \sqrt{3})(3 \tan x - \sqrt{3})$$

is not defined. From the given definitions of the trigonometric functions, $f\left(\dfrac{\pi}{2}\right)$ is not defined, since $\tan x$ is not defined for $x = \dfrac{\pi}{2}$ (or for any odd multiple of $\dfrac{\pi}{2}$).

4.2   Inverse Trigonometric Functions

Inverse Function	Domain	Range
$y = \arccos x$, or $y = \cos^{-1} x$	$-1 \le x \le 1$	$0 \le y \le \pi$
$y = \arcsin x$, or $y = \sin^{-1} x$	$-1 \le x \le 1$	$-\dfrac{\pi}{2} \le y \le \dfrac{\pi}{2}$
$y = \arctan x$, or $y = \tan^{-1} x$	All reals	$-\dfrac{\pi}{2} < y < \dfrac{\pi}{2}$
$y = \text{arccot}\, x$, or $y = \cot^{-1} x$	All reals	$0 < y < \pi$
$y = \text{arcsec}\, x$, or $y = \sec^{-1} x$	$\|x\| \ge 1$	$0 \le y \le \pi, y \ne \dfrac{\pi}{2}$
$y = \text{arccsc}\, x$, or $y = \csc^{-1} x$	$\|x\| \ge 1$	$-\dfrac{\pi}{2} \le y \le \dfrac{\pi}{2}, y \ne 0$

The principal values of the inverse trigonometric functions are those values defined by these inverse trigonometric functions. The principal values are the values obtained from a calculator.

4.3   Evaluating Trigonometric Functions

REDUCTION PRINCIPLE

If t represents any of the six trigonometric functions, then $t(\theta) = \pm t(\theta')$, where the sign depends on the quadrant and θ' is the reference angle of θ.

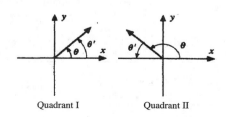

Quadrant I   Quadrant II

All of the trigonometric functions are positive in the first quadrant, sine and cosecant are positive in the second quadrant, tangent and cotangent are positive in the third quadrant, and cosine and secant are positive in the fourth quadrant.

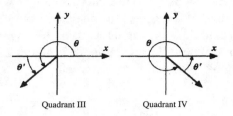

Quadrant III   Quadrant IV

BY CALCULATOR

$\cos\theta$ $\boxed{\theta}$ $\boxed{\cos}$ $\sec\theta$ $\boxed{\theta}$ $\boxed{\sin}$ $\boxed{1/x}$ $\cos^{-1}\theta$ $\boxed{\theta}$ $\boxed{\text{inv}}$ $\boxed{\cos}$

$\sec^{-1}\theta$ $\boxed{\theta}$ $\boxed{1/x}$ $\boxed{\text{inv}}$ $\boxed{\cos}$

$\sin\theta$ $\boxed{\theta}$ $\boxed{\sin}$ $\csc\theta$ $\boxed{\theta}$ $\boxed{\sin}$ $\boxed{1/x}$ $\sin^{-1}\theta$ $\boxed{\theta}$ $\boxed{\text{inv}}$ $\boxed{\sin}$

$\csc^{-1}\theta$ $\boxed{\theta}$ $\boxed{1/x}$ $\boxed{\text{inv}}$ $\boxed{\sin}$

$\tan\theta$ $\boxed{\theta}$ $\boxed{\tan}$ $\cot\theta$ $\boxed{\theta}$ $\boxed{\tan}$ $\boxed{1/x}$ $\tan^{-1}\theta$ $\boxed{\theta}$ $\boxed{\text{inv}}$ $\boxed{\tan}$

$\cot^{-1}\theta$:

if $\theta > 0$; $\boxed{\theta}$ $\boxed{1/x}$ $\boxed{\text{inv}}$ $\boxed{\tan}$

if $\theta < 0$; $\boxed{\theta}$ $\boxed{1/x}$ $\boxed{\text{inv}}$ $\boxed{\tan}$ $\boxed{+}$ $\boxed{\pi}$ $\boxed{=}$

BY TABLE

Angle θ	0	$\dfrac{\pi}{6}$	$\dfrac{\pi}{4}$	$\dfrac{\pi}{3}$	$\dfrac{\pi}{2}$	π	$\dfrac{3\pi}{2}$
$\cos\theta$	1	$\dfrac{\sqrt{3}}{2}$	$\dfrac{\sqrt{2}}{2}$	$\dfrac{1}{2}$	0	-1	0
$\sin\theta$	0	$\dfrac{1}{2}$	$\dfrac{\sqrt{2}}{2}$	$\dfrac{\sqrt{3}}{2}$	1	0	-1
$\tan\theta$	0	$\dfrac{\sqrt{3}}{3}$	1	$\sqrt{3}$	undefined	0	undefined
$\sec\theta$	1	$\dfrac{2}{\sqrt{3}}$	$\dfrac{2}{\sqrt{2}}$	2	undefined	-1	undefined
$\csc\theta$	undefined	2	$\dfrac{2}{\sqrt{2}}$	$\dfrac{2}{\sqrt{3}}$	1	undefined	-1
$\cot\theta$	undefined	$\sqrt{3}$	1	$\dfrac{1}{\sqrt{3}}$	0	undefined	0

$\boxed{\text{sMH}}$

Knowledge of these exact values is assumed in calculus.

$\boxed{\text{sMh}}$ *This table of exact values can be extended by using one or more of the trigonometric identities listed in Section 4.5 of this handbook. The next example is similar to Problems 43–46 in Problem Set 1.1.*

EXAMPLE 4.1   Exact values

Find the exact value of $\sin\left(-\dfrac{5\pi}{12}\right)$.

Solution   First, use the reduction principle to write

$$\sin\left(-\frac{5\pi}{12}\right) = -\sin\frac{\pi}{12}$$

↑

Negative because the angle is in Quadrant III

Then, notice that, since $\dfrac{\pi}{12} = 15° = 45° - 30°$, we have $\dfrac{\pi}{12} = \dfrac{\pi}{4} - \dfrac{\pi}{6}$. Thus,

$$-\sin\frac{\pi}{12} = -\sin\left(\frac{\pi}{4} - \frac{\pi}{6}\right)$$

$$= -\left[\sin\frac{\pi}{4}\cos\frac{\pi}{6} - \cos\frac{\pi}{4}\sin\frac{\pi}{6}\right] \qquad \textit{Identity 18}$$

$$= -\left[\frac{\sqrt{2}}{2}\cdot\frac{\sqrt{3}}{2} - \frac{\sqrt{2}}{2}\cdot\frac{1}{2}\right]$$

$$= -\left[\frac{\sqrt{6} - \sqrt{2}}{4}\right]$$

$$= \frac{\sqrt{2} - \sqrt{6}}{4} \qquad\qquad\qquad \square$$

4.4   Trigonometric Graphs

TRIGONOMETRIC FUNCTIONS

Cosine $y = \cos x$

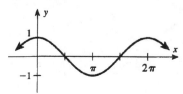

Sine $y = \sin x$

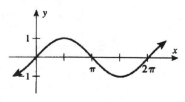

Secant $y = \sec x$

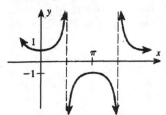

Cosecant $y = \csc x$

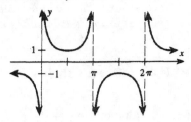

Tangent $y = \tan x$

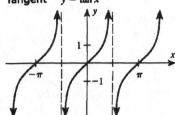

Cotangent $y = \cot x$

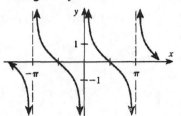

INVERSE TRIGONOMETRIC FUNCTIONS

Arccosine $y = \text{Cos}^{-1}x$

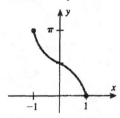

Arcsine $y = \text{Sin}^{-1}x$

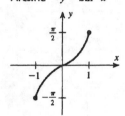

Arcsecant $y = \text{Sec}^{-1}x$

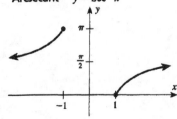

Arccosecant $y = \text{Csc}^{-1}x$

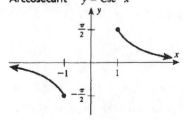

Arctangent $y = \text{Tan}^{-1}x$

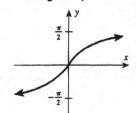

Arccotangent $y = \text{Cot}^{-1}x$

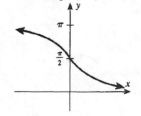

GENERAL TRIGONOMETRIC GRAPHS

SMH *You are expected to be able to graph trigonometric functions. Problem Set 1.1 (Problems 51–56) and Problem Set 4 (Problems 12–21) should give you some practice.* To graph a general trigonometric curve, begin by drawing a frame:

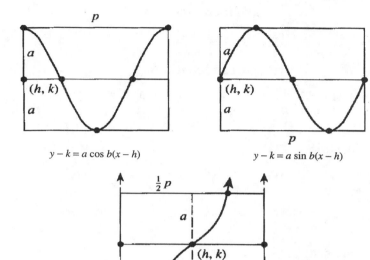

$$y - k = a \cos b(x - h)$$

$$y - k = a \sin b(x - h)$$

$$y - k = a \tan b(x - h)$$

1. Algebraically, put the equation into one of the preceding general forms.
2. Identify (by inspection) the following values: (h, k), a, and b. Then calculate $p = \dfrac{2\pi}{b}$ for the cosine and sine and $p = \dfrac{\pi}{b}$ for the tangent.
3. Draw a frame:
   a. Plot (h, k); this is the starting point.
   b. Draw a; the *height of the frame* is $2|a|$, up and down a units from (h, k).
   c. Draw p, the *length of the frame*.
4. Plot the endpoints, midpoints, and quarter points for each curve as shown in the illustrations. You do not need to know the coordinates of these points. Draw a sketch of the curve, using the plotted points.

4.5   Trigonometric Identities

Fundamental identities

Reciprocal identities

1. $\sec\theta = \dfrac{1}{\cos\theta}$ **2.** $\csc\theta = \dfrac{1}{\sin\theta}$ **3.** $\cot\theta = \dfrac{1}{\tan\theta}$

Ratio identities

4. $\tan\theta = \dfrac{\sin\theta}{\cos\theta}$ **5.** $\cot\theta = \dfrac{\cos\theta}{\sin\theta}$

Pythagorean identities

6. $\cos^2\theta + \sin^2\theta = 1$ **7.** $1 + \tan^2\theta = \sec^2\theta$

8. $\cot^2\theta + 1 = \csc^2\theta$

Cofunction identities

9. $\cos\left(\dfrac{\pi}{2} - \theta\right) = \sin\theta$ **10.** $\sin\left(\dfrac{\pi}{2} - \theta\right) = \cos\theta$

11. $\tan\left(\dfrac{\pi}{2} - \theta\right) = \cot\theta$

Opposite-angle identities

12. $\cos(-\theta) = \cos\theta$ **13.** $\sin(-\theta) = -\sin\theta$

14. $\tan(-\theta) = -\tan\theta$

Addition laws

15. $\cos(\alpha + \beta) = \cos\alpha\cos\beta - \sin\alpha\sin\beta$

16. $\cos(\alpha - \beta) = \cos\alpha\cos\beta + \sin\alpha\sin\beta$

17. $\sin(\alpha + \beta) = \sin\alpha\cos\beta + \cos\alpha\sin\beta$

18. $\sin(\alpha - \beta) = \sin\alpha\cos\beta - \cos\alpha\sin\beta$

19. $\tan(\alpha + \beta) = \dfrac{\tan\alpha + \tan\beta}{1 - \tan\alpha\tan\beta}$

20. $\tan(\alpha - \beta) = \dfrac{\tan\alpha - \tan\beta}{1 + \tan\alpha\tan\beta}$

Double-angle identities

21. $\cos 2\theta = \cos^2\theta - \sin^2\theta$ **22.** $\sin 2\theta = 2\sin\theta\cos\theta$

$\qquad\qquad = 2\cos^2\theta - 1$

$\qquad\qquad = 1 - 2\sin^2\theta$

23. $\tan 2\theta = \dfrac{2\tan\theta}{1 - \tan^2\theta}$

Half-angle identities

24. $\cos \frac{1}{2}\theta = \pm\sqrt{\dfrac{1+\cos\theta}{2}}$ **25.** $\sin \frac{1}{2}\theta = \pm\sqrt{\dfrac{1-\cos\theta}{2}}$

26. $\tan \frac{1}{2}\theta = \dfrac{1-\cos\theta}{\sin\theta}$

$\phantom{\tan \frac{1}{2}\theta} = \dfrac{\sin\theta}{1+\cos\theta}$

Product-to-sum identities

27. $2\cos\alpha\cos\beta = \cos(\alpha-\beta)+\cos(\alpha+\beta)$
28. $2\sin\alpha\sin\beta = \cos(\alpha-\beta)-\cos(\alpha+\beta)$
29. $2\sin\alpha\cos\beta = \sin(\alpha+\beta)+\sin(\alpha-\beta)$
30. $2\cos\alpha\sin\beta = \sin(\alpha+\beta)-\sin(\alpha-\beta)$

Sum-to-product identities

31. $\cos\alpha+\cos\beta = 2\cos\left(\dfrac{\alpha+\beta}{2}\right)\cos\left(\dfrac{\alpha-\beta}{2}\right)$

32. $\cos\alpha-\cos\beta = -2\sin\left(\dfrac{\alpha+\beta}{2}\right)\sin\left(\dfrac{\alpha-\beta}{2}\right)$

33. $\sin\alpha+\sin\beta = 2\sin\left(\dfrac{\alpha+\beta}{2}\right)\cos\left(\dfrac{\alpha-\beta}{2}\right)$

34. $\sin\alpha-\sin\beta = 2\sin\left(\dfrac{\alpha-\beta}{2}\right)\cos\left(\dfrac{\alpha+\beta}{2}\right)$

Hyperbolic identities

35. $\operatorname{sech} x = \dfrac{1}{\cosh x}$ **36.** $\operatorname{csch} x = \dfrac{1}{\sinh x}$

37. $\coth x = \dfrac{1}{\tanh x}$ **38.** $\tanh x = \dfrac{\sinh x}{\cosh x}$

39. $\coth x = \dfrac{\cosh x}{\sinh x}$ **40.** $\cosh^2 x - \sinh^2 x = 1$

41. $1 - \tanh^2 x = \operatorname{sech}^2 x$ **42.** $\coth^2 x - 1 = \operatorname{csch}^2 x$

43. $\sinh(-x) = -\sinh x$ **44.** $\cosh(-x) = \cosh x$

45. $\tanh(-x) = -\tanh x$

46. $\sinh(x \pm y) = \sinh x \cosh y \pm \cosh x \sinh y$

47. $\cosh(x \pm y) = \cosh x \cosh y \pm \sinh x \sinh y$

48. $\tanh(x \pm y) = \dfrac{\tanh x \pm \tanh y}{1 \pm \tanh x \tanh y}$

49. $\cosh 2x = \cosh^2 x + \sinh^2 x$

$$= 2\cosh^2 x - 1$$

$$= 1 + 2\sinh^2 x$$

50. $\sinh 2x = 2\sinh x \cosh x$

51. $\tanh 2x = \dfrac{2\tanh x}{1 + \tanh^2 x}$

52. $\cosh \frac{1}{2}x = \pm\sqrt{\dfrac{\cosh x + 1}{2}}$

53. $\sinh \frac{1}{2}x = \pm\sqrt{\dfrac{\cosh x - 1}{2}}$

54. $\tanh \frac{1}{2}x = \dfrac{\cosh x - 1}{\sinh x} = \dfrac{\sinh x}{\cosh x + 1}$

55. $\sinh^{-1} x = \ln(x + \sqrt{x^2 + 1})$

56. $\operatorname{csch}^{-1} x = \ln\left(\dfrac{1 + \sqrt{1 + x^2}}{x}\right)$ if $x > 0$

57. $\cosh^{-1} x = \ln(x + \sqrt{x^2 - 1})$

58. $\operatorname{sech}^{-1} x = \ln\left(\dfrac{1 + \sqrt{1 - x^2}}{x}\right)$ if $0 < x \le 1$

59. $\tanh^{-1} x = \frac{1}{2}\ln\left(\dfrac{1 + x}{1 - x}\right)$ if $-1 < x < 1$

60. $\coth^{-1} x = \frac{1}{2}\ln\left(\dfrac{x + 1}{x - 1}\right)$ if $x^2 > 1$

[SMH] *The following example is similar to Problems 25–30 in Problem Set 1.4 and Problems 32–33 of Problem Set 4.*

EXAMPLE 4.2   Finding an exact value

Find the exact value of $\sin\left(\cos^{-1}\frac{5}{6}\right)$.

Solution   Let $\alpha = \cos^{-1}\frac{5}{6}$, so that $\cos\alpha = \frac{5}{6}$. We restate the given trigonometric expression as

$$\sin\left(\cos^{-1}\tfrac{5}{6}\right) = \sin\alpha$$

$$= \pm\sqrt{1 - \cos^2\alpha} \quad \textit{Since } \sin^2\alpha + \cos^2\alpha = 1$$

$$= +\sqrt{1 - \left(\frac{5}{6}\right)^2} \quad \begin{array}{l}\textit{Positive, since the inverse}\\ \textit{cosine is positive in Quadrant I.}\end{array}$$

$$= \sqrt{\frac{36}{36} - \frac{25}{36}}$$

$$= \frac{\sqrt{11}}{6} \qquad\qquad\qquad\qquad\qquad\qquad \square$$

4.6   Solving Triangles

The following results hold for any plane triangle ABC with sides a, b, c and angles α, β, γ.

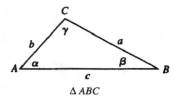

$\triangle ABC$

Pythagorean theorem

In a right triangle with right angle at C,
$c^2 = a^2 + b^2$

Law of cosines

$$a^2 = b^2 + c^2 - 2bc\cos\alpha \qquad\qquad b^2 = a^2 + c^2 - 2ac\cos\beta$$

$$\cos\alpha = \frac{b^2 + c^2 - a^2}{2bc} \qquad\qquad \cos\beta = \frac{a^2 + c^2 - b^2}{2ac}$$

$$c^2 = a^2 + b^2 - 2ab\cos\gamma$$

$$\cos\gamma = \frac{a^2 + b^2 - c^2}{2ab}$$

Law of sines

$$\frac{\sin\alpha}{a} = \frac{\sin\beta}{b} = \frac{\sin\gamma}{c}$$

Law of tangents

$$\frac{a+b}{a-b} = \frac{\tan\frac{1}{2}(\alpha+\beta)}{\tan\frac{1}{2}(\alpha-\beta)}$$

with similar relations involving the other sides and angles

AREA FORMULAS

Two sides and the included angle are known:

$$\text{Area} = \tfrac{1}{2}ab \sin \gamma = \tfrac{1}{2}ac \sin \beta = \tfrac{1}{2}bc \sin \alpha$$

Two angles and the included side are known:

$$\text{Area} = \frac{a^2 \sin \beta \sin \gamma}{2 \sin \alpha} = \frac{b^2 \sin \alpha \sin \gamma}{2 \sin \beta} = \frac{c^2 \sin \alpha \sin \beta}{2 \sin \gamma}$$

Three sides are known:

$$\text{Area} = \sqrt{s(s-a)(s-b)(s-c)}, \text{ where } s = \tfrac{1}{2}(a+b+c)$$

Area of a sector

$$\text{Area} = \tfrac{1}{2}\theta r^2 \text{ for central angle } \theta$$

PROCEDURE FOR SOLVING TRIANGLES

Given	Conditions on the given information	Method of Solution
1. AAA		No solution
2. SSS	**More than one side given:**	**Law of Cosines**
	a. The sum of the lengths of the two smaller sides is less than or equal to the length of the larger side.	No solution
	b. The sum of the lengths of the two smaller sides is greater than the length of the larger side.	Law of Cosines
3. SAS	**a.** The given angle is greater than or equal to 180°.	No solution
	b. The given angle is less than 180°.	Law of Cosines
3. SSA	**a.** The given angle is greater than or equal to 180°.	No solution
	b. There are no solutions, one solution, or two solutions, as determined by the quadratic formula.	Law of Cosines

4. ASA or AAS	**More than one angle given:**	**Law of Sines**
	a. The sum of the given angles is greater than or equal to 180°.	No solution
	b. The sum of the given angles is less than 180°.	**Law of Sines**

4.7 Trigonometric Equations

[SMH] *You will find a couple of these in Problem Set 1.1 of the text.*

PROCEDURE FOR SOLVING TRIGONOMETRIC EQUATIONS

1. Solve for a single trigonometric function. You may use trigonometric identities, factoring, or the quadratic formula.
2. Solve for the angle. You will use the definitions of the inverse trigonometric functions for this step.
3. Solve for the unknown.

PRINCIPAL VALUES

EXAMPLE 4.3   Linear trigonometric equation

Solve the equations for the principal value of θ. Compare the solutions of these similar problems.

a. $5\sin(\theta + 1) = \frac{1}{2}$ 　　　　　**b.** $\sin 5(\theta + 1) = \frac{1}{2}$

Solution

a. $5\sin(\theta + 1) = \frac{1}{2}$

$\sin(\theta + 1) = \dfrac{1}{10}$ 　　　　*Solve for the function*

$\theta + 1 = \sin^{-1} 0.1$ 　　　　*Solve for the angle*

$\theta = -1 + \sin^{-1} 0.1$ 　　*Solve for the unknown*

≈ -0.8998326 　　*We use radians (real numbers) unless otherwise specified*

b. $\sin 5(\theta + 1) = \frac{1}{2}$ *The equation is solved for*
the function

$$5(\theta + 1) = \sin^{-1}\left(\tfrac{1}{2}\right)$$ *Solve for the angle*

$$5\theta = -5 + \frac{\pi}{6}$$ *Solve for the unknown*

$$= -1 + \frac{\pi}{30}$$

$$\approx -0.8952802$$

Notice that these two answers are *not* the same.   □

EXAMPLE 4.4   Quadratic trigonometric equation by factoring

Find the principal values of θ for $15\cos^2\theta - 2\cos\theta - 8 = 0$.

Solution

$$15\cos^2\theta - 2\cos\theta - 8 = 0$$

$$(3\cos\theta + 2)(5\cos\theta - 4) = 0 \quad \textit{Factor if possible}$$

The last equation is solved by setting each factor equal to zero (factor theorem):

$3\cos\theta + 2 = 0$ $5\cos\theta - 4 = 0$

$\cos\theta = -\dfrac{2}{3}$ $\cos\theta = \dfrac{4}{5}$

$\theta = \cos^{-1}\left(-\dfrac{2}{3}\right)$ $\theta = \cos^{-1}\left(\dfrac{4}{5}\right)$

≈ 2.300524 ≈ 0.6435011 □

EXAMPLE 4.5   Quadratic trigonometric equation by quadratic formula

Find the principal values of θ for $\tan^2\theta - 5\tan\theta - 4 = 0$.

Solution

$$\tan^2\theta - 5\tan\theta - 4 = 0 \quad \textit{Factor if possible}$$

$$\tan\theta = \frac{5 \pm \sqrt{25 - 4(1)(-4)}}{2}$$

$$= \frac{5 \pm \sqrt{41}}{2} \qquad \textit{Quadratic formula if the}$$
$$\textit{equation cannot be factored}$$

$$\theta = \tan^{-1}\left(\frac{5 \pm \sqrt{41}}{2}\right)$$

$$\approx \tan^{-1}(5.7015621), \tan^{-1}(-0.7015621)$$

$$\approx 1.3971718, -0.6117736 \qquad \square$$

GENERAL SOLUTION

The procedure for finding the general solution of a trigonometric equation is to first find the reference angle, by using the table of exact values or a calculator. Then find two values less than one revolution apart, using the reference angle:

For $y = \arccos x$ or $y = \text{arcsec } x$,
    if y is positive, then the inverse function is in Quadrants I and IV
    if y is negative, then the inverse function is in Quadrants II and III

For $y = \arcsin x$ or $y = \text{arccsc } x$,
    if y is positive, then the inverse function is in Quadrants I and II
    if y is negative, then the inverse function is in Quadrants III and IV

For $y = \arctan x$ or $y = \text{arccot } x$,
    if y is positive, then the inverse function is in Quadrants I and III
    if y is negative, then the inverse function is in Quadrants II and IV

The foregoing information is summarized in Figure 4.1.
    After you have found the two values less than one revolution apart, the entire solution is found by using the period of the function:

    For cosine, sine, secant and cosecant: add multiples of 2π
    For tangent and cotangent: add multiples of π

EXAMPLE 4.6   General linear trigonometric equation

a. Solve $\cos \theta = \frac{1}{2}$.   **b.** Solve $\cos \theta = -\frac{1}{2}$.

Sine and cosecant positive	**A**ll positive
Tangent and cotangent positive	**C**osine and secant positive

Figure 4.1   Signs of the trigonometric functions

94   Chapter 4

Solution

a. Reference angle $\theta' = \operatorname{Arccos} \left| \frac{1}{2} \right| = \frac{\pi}{3}$; angles less than one revolution apart with a reference angle of $\frac{\pi}{3}$ are $\frac{\pi}{3}$ (Quadrant I) and $\frac{5\pi}{3}$ (Quadrant IV). The solution is infinite, so to find all solutions, add multiples of 2π to these values: $\theta = \frac{\pi}{3} + 2k\pi, \frac{5\pi}{3} + 2k\pi$, for any integral value of k.

b. $\theta' = \operatorname{Arccos} \left| -\frac{1}{2} \right| = \frac{\pi}{3}$. Reference angle is in Quadrants II and III: $\theta = \frac{2\pi}{3} + 2k\pi, \frac{4\pi}{3} + 2k\pi$. $\square$

EXAMPLE 4.7   Approximate values of a linear trigonometric function

Solve $\sin x = \frac{2}{\pi}$ for $0 \le x \le 2\pi$.

Solution $x = \operatorname{Arcsin} \left(\frac{2}{\pi} \right) \approx 0.6901071$. The solution is in Quadrants I and II $\left(\frac{2}{\pi} \text{ is positive} \right)$: $x \approx 0.6901071, 2.4514856$. $\square$

EXAMPLE 4.8   Trigonometric equation using an identity

Solve $-\frac{1}{2} \cos 2t = -2 \sin t$.

Solution

$$-\tfrac{1}{2} \cos 2t = -2 \sin t$$
$$\cos 2t = 4 \sin t$$
$$1 - 2 \sin^2 t = 4 \sin t$$
$$2 \sin^2 t + 4 \sin t - 1 = 0$$
$$\sin t = \frac{-4 \pm \sqrt{4^2 - 4(2)(-1)}}{2(2)}$$
$$= \frac{-4 \pm 2\sqrt{6}}{4}$$
$$= \frac{-2 \pm \sqrt{6}}{2}$$

$$\approx 0.2247448714, -2.224744871$$

$$\uparrow$$

$$\text{Reject } (\sin t \geq -1)$$

$$t \approx \text{Arcsin}(0.227448714)$$

$$\approx 0.2266812, 2.914911452 \qquad \square$$

4.8   PROBLEM SET 4

Find the radian measure of each angle in Problems 1–4.

1. $\theta = 6°$ **2.** $\theta = 270°$ **3.** $\theta = 100°$ **4.** $\theta = 2\pi°$

Find the degree measure of each angle in Problems 5–8.

5. $\theta = \dfrac{2\pi}{3}$ **6.** $\theta = \dfrac{n\pi}{4}$ **7.** $\theta = 4.2$ **8.** $\theta = 120$

9. Evaluate: **a.** $\cos \pi$ **b.** $\cos \dfrac{3\pi}{2}$

   c. $\cos 2\pi$ **d.** $\sin \pi$ **e.** $\sin \dfrac{3\pi}{2}$

10. Evaluate: **a.** $\sin \dfrac{3\pi}{4}$ **b.** $\cos \dfrac{3\pi}{4}$

   c. $\sin \dfrac{5\pi}{4}$ **d.** $\cos \dfrac{5\pi}{4}$ **e.** $\sin 2\pi$

11. Find $\sin^2\left(\dfrac{7\pi x}{8}\right) + \cos^2\left(\dfrac{7\pi x}{8}\right)$.

Graph the functions in Problems 12–21.

12. $f(x) = \sin\left(x - \dfrac{\pi}{3}\right)$ **13.** $f(x) = 3 \sin x$

14. $y - 2 = \sin\left(x - \dfrac{\pi}{2}\right)$ **15.** $y - 1 = 2 \cos\left(x - \dfrac{\pi}{4}\right)$

16. $f(x) = 2 \cos(3x + 2\pi) - 2$ **17.** $f(x) = \tan\left(x + \dfrac{\pi}{4}\right) - 2$

18. $y - 3 = \sin(\pi - x)$ **19.** $y + 1 = -\tan\left(x - \dfrac{\pi}{6}\right)$

20. $f(x) = 2 \sec(x + 1)$ **21.** $f(x) = 2 \cot\left(x - \dfrac{\pi}{6}\right) - 1$

In Problems 22–25, use the addition formulas to find the exact value.

22. $\cos(75°) = \cos(45° + 30°)$ **23.** $\sin 15°$
24. $\sin(105°) = \sin(60° + 45°)$ **25.** $\sin 195°$
26. Show that $\sin 2x = 2 \sin x \cos x$
27. Show that, for any integer n, $\sin(x + n\pi) = (-1)^n \sin x$
28. Show that, for any integer n, $\cos(x + n\pi) = (-1)^n \cos x$
29. Show that $2 \sin x \cos y = \sin(x + y) + \sin(x - y)$
30. Show that $2 \cos x \sin y = \sin(x + y) - \sin(x - y)$

96   Chapter 4

31. Use the result of Problem 29 to show that

$$\sin A + \sin B = 2 \sin \left(\frac{A+B}{2}\right) \cos \left(\frac{A-B}{2}\right)$$

32. If $\sin^{-1}\frac{1}{5}$ is the angle whose sine is $\frac{1}{5}$ and $\cos^{-1}\frac{1}{5}$ is the angle whose cosine is $\frac{1}{5}$, find the exact value of

$$\cos \left(\sin^{-1}\frac{1}{5} + 2\cos^{-1}\frac{1}{5}\right)$$

[SMH] *From Problem Set 1.4, Problem 29, of text.*

33. If $\sin^{-1}\frac{1}{5}$ is the angle whose sine is $\frac{1}{5}$ and $\cos^{-1}\frac{1}{4}$ is the angle whose cosine is $\frac{1}{4}$, find the exact value of

$$\sin \left(\sin^{-1}\frac{1}{5} + \cos^{-1}\frac{1}{4}\right)$$

[SMH] *From Problem Set 1.4, Problems 30, of text.*

Solve the equations in Problems 34–52 for $0 \le x < 2\pi$. In Problems 42–52, give answers correct to two decimal places.

34. $\sin x = 0.5$ **35.** $\sin x = -0.5$
36. $(\sin x)(\cos x) = 0$ **37.** $(\sin x)(\tan x) = 0$
38. $(2\cos x + \sqrt{2})(2\cos x - 1) = 0$
39. $(3\tan x + \sqrt{3})(3\tan x - \sqrt{3}) = 0$
40. $\tan^2 x = \tan x$ **41.** $\tan^2 x = \sqrt{3}\tan x$
42. $\cos^2 x - 1 - \cos x = 0$ **43.** $\sin^2 x - \sin x - 2 = 0$
44. $\tan^2 x - 3\tan x + 1 = 0$ **45.** $\csc^2 x - \csc x - 1 = 0$
46. $\cos 3x + 2\sin 2x \cos 3x = 0$ **47.** $\sin 2x + 2\cos x \sin 2x = 0$
48. $\cos(3x - 1) = \frac{1}{2}$ **49.** $\tan(2x + 1) = \sqrt{3}$
50. $\sin 2x + 1 = \sqrt{3}$
51. $\sin^2 3x + \sin 3x + 1 = 1 - \sin^2 3x$
52. $\sin^2 3x + \sin 3x = \cos^2 3x - 1$

CHAPTER 5

Polar Coordinates

5.1   Plotting Points in Polar Coordinates

PLOTTING POLAR-FORM POINTS

In a **polar coordinate system**, points are plotted in relation to a fixed point O, called the origin or **pole**, and a fixed ray emanating from the origin, called the **polar axis**. We then associate with each point P in the plane an ordered pair of numbers $P(r, \theta)$, where r is the distance from O to P and θ is the angle measured from the polar axis to the ray OP, as shown in Figure 5.1. The number r is called the **radial coordinate** of P, and θ is the **polar angle**. The polar angle is regarded as positive if measured counterclockwise up from the polar axis and negative if measured clockwise. The origin O has radial coordinate 0, and it is convenient to say that O has polar coordinates $(0, \theta)$, for all angles θ.

If the point P has polar coordinates (r, θ), we say that the point Q obtained by reflecting P in the origin O has coordinates $(-r, \theta)$. Thus, if you think of a pencil lying along the directed line segment $\overline{OP}$ with its midpoint at O and tip at $P(r, \theta)$, then the eraser will be at $Q(-r, \theta)$, as illustrated in the figure. The general procedure for plotting points in polar coordinates is demonstrated in the next example.

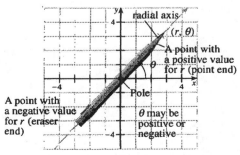

Figure 5.1   Polar-form points

EXAMPLE 5.1   Plotting polar-form points

Plot each of the following polar-form points: $A\left(4, \frac{\pi}{3}\right)$, $B\left(-4, \frac{\pi}{3}\right)$, $C\left(3, -\frac{\pi}{6}\right)$, $D\left(-3, -\frac{\pi}{6}\right)$, $E(-3, 3)$, $F(-3, -3)$, $G(-4, -2)$, $H\left(5, \frac{3\pi}{2}\right)$, $I\left(-5, \frac{\pi}{2}\right)$, $J\left(5, -\frac{\pi}{2}\right)$.

Solution   Points *A, B, C,* and *D* illustrate the basic ideas of plotting polar-form points.

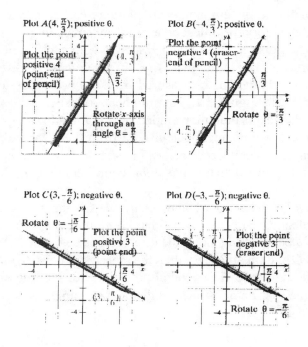

Points *E, F, G, H, I,* and *J* illustrate common situations that can sometimes be confusing (see figure at top of next page). Make sure you take time with each example.   □

In Example 5.1, we found that $\left(5, \frac{3\pi}{2}\right)$, $\left(-5, \frac{\pi}{2}\right)$, and $\left(5, -\frac{\pi}{2}\right)$ all represent the same point in polar coordinates. Indeed, every point in the plane has infinitely many polar representations. This property of the polar coordinate system causes some difficulties, but nothing that cannot be handled by exercising a little caution. We shall point out situations in our examples in which the nonuniqueness of the polar representation must be taken into account.

Plot $E(-3, 3)$.

Plot $F(-3, -3)$.

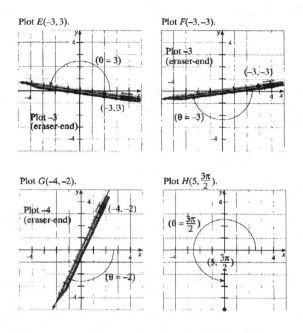

$I\left(-5, \dfrac{\pi}{2}\right)$, $J\left(5, -\dfrac{\pi}{2}\right)$, and $H\left(5, \dfrac{3\pi}{2}\right)$ all represent the same point.

5.2   Relationship Between Polar and Rectangular Coordinates

The relationship between polar and rectangular coordinates can be found by using trigonometric functions. The origin of the rectangular coordinate system is the pole, and the x-axis is the polar axis.

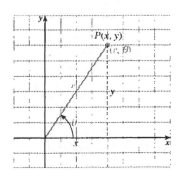

RELATIONSHIP BETWEEN RECTANGULAR AND POLAR COORDINATES

1. To change *from polar to rectangular coordinates,*

$$x = r\cos\theta \quad y = r\sin\theta$$

2. To change *from rectangular to polar coordinates,*

$$r = \sqrt{x^2 + y^2} \quad \bar{\theta} = \tan^{-1}\left|\frac{y}{x}\right|, x \neq 0$$

where $\bar{\theta}$ is the reference angle for θ. Place θ in the proper quadrant by noting the signs of x and y. If $x = 0$, then $\bar{\theta} = \dfrac{\pi}{2}$.

What this says: The reference angle $\bar{\theta}$ for a standard-position angle θ is defined to be the smallest positive angle that the angle θ makes with the x-axis.

EXAMPLE 5.2   Converting from polar to rectangular coordinates

Change the polar coordinates $\left(-2, \dfrac{5\pi}{6}\right)$ to rectangular coordinates.

Solution

$$x = -2\cos\frac{5\pi}{6} = -2\left(-\frac{\sqrt{3}}{2}\right) = \sqrt{3}$$

$$y = -2\sin\frac{5\pi}{6} = -2\left(\frac{1}{2}\right) = -1$$

The rectangular coordinates are $(\sqrt{3}, -1)$.   □

EXAMPLE 5.3   Converting from rectangular coordinates to polar coordinates

Write polar-form coordinates for the point with rectangular coordinates $\left(-\frac{5}{2}, -\frac{5}{2}\right)$.

Solution

$$r = \sqrt{\left(-\frac{5}{2}\right)^2 + \left(-\frac{5}{2}\right)^2} = \sqrt{\frac{25}{4} + \frac{25}{4}} = \frac{5}{2}\sqrt{2}$$

Note that θ is in Quadrant III because x is negative and y is negative.

$$\bar{\theta} = \tan^{-1}\left|\frac{-\frac{5}{2}}{-\frac{5}{2}}\right| = \tan^{-1}(1) = \frac{\pi}{4}; \text{thus, } \theta = \frac{5\pi}{4}(\text{ Quadrant III})$$

Polar-form coordinates are $\left(\frac{5}{2}\sqrt{2}, \frac{5\pi}{4}\right)$.   □

5.3   Polar Graphs

The **graph** of an equation in polar coordinates is the set of all points P whose polar coordinates (r, θ) satisfy the given equation. Circles, lines through the origin, and rays emanating from the origin have particularly simple equations in polar coordinates: Circles centered at the pole with radius a have equations of the form $r = a$; lines (or rays emanating from the origin) have equations of the form $\theta = k$, for some constant k.

As with other equations, we begin graphing polar-form curves by plotting some points. However, you must first be able to recognize whether a point in polar form satisfies a given equation.

EXAMPLE 5.4   Verifying that polar coordinates satisfy an equation

Show that each of the following points lies on the polar graph whose equation is

$$r = \frac{2}{1 - \cos\theta}$$

a. $\left(2, \frac{\pi}{2}\right)$ **b.** $\left(-2, \frac{3\pi}{2}\right)$ **c.** $(-1, 2\pi)$

Solution   Begin by substituting the given coordinates into the equation:

a. $\boxed{2} \overset{?}{=} \dfrac{2}{1 - \cos\boxed{\frac{\pi}{2}}} = \dfrac{2}{1 - 0} = 2;$

$\left(2, \dfrac{\pi}{2}\right)$ is on the curve, because it satisfies the equation.

b. $\boxed{-2} \overset{?}{=} \dfrac{2}{1 - \cos \boxed{\frac{3\pi}{2}}}$

$= \dfrac{2}{1 - 0} = 2$

*Although the equation is not satisfied, we **cannot** say that the point is not on the curve. Indeed, we see from part **a** that it is on the curve, because $\left(-2, \dfrac{3\pi}{2}\right)$ and $\left(2, \dfrac{\pi}{2}\right)$ name the same point!*

What this says: Even if one representation of a point does not satisfy the equation, we must still check equivalent representations of the point.

---

c. For $(-1, 2\pi)$, $\boxed{-1} \overset{?}{=} \dfrac{2}{1 - \cos \boxed{2\pi}} = \dfrac{2}{1 - 1}$, which is undefined.

Next, check the equivalent representation $(1, \pi)$:

$$\boxed{1} \overset{?}{=} \dfrac{2}{1 - \cos \pi} = \dfrac{2}{1 - (-1)} = 1$$

Thus, the point $(-1, 2\pi)$ is on the curve.   □

We will discuss the graphing of polar-form curves in the next section. Sometimes, though, a polar-form equation can be graphed by changing it to rectangular form.

EXAMPLE 5.5   Polar-form graphing by changing to rectangular form

Graph the following polar-form curves by changing to rectangular form:

a. $r = 3 \cos \theta$ **b.** $r = 4 \sec \theta$ **c.** $r = \dfrac{6}{2 \sin \theta + \cos \theta}$

Solution

a.	$r = 3 \cos \theta$	*Given equation*
	$r^2 = 3r \cos \theta$	*Multiply by r.*
	$x^2 + y^2 = 3x$	*Because $x = r \cos \theta$ and $r^2 = x^2 + y^2$*

$$\left[x^2 - 3x + \left(\tfrac{3}{2}\right)^2\right] + y^2 = \tfrac{9}{4} \qquad \textit{Complete the square.}$$

$$\left(x - \tfrac{3}{2}\right)^2 + y^2 = \tfrac{9}{4}$$

We see that this is the equation of a circle with center at $\left(\tfrac{3}{2}, 0\right)$ and radius $\tfrac{3}{2}$. The graph is shown in Figure 5.2a.

b. Because $r = 4 \sec \theta$ can be expressed as $r \cos \theta = 4$, the given equation can be written $x = 4$, whose graph is a vertical line (Figure 5.2b).

c. $r = \dfrac{6}{2 \sin \theta + \cos \theta}$

Given equation

$$2r \sin \theta + r \cos \theta = 6$$

$$2y + x = 6 \qquad \textit{Because } x = r \cos \theta, \; y = r \sin \theta$$

We recognize this equation as that of as a line with y-intercept 3 and slope $-\frac{1}{2}$ (Figure 5.2c). $\qquad\qquad \square$

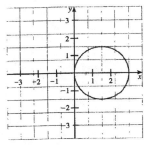

5.2a. Graph of $r = 3 \cos \theta$

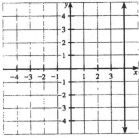

5.2b. Graph of $r \cos \theta = 4$

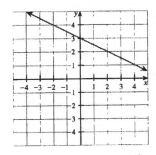

5.2c. Graph of $r = \dfrac{6}{2 \sin \theta + \cos \theta}$

Figure 5.2   Polar-form graphs

5.4   GRAPHING BY PLOTTING POINTS

We have examined polar forms for lines and circles, and in this section we shall examine curves that are more easily represented in polar coordinates than in rectangular coordinates. We begin with a simple spiral.

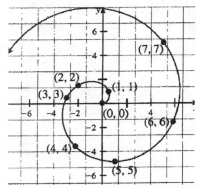

Figure 5.3   Graph of $r = \theta$

EXAMPLE 5.6   A spiral by plotting points

Graph $r = \theta$ for $\theta \geq 0$.

Solution   Set up a table of values:

θ	r
0	0
1	1
2	2
3	3
4	4
5	5
6	6

Choose a θ, and then find a corresponding r so that (r, θ) satisfies the equation. Plot each of these points and connect them, as shown in Figure 5.3.

Notice that as θ increases, r must also increase.   □

In Example 5.6, in the polar equation $r = \theta$, we see that there is exactly one value of r for each value of θ. Thus, the relationship given by $r = \theta$ is a function of θ, and we can write the polar form $r = f(\theta)$, where $f(\theta) = \theta$. A function of the form $r = f(\theta)$, where θ is a polar angle and r is the corresponding radial distance, is called a **polar function**.

5.5   Cardioids

Next, we examine a class of polar curves called **cardioids** because of their heartlike shape.

EXAMPLE 5.7   A cardioid by plotting points

Graph $r = 1 - \cos\theta$.

Solution   Construct a table of values by choosing values for θ and approximating the corresponding values for r:

θ	r
0	0
1	0.4597
2	1.4161
3	1.9900
4	1.6536
5	0.7164
6	0.3983

Note that if $\theta = \dfrac{\pi}{2}$, then $r = 1$, and if $\theta = \pi$, then $r = 2$. The points are connected as shown in Figure 5.4.   □

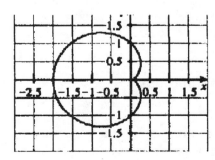

Figure 5.4   Graph of $r = 2(1 - \cos\theta)$

The general form for a cardioid in standard position is given in the following box.

STANDARD-POSITION CARDIOID

$$r = a(1 - \cos\theta)$$

In general, a cardioid in standard position can be completely determined by plotting four particular points:

θ	$r = a(1 - \cos\theta)$	Point
0	$r = a(1 - \cos 0) = a(1 - 1) = 0$	$(0, 0)$
$\dfrac{\pi}{2}$	$r = a\left(1 - \cos\dfrac{\pi}{2}\right) = a(1 - 0) = a$	$\left(a, \dfrac{\pi}{2}\right)$
π	$r = a(1 - \cos\pi) = a(1 + 1) = 2a$	$(2a, \pi)$
$\dfrac{3\pi}{2}$	$r = a\left(1 - \cos\dfrac{3\pi}{2}\right) = a(1 - 0) = a$	$\left(a, \dfrac{3\pi}{2}\right)$

These four points are all that you need to graph other standard-position cardioids, because all cardioids have the same shape as the one shown in Figure 5.4.

WHAT DOES THIS SAY? Remember, just as when you graph rectangular curves, the key is not in plotting many points, but in recognizing the type of curve and then plotting a few key points.

5.6   Symmetry and Rotations

In sketching a polar graph, it is often useful to determine whether the graph has been rotated or whether it has any symmetry.

If an angle α is subtracted from θ in a polar-form equation, the effect is to rotate the curve.

ROTATION OF POLAR-FORM GRAPHS

> The polar graph of $r = f(\theta - \alpha)$ is the same as the polar graph of $r = f(\theta)$, only rotated through an angle α. If α is positive, the rotation is counterclockwise, and if α is negative, then the rotation is clockwise.

EXAMPLE 5.8   Rotated cardioid

Graph $r = 3 - 3\cos\left(\theta - \dfrac{\pi}{6}\right)$.

Solution   Recognize this as a cardioid with $a = 3$ and a rotation of $\dfrac{\pi}{6}$. Plot the four points shown in Figure 5.5, and draw the cardioid. $\square$

If the rotation is $90°$, the equation simplifies considerably. We have

$$r = 3 - 3\cos\left(\theta - \frac{\pi}{2}\right)$$

$$= 3 - 3\left[\cos\theta\cos\frac{\pi}{2} + \sin\theta\sin\frac{\pi}{2}\right]$$

Standard cardioid with 90° rotation $\cos(\alpha - \beta) = \cos\alpha\cos\beta + \sin\alpha\sin\beta$

$$= 3 - 3\left[\cos\theta(0) + \sin\theta(1)\right]$$

$$= 3 - 3\sin\theta$$

Compare this equation with that of Example 5.8, and you will see that the only difference is a $90°$ rotation instead of a $30°$ rotation. This means that the graph of an equation of the form

$$r = a(1 - \sin\theta)$$

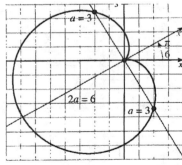

Figure 5.5   Graph of $r = 3 - 3\cos\left(\theta - \dfrac{\pi}{6}\right)$

instead of $r = a(1 - \cos\theta)$ is a standard-form cardioid with a 90° rotation. Similarly,

$r = a(1 + \cos\theta)$ is a standard-form cardioid with a 180° rotation.

$r = a(1 + \sin\theta)$ is a standard-form cardioid with a 270° rotation.

The cardioid is only one of the polar-form curves that we will consider. Before sketching other curves, let us examine symmetry. There are three important kinds of polar symmetry, which are described in the following box and are demonstrated in Figure 5.6:

SYMMETRY IN THE GRAPH OF THE POLAR FUNCTION $r = f(\theta)$

A polar-form graph $r = f(\theta)$ is symmetric with respect to ...	... if the equation $r = f(\theta)$ is unchanged when (r, θ) is replaced by ...
x-axis	$(r, -\theta)$
y-axis	$(r, \pi - \theta)$
origin or, alternatively	$(-r, \theta)$
x-axis	$(-r, \pi - \theta)$
y-axis	$(-r, -\theta)$

5.7   Limaçons

We will illustrate symmetry in polar-form curves by graphing a curve called a *limaçon*.

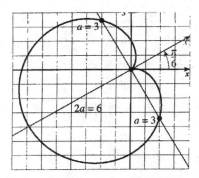

Figure 5.6a.   Symmetry with respect to the *x*-axis

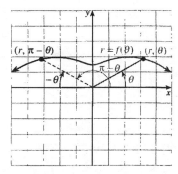

Figure 5.6b. Symmetry with respect to the y-axis

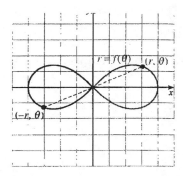

Figure 5.6c. Symmetry with respect to the origin

EXAMPLE 5.9   Graphing a limaçon by using symmetry

Graph $r = 3 + 2\cos\theta$.

Solution   Let $f(\theta) = 3 + 2\cos\theta$.
Symmetry with respect to the x-axis

$$f(-\theta) = 3 + 2\cos(-\theta) = 3 + 2\cos\theta = f(\theta)$$

Yes, the curve is symmetric, so it is enough to graph f for θ between 0 and π.
Symmetry with respect to the y-axis

$$f(\pi - \theta) = 3 + 2\cos(\pi - \theta)$$

$$= 3 + 2[\cos\pi\cos\theta + \sin\pi\sin\theta]$$

$$= 3 - 2\cos\theta$$

After checking the other primary representation, we find that it is not symmetric with respect to the y-axis.

Symmetry with respect to the origin

$-r \neq f(\theta)$ and $r \neq f(\theta + \pi)$; the curve is not symmetric

with respect to the origin.

The graph is shown in Figure 5.7; note that we sketch the top half of the graph (for $0 \leq \theta \leq \pi$) by plotting points and then complete the sketch by reflecting the graph in the x-axis. Because $\cos \theta$ decreases steadily from its largest value of 1 at $\theta = 0$ to its smallest value of -1 at $\theta = \pi$, the radial distance $r = 3 + 2\cos \theta$ will also steadily decrease as θ increases from 0 to π. The largest value of r is $r = 3 + 2(1) = 5$ at $\theta = 0$, and the smallest value of r is $r = 3 + 2(-1) = 1$ at $\theta = \pi$.□

The graph of any polar equation of the general form

$$r = b \pm a \cos \theta \text{ or } r = b \pm a \sin \theta$$

is called a **limaçon** (derived from the Latin word *limax*, which means "slug"; in French, it is the word for "*snail*"). The special case where $a = b$ is the *cardioid*. Figure 5.8 shows four different kinds of limaçons that can occur. Note how the appearance of the graph depends on the ratio a/b. We have discussed cases II and III in Examples 5.8 and 5.9. Case I (the "inner loop" case) and case IV (the "convex") case are examined in the problem set.
Just as with the cardioid, we designate a standard-form limaçon and consider the others as rotations thereof:

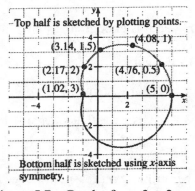

Figure 5.7   Graph of $r = 3 + 2\cos \theta$

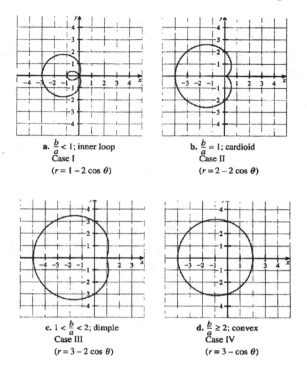

a. $\frac{b}{a} < 1$; inner loop
Case I
$(r = 1 - 2\cos\theta)$

b. $\frac{b}{a} = 1$; cardioid
Case II
$(r = 2 - 2\cos\theta)$

c. $1 < \frac{b}{a} < 2$; dimple
Case III
$(r = 3 - 2\cos\theta)$

d. $\frac{b}{a} \geq 2$; convex
Case IV
$(r = 3 - \cos\theta)$

Figure 5.8   Limaçons: $r = b \pm a\cos\theta$ or $r = b \pm a\sin\theta$

STANDARD-POSITION LIMAÇON

$$r = b - a\cos\theta$$

$r = b - a\cos\theta$ **Standard form**
$r = b - a\sin\theta$ 90° rotation
$r = b + a\cos\theta$ 180° rotation
$r = b + a\sin\theta$ 270° rotation

5.8   Rose Curves

There are several polar-form curves known as **rose curves**, which consist of several loops, called **leaves** or **petals**.

EXAMPLE 5.10   Graphing a four-leaved rose

Graph $r = 4\cos 2\theta$.

Solution   Let $f(\theta) = 4\cos 2\theta$.

Symmetry with respect to the x-axis

$f(-\theta) = 4\cos 2(-\theta) = 4\cos 2\theta = f(\theta)$; Yes, the curve is symmetric with respect to the x-axis.

Symmetry with respect to the y-axis $f(\pi - \theta) = 4\cos 2(\pi - \theta)$ $= 4\cos(2\pi - 2\theta) = 4\cos(-2\theta) = 4\cos 2\theta = f(\theta)$; Yes, the curve is symmetric with respect to the y-axis.

Because of this symmetry, we shall sketch the graph of $r = f(\theta)$ for θ between 0 and $\dfrac{\pi}{2}$ and then use symmetry to complete the graph.

θ	$f(\theta)$
0	4
0.2	3.684244
0.4	2.786827
0.6	1.449431
0.8	−0.1167981
1	−1.664587
1.2	−2.949575
1.4	−3.768889

When $\theta = 0$, $r = 4$, and as θ increases from 0 to $\dfrac{\pi}{4}$, the radial distance r decreases from 4 to 0. Then, as θ increases from $\dfrac{\pi}{4}$ to $\dfrac{\pi}{2}$, r becomes negative and decreases from 0 to −4. A table of values is given in the margin.

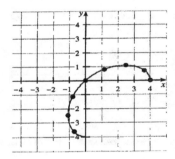

The next part of the graph is obtained by first reflecting in the y-axis:

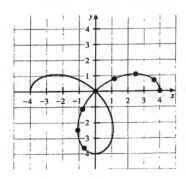

The last part of the graph is found by reflecting in the x-axis:

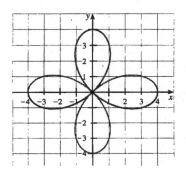

In general, $r = a \cos n\theta$ is the equation of a rose curve in which each petal has length a. If n is an even number, the rose has $2n$ petals; if n is odd, the number of petals is n. The tips of the petals are equally spaced on a circle of radius a. Equations of the form $r = a \sin n\theta$ are handled as rotations.

STANDARD-POSITION ROSE CURVE

$$r = a \cos n\theta$$

EXAMPLE 5.11   Graphing a rose curve by using a rotation

Graph $r = 5 \sin 4\theta$.

Solution   We begin by finding the amount of rotation:

$$r = 5 \sin 4\theta$$

$$= 5 \cos \left(\frac{\pi}{2} - 4\theta \right) \quad \textit{Cofunctions of complementary angles}$$

$$= 5 \cos \left(4\theta - \frac{\pi}{2} \right) \quad \textit{Remember, } \cos(-\theta) = \cos \theta.$$

$$= 5 \cos 4 \left(\theta - \frac{\pi}{8} \right)$$

We recognize this as a rose curve rotated $\dfrac{\pi}{8}$. There are $2(4) = 8$ petals of length 5. The petals are a distance of $\dfrac{\pi}{4}$ (one revolution $= 2\pi$

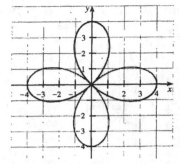

Figure 5.9   Graph of $r = 5 \sin 4\theta$

divided by the number of petals) apart. The graph is shown in Figure 5.9.   □

The graph of the eight-leaved rose in Example 5.11 provides a good illustration of why the alternative criteria for symmetry are given. It is obvious from the figure that the curve is symmetric with respect to the x-axis, but if $f(\theta) = 5 \sin 4\theta$, we have

$$f(-\theta) = 5 \sin 4(-\theta) = -5 \sin 4\theta \neq f(\theta)$$

which means the primary criterion for symmetry with respect to the x-axis fails. However,

$$
\begin{aligned}
f(\pi - \theta) &= 5 \sin 4(\pi - \theta) \\
&= 5[\sin 4\pi \cos(-4\theta) + \cos 4\pi \sin(-4\theta)] \\
&= -5 \sin 4\theta \\
&= -f(\theta)
\end{aligned}
$$

so when (r, θ) is on the graph, so is $(-r, \pi - \theta)$. Thus, the alternative criterion confirms that the graph is indeed symmetric with respect to the x-axis.

5.9   Lemniscates

The last general type of polar-form curve we will consider is called a **lemniscate**.

STANDARD-POSITION LEMNISCATE

$$r^2 = a^2 \cos 2\theta$$

EXAMPLE 5.12   Graphing a lemniscate

Graph $r^2 = 9\cos 2\theta$.

Solution   As before, when graphing a curve for the first time, begin by checking symmetry and plotting points. For this example, note that you obtain two values for r when solving the quadratic equation. For example, if $\theta = 0$, then $\cos 2\theta = 1$ and $r^2 = 9$, so $r = 3$ or -3.

Symmetry with respect to the *x*-axis
$9\cos[2(-\theta)] = 9\cos 2\theta$, so $r^2 = 9\cos 2\theta$ is not affected when θ is replaced by $-\theta$; yes, the curve is symmetric with respect to the *x*-axis.

Symmetry with respect to the *y*-axis
$9\cos[2(\pi - \theta)] = 9\cos(2\pi - 2\theta) = 9\cos(-2\theta) = 9\cos 2\theta$; yes, the curve is symmetric with respect to the *y*-axis.

Symmetry with respect to the origin
$(-r)^2 = r^2$ so $r^2 = 9\cos 2\theta$ is not affected when r is replaced by $-r$; yes, the curve is symmetric with respect to the origin.
Note that because $r^2 \geq 0$, the equation has a solution only when $\cos 2\theta \geq 0$; that is,

$$-\frac{\pi}{4} \leq \theta \leq \frac{\pi}{4}; \frac{3\pi}{4} \leq \theta \leq \frac{5\pi}{4}; \ldots$$

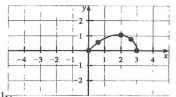

We begin by restricting our attention to the interval $0 \leq \theta \leq \frac{\pi}{4}$.
Note that $\sqrt{9\cos 2\theta}$ decreases steadily from 3 to 0 as θ varies from 0 to $\frac{\pi}{4}$:

A second step is to use symmetry to reflect the curve in the *x*-axis:

Finally, obtain the rest of the graph by reflecting the curve in the *y*-axis:

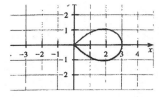

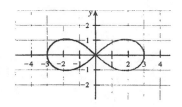

□

5.10   PROBLEM SET 5

In Problems 1–3, plot each of the given polar-form points and give equivalent rectangular coordinates.

1. **a.** $\left(4, \dfrac{\pi}{4}\right)$ **b.** $\left(6, \dfrac{\pi}{3}\right)$ **c.** $\left(5, \dfrac{2\pi}{3}\right)$

2. **a.** $\left(3, -\dfrac{\pi}{6}\right)$ **b.** $\left(\dfrac{3}{2}, -\dfrac{5\pi}{6}\right)$ **c.** $(-4, 4)$

3. **a.** $(1, 3\pi)$ **b.** $\left(-2, -\dfrac{3\pi}{2}\right)$ **c.** $(0, -3)$

Plot the rectangular-form points in Problems 4–6, and give a polar form.

4. **a.** $(5, 5)$ **b.** $(-1, \sqrt{3})$ **c.** $(2, -2\sqrt{3})$

5. **a.** $(-2, -2)$ **b.** $(3, -3)$ **c.** $(3, 7)$

6. **a.** $(3, -3\sqrt{3})$ **b.** $(\sqrt{3}, -1)$ **c.** $(-3, 0)$

Write each equation given in Problems 7–14 in rectangular coordinates.

7. $r = 4 \sin\theta$ 8. $r = 16$

9. $r = 1 - \sin\theta$ 10. $r = 2\cos\theta$

11. $r = \sec\theta$ 12. $r = 4\tan\theta$

13. $r^2 = \dfrac{2}{1 + \sin^2\theta}$ 14. $r^2 = \dfrac{2}{3\cos^2\theta - 1}$

In Problems 15–20, tell whether each of the given points lies on the curve

$$r = \dfrac{5}{1 - \sin\theta}$$

15. $\left(10, \dfrac{\pi}{6}\right)$ 16. $\left(5, \dfrac{\pi}{2}\right)$

17. $\left(-10, \dfrac{5\pi}{6}\right)$ 18. $\left(-\dfrac{10}{3}, \dfrac{5\pi}{6}\right)$

19. $\left(20 + 10\sqrt{3}, \dfrac{\pi}{3}\right)$ 20. $\left(-10, \dfrac{\pi}{3}\right)$

In Problems 21–28, tell whether each of the given points lies on the curve $r = 2(1 - \cos\theta)$.

21. $\left(1, \dfrac{\pi}{3}\right)$ **22.** $\left(1, -\dfrac{\pi}{3}\right)$

23. $\left(-1, \dfrac{\pi}{3}\right)$ **24.** $\left(-2, \dfrac{\pi}{2}\right)$

25. $\left(2 + \sqrt{2}, \dfrac{\pi}{4}\right)$ **26.** $\left(-2 - \sqrt{2}, \dfrac{\pi}{4}\right)$

27. $\left(0, \dfrac{\pi}{4}\right)$ **28.** $\left(0, -\dfrac{2\pi}{3}\right)$

Sketch the graph of each equation given in Problems 29–42.

29. $r = \dfrac{3}{2}$ **30.** $r = \dfrac{3}{2}, 0 \le \theta \le 2$

31. $r = \sqrt{2}, 0 \le \theta \le 2$ **32.** $r = 4$

33. $\theta = 1$ **34.** $\theta = 1, r \ge 0$

35. $\theta = \dfrac{\pi}{6}, r < 0$ **36.** $\theta = \dfrac{\pi}{2}$

37. $r = 3\cos 3\theta$ **38.** $r^2 = 9\cos 2\theta$

39. $r^2 = 9\sin 2\theta$ **40.** $r = 2\cos 2\left(\theta + \dfrac{\pi}{3}\right)$

41. $r = \sin 3\left(\theta + \dfrac{\pi}{6}\right)$ **42.** $r = 1 + \cos\theta$

In Problems 43–48, graph the given pair of curves on the same coordinate axes. The first equation uses rectangular coordinates (x, y) and the second uses polar coordinates (r, θ).

43. $y = \cos x$ and $r = \cos\theta$

44. $y = \sin x$ and $r = \sin\theta$

45. $y = \tan x$ and $r = \tan\theta$

46. $y = \sec x$ and $r = \sec\theta$

47. $y = \csc x$ and $r = \csc\theta$

48. $y = \cot x$ and $r = \cot \theta$

49.   Show that the polar equations $r = \cos \theta + 1$ and $r = \cos \theta - 1$ have the same graph in the xy-plane.

50.   Show that the graph of the polar equation $r = a \sin \theta + b \cos \theta$ is a circle. Find its center and radius.

CHAPTER 6
Conic Sections: The Parabola

Consider the general second-degree equation

$$Ax^2 + Bxy + Cy^2 + Dx + Ey + F = 0$$

for any constants A, B, C, D, E, and F. If $A = B = C = 0$, the equation is not quadratic, but linear (first degree); but if at least one of A, B, and C is not zero, then the equation is quadratic. Historically, second-degree equations in two variables were first considered in a geometric context and were called **conic sections**, because the curves they represent can be described as the intersections of a double-napped right circular cone with a plane. (See Figure 6.1.)

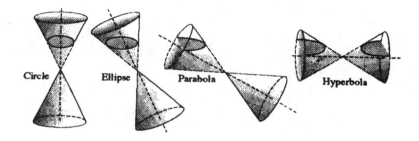

Figure 6.1   Conic sections

[sMH]   *The text assumes that you are familiar with the parabola, circle, ellipse, and hyperbola in standard position, as well as those translated to (h, k). In other words, you need to be familiar with the conic sections in this chapter.*

6.1   Standard-Position Parabolas

We shall use the following definition of a parabola:

PARABOLA

> A **parabola** is the set of all points in the plane that are equidistant from a fixed point (called the **focus**) and a fixed line (called the **directrix**).

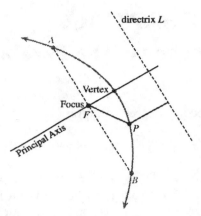

Figure 6.2   Parabola

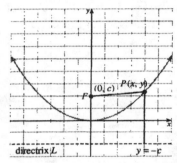

Figure 6.3   Graph of the parabola $x^2 = 4cy$

The line through the focus perpendicular to the directrix is called the **principal axis** of the parabola, and the point where the axis intersects the parabola is called the **vertex**. The line segment that passes through the focus perpendicular to the axis and with endpoints on the parabola is called the **focal chord**. This terminology is shown in Figure 6.2.

To obtain the equation of a parabola, first consider a special case: a parabola with focus $F(0, c)$ and directrix $y = -c$, where c is any positive number. This parabola must have its vertex at the origin (the vertex is halfway between the focus and the directrix) and must open upward, as shown in Figure 6.3.

Let (x, y) be any point on the parabola. Then, from the definition of a parabola,

DISTANCE FROM (x, y) to $(0, c)$ = DISTANCE FROM (x, y) TO THE DIRECTRIX

$$\sqrt{(x - 0)^2 + (y - c)^2} = y + c$$

$$x^2 + y^2 - 2cy + c^2 = y^2 + 2cy + c^2 \qquad \textit{Square both sides.}$$

$$x^2 = 4cy$$

This is the equation of the parabola with vertex (0, 0) and directrix $y = -c$.

You can repeat the preceding argument (see Problems 56–58) for parabolas that have their vertex at the origin and open downward, to the left, and to the right to obtain the results summarized next.

STANDARD-FORM EQUATIONS FOR PARABOLAS

Parabola	Focus	Directrix	Vertex
Upward: $x^2 = 4cy$	$(0, c)$	$y = -c$	$(0, 0)$
Downward: $x^2 = -4cy$	$(0, -c)$	$y = c$	$(0, 0)$
Right: $y^2 = 4cx$	$(c, 0)$	$x = -c$	$(0, 0)$
Left: $y^2 = -4cx$	$(-c, 0)$	$x = c$	$(0, 0)$

The length of the *focal chord* is the coefficient $4c$.

To graph a parabola, find and plot its vertex, determine c (usually by inspection), and count out c units from the vertex *in the appropriate direction*, as determined by the form of the equation. Finally, it is shown in the problem set that the length of the focal chord is $4c$, and we use this number to determine the width of the parabola, as in the following example.

EXAMPLE 6.1   Graphing a standard-form parabola

Graph $2y^2 - 5x = 0$.

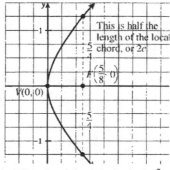

Figure 6.4   Graph of the parabola $2y^2 - 5x = 0$

Solution   First, algebraically change the equation so that it is in standard form by solving for the second-degree term:

$$y^2 = \tfrac{5}{2}x$$

The vertex is (0, 0) and

$$4c = \tfrac{5}{2}, \quad \text{so} \quad c = \tfrac{5}{8}$$

Thus, the parabola opens to the right, the focus is $\left(\tfrac{5}{8}, 0\right)$, and the length of the focal chord is $4c = \tfrac{5}{2}$, as shown in Figure 6.4.   □

There are two basic types of problems in analytic geometry:

1. Given the equation, draw the graph; this is what we did in Example 6.1.
2. Given the graph (or information about the graph), write the equation. The next example is of this type.

EXAMPLE 6.2   Writing the equation of a parabola

Find an equation of a parabola with focus $F(0, -2)$ and directrix $y = 2$.

Solution   This is the curve drawn in Figure 6.5. We see that the curve is a parabola which opens downward with vertex at the origin. By inspection, $c = 2$. The form of the equation is $x^2 = -4cy$, so the desired equation is

$$x^2 = -8y$$

6.2   TRANSLATION OF PARABOLAS

If a parabola is not in standard position, but its axis is parallel to one of the coordinate axes, it can be put into standard form by a change of variable of the form $X = x - h$, $Y = y - k$. Such a change in variable is called a **translation**, and it has the general effect shown in Figure 6.6.

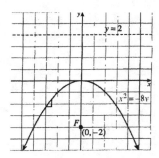

Figure 6.5   Graph of the parabola with focus $(0, -2)$ and directrix $y = 2$

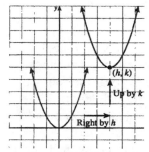

Figure 6.6 Translation of a parabola; vertex is at (h, k).

Suppose $(h, k) = (4, 5)$; then the coordinates of P are $(x, y) = (6, 9)$ and $(X, Y) = (2, 4)$; check:

$$X = x - h = 6 - 4 = 2$$

$$Y = y - k = 9 - 5 = 4$$

EFFECT OF A TRANSLATION

Replacing $x - h$ by X and $y - k$ by Y in an equation has the effect of translating the graph of the equation

h units horizontally (**right** if $h > 0$ and **left** if $h < 0$)

k units vertically (**up** if $k > 0$ and **down** if $k < 0$)

This means that the equations for parabolas with **vertex** (h, k) are as follows:

$$(x - h)^2 = 4c(y - k), \qquad X^2 = 4cY$$
$$(x - h)^2 = -4c(y - k), \qquad X^2 = -4cY$$
$$(y - k)^2 = 4c(x - h), \qquad Y^2 = 4cX$$
$$(y - k)^2 = -4c(x - h), \qquad Y^2 = -4cX$$

EXAMPLE 6.3   Graphing a parabola by using a translation

Sketch the parabola $y = x^2 + 2x + 3$. Find the vertex, c, and the length of the focal chord. Also, find the focus and the equation of the directrix.

Solution   First, complete the square:

$$y = x^2 + 2x + 3$$

$$y - 3\boxed{+1} = x^2 + 2x\boxed{+1}$$

$$y - 2 = (x + 1)^2$$

Next, plot the vertex $(-1, 2)$. If we replace $y - 2$ by Y and $x + 1$ by X, we have $Y = X^2$, which tells us that the parabola opens upward. Also, $4c = 1$, so $c = \frac{1}{4}$. Thus, plot the focus by counting up $\frac{1}{4}$ unit, and then draw the focal chord with length 1. Because these points are fairly close on the chosen scale, we plot an additional point, say, the y-intercept: If $x = 0$, then $y = 0^2 + 2(0) + 3 = 3$. (See Figure 6.7.)

Notice that we do not need to know the coordinates of the focus or the directrix to draw the graph. We needed to know only the vertex, the distance c, and the length of the focal chord, $4c$. If c is small relative to the vertex, it may be necessary to plot an additional point.

However, we may need to know the coordinates of the focus and directrix for further analysis. To find these numbers, we can use the reverse translation $x = X + h$, $y = Y + k$:

	XY-coordinates	xy-coordinates
Vertex	$(0, 0)$	$(-1, 2)$
focus	$(0, \frac{1}{4})$	$(-1, \frac{9}{4})$
directrix	$Y = -\frac{1}{4}$	$y = \frac{7}{4}$

EXAMPLE 6.4   Finding the equation of a translated parabola

Find an equation for the parabola with focus $(4, -3)$ and whose directrix is the line $x + 2 = 0$.

Solution   Sketch the information as shown in Figure 6.8. The vertex is $(1, -3)$, because it must be equidistant from F and the directrix. Note that $c = 3$. Thus, substitute into the equation of a parabola that

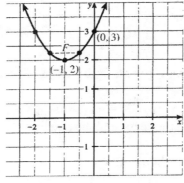

Figure 6.7   Graph of $y = x^2 + 2x + 3$

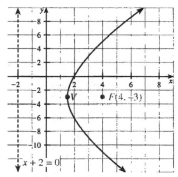

Figure 6.8   Graph of a parabola with focus $(4, -3)$ and directrix $x + 2 = 0$.

opens to the right, namely $y^2 = 4cx$, and then translate to the point (h, k) to obtain the equation

$$(y - k)^2 = 4c(x - h)$$

Because $(h, k) = (1, -3)$, the desired equation is

$$(y + 3)^2 = 12(x - 1) \qquad \square$$

6.3   REPRESENTATION IN POLAR COORDINATES

Next, we shall see how a parabola can be represented in polar coordinates. Let a parabola be given in the plane. Place the x-axis along the principal axis of the parabola, and place the pole at the focus, as shown in Figure 6.9. We refer to this position as **standard polar position** for the parabola. Assume that the parabola opens to the right and that the directrix L is the vertical line $x = -p$, where $p > 0$ is the distance from the focus to the directrix.

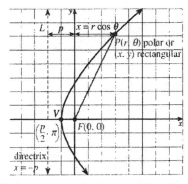

Figure 6.9   A standard polar position for a parabola

If P is a point on the parabola with rectangular coordinates (x, y) and polar coordinates (r, θ), we must have

$$\text{DISTANCE P TO F} = \text{DISTANCE P TO L}$$

$$|r| = |p + r\cos\theta|$$

$$r = \pm(p + r\cos\theta)$$

$$r = \frac{p}{1 - \cos\theta} \quad - \quad r = \frac{p}{1 + \cos\theta}$$

It can be shown that these two equations represent the same graph, so we shall use the one on the left to represent the given parabola. We can similarly derive equations for parabolas that open downward, left, or to the right. These graphs are shown in Figure 6.10.

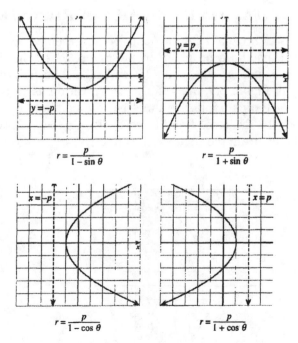

$$r = \frac{p}{1 - \sin\theta} \qquad\qquad r = \frac{p}{1 + \sin\theta}$$

$$r = \frac{p}{1 - \cos\theta} \qquad\qquad r = \frac{p}{1 + \cos\theta}$$

Figure 6.10   Standard position polar-form parabolas $(0 < \dfrac{p}{2} < 1)$

STANDARD POLAR EQUATIONS FOR PARABOLAS

	Parabola	Focus	Directrix Rectangular-form*	Vertex, Polar-form
Upward:	$r = \dfrac{p}{1 - \sin\theta}$	$(0, 0)$	$y = -p$	$\left(\dfrac{p}{2}, \dfrac{3\pi}{2}\right)$
Downward:	$r = \dfrac{p}{1 + \sin\theta}$	$(0, 0)$	$y = p$	$\left(\dfrac{p}{2}, \dfrac{\pi}{2}\right)$
Right:	$r = \dfrac{p}{1 - \cos\theta}$	$(0, 0)$	$x = -p$	$\left(\dfrac{p}{2}, \pi\right)$
Left:	$r = \dfrac{p}{1 + \cos\theta}$	$(0, 0)$	$x = p$	$\left(\dfrac{p}{2}, 0\right)$

EXAMPLE 6.5   Graphing a polar-form parabola

Describe and sketch the graph of the equation

$$r = \frac{4}{3 - 3\cos\theta}$$

Solution

$$r = \frac{4}{3 - 3\cos\theta} \cdot \frac{\frac{1}{3}}{\frac{1}{3}} = \frac{\frac{4}{3}}{1 - \cos\theta}$$

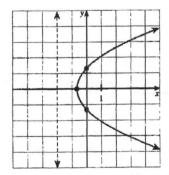

Figure 6.11   Graph of $r = \dfrac{4}{3 - 3\cos\theta}$

* We could, of course, state these equations of lines in polar form. For example, $y = -p$ is $r\sin\theta = -p$, but we prefer writing the equation of the directrix in rectangular form.

By inspection, you can now see (Figure 6.11) that the parabola opens to the right and that $p = \frac{4}{3}$. Thus, the vertex is

$$\left(\frac{p}{2}, \pi\right) = \left(\frac{2}{3}, \pi\right)$$

Plot the vertex and the line $x = -\frac{4}{3}$, as shown in the margin. You can plot other points that are easy to calculate, such as the points where $\theta = \dfrac{\pi}{2}$ and $\theta = \pi$ or $\theta = \dfrac{3\pi}{2}$.   □

EXAMPLE 6.6   Finding a polar-form equation of a parabola

Find a polar-form equation for the parabola with focus at the origin and vertex at the polar-form point $(3, \pi)$.

Solution   The vertex $(3, \pi)$ is on the x-axis and to the left of the focus (the pole). Thus, the parabola opens to the right and has a polar-form equation

$$r = \frac{p}{1 - \cos\theta}$$

where p is the distance from the focus to the directrix. Because the vertex $(3, \pi)$ is halfway between the focus and the directrix, we must have $p = 6$, so that the required equation is

$$r = \frac{6}{1 - \cos\theta}$$ □

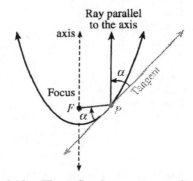

Figure 6.12   The reflection property of parabolas

6.4   PARABOLIC REFLECTORS*

Parabolic curves are used in the design of lighting systems, telescopes, and radar antennas, mainly because of the property illustrated in Figure 6.12 and described more formally in Handbook Theorem 3.

HANDBOOK THEOREM 3   Reflection property of parabolas
Let P be a point on a parabola in the plane, and let T be the tangent line to the parabola at P. Then the angle between T and the line through P parallel to the principal axis of the parabola equals the angle between T and the line connecting P to the focus.   ■

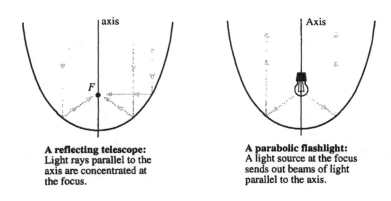

A reflecting telescope:
Light rays parallel to the axis are concentrated at the focus.

A parabolic flashlight:
A light source at the focus sends out beams of light parallel to the axis.

As an illustration of how this property is used, let us examine its application to reflecting telescopes. The eyepiece of such a telescope is placed at the focus of a parabolic mirror. Light enters the telescope in rays that are parallel to the axis of the parabola. It is a principle of physics that when light is reflected, the angle of incidence equals the angle of reflection. Hence, the parallel rays of light strike the parabolic mirror so that they all reflect through the focus, which means that the parallel rays are concentrated at the eyepiece located at the focus.

---

* Since these reflectors are three dimensional, the precise word is *paraboloidal*, but the most common usage refers to the cross-sectional shape, which is parabolic.

Flashlights and automobile headlights simply reverse the process: A light source is placed at the focus of a parabolic mirror, the light rays strike the mirror with angle of incidence equal to the angle of reflection, and each ray is reflected along a path parallel to the axis, thus emitting a light beam of parallel rays.

Radar utilizes both of these properties. First, a pulse is transmitted from the focus to a parabolic surface. As with a reflecting telescope, parallel pulses are transmitted in this way. The reflected pulses then strike the parabolic surface and are sent back to be received at the focus.

6.5   PROBLEM SET 6

Sketch the curves in Problems 1–22. Find the vertex V and c.

1. $y^2 = 8x$
2. $y^2 = -12x$
3. $y^2 = -20x$
4. $4x^2 = 10y$
5. $3x^2 = -12y$
6. $2x^2 = -4y$
7. $2x^2 + 5y = 0$
8. $5y^2 + 15x = 0$
9. $3y^2 - 15x = 0$
10. $4y^2 + 3x = 12$
11. $5x^2 + 4y = 20$
12. $4x^2 + 3y = 12$
13. $(y - 1)^2 = 2(x + 2)$
14. $(y + 3)^2 = 3(x - 1)$
15. $(x + 2)^2 = 2(y - 1)$
16. $(x - 1)^2 = 3(y + 3)$
17. $y^2 + 4x - 3y + 1 = 0$
18. $y^2 - 4x + 10y + 13 = 0$
19. $y^2 + 4y - 10x + 74 = 0$
20. $x^2 + 9y - 6x + 18 = 0$
21. $9x^2 + 6x + 18y - 23 = 0$
22. $9x^2 + 6y + 18x - 23 = 0$
23. Graph $f(x) = x^2 - 4x + 7$
    [sMH] *From Example 2, Section 3.4, of text.*
24. Graph $P(x) = 400(10 - x)(2 + x)$
    [sMH] *From Example 1, Section 4.7, of text.*

[sMH]

Find an equation for each curve in Problems 25–32.

25. Directrix $x = 0$; focus $(5, 0)$
26. Directrix $y = 0$; focus $(0, -3)$
27. Directrix $x - 3 = 0$; vertex $(-1, 2)$
28. Directrix $y + 4 = 0$; vertex $(4, -1)$
29. Vertex $(-2, -3)$; focus $(-2, 3)$
30. Vertex $(-3, 4)$; focus $(1, 4)$
31. Vertex $(-3, 2)$ and passing through $(-2, -1)$; axis parallel to the y-axis
32. Vertex $(4, 2)$ and passing through $(-3, -4)$; axis parallel to the x-axis

Sketch the graph of the polar-form parabola in Problems 33–38. Check your work by finding an equivalent Cartesian equation.

33. $r = \dfrac{6}{1 + \cos\theta}$ **34.** $r = \dfrac{4}{1 - \sin\theta}$

35. $r = \dfrac{-9}{1 + \sin\theta}$ **36.** $r = \dfrac{-2}{1 - \cos\theta}$

37. $r = \dfrac{8}{2 - 2\cos\theta}$ **38.** $r = \dfrac{9}{3 + 3\cos\theta}$

In Problems 39–42, find a polar equation for a parabola with its focus at the pole and with the given property.

39. vertex at the polar-form point $(4, 0)$
40. vertex at the polar-form point $(2, \pi)$
41. directrix at $y = -4$ **42.** directrix at $x = 3$

In Problems 43–46, find a polar equation for the parabola with the given Cartesian equation given.

43. $y^2 = 4x$ **44.** $x^2 = -2y$

45. $4x^2 = y - 3$ **46.** $x + 1 = 2(y - 3)^2$

47. Find the point(s) on the parabola $y^2 = 9x$ that is (are) closest to $(2, 0)$.
48. Find the point(s) on the parabola $x^2 = 4cy$ that is (are) closest to the focus.
49. Find the equation for the tangent line and the line perpendicular to the parabola $y^2 = 4x$ at the point $(1, -2)$.
50. Find the equation of the set of all points with distances from $(4, 3)$ that equal their distances from $(0, 3)$.
51. Find the equation of the set of all points with distances from $(4, 3)$ that equal their distances from $(-2, 1)$.

132   Chapter 6

52. Find an equation for a parabola that opens to the right with focal chord length 6 if it is known that the parabola has focus $(4, -2)$.

53. A parabolic archway has the dimensions shown in Figure 6.13. Find the equation of the parabolic portion.

54. Beams of light parallel to the axis of the parabolic mirror shown in Figure 6.14 strike the mirror and are reflected. Find the distance from the vertex to the point where the beams concentrate if the radius at the top of the dish is 4 ft.

55. A radar antenna is constructed so that a cross section along its axis is a parabola with the receiver at the focus. Find the focus if the antenna is 12 m across and its depth is 4 m. (See Figure 6.15.)

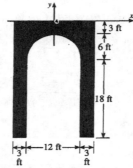

Figure 6.13   A parabolic archway

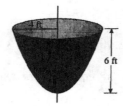

Figure 6.14   A parabolic mirror

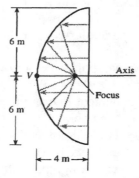

Figure 6.15   Dimensions for a radar antenna

56. Derive the equation of a parabola with $F(0, -c)$, where c is a positive number and the directrix is the line $y = c$.

57. Derive the equation of a parabola with $F(c, 0)$, where c is a positive number and the directrix is the line $x = -c$.

58. Derive the equation of a parabola with $F(-c, 0)$, where c is a positive number and the directrix is the line $x = c$.

59. Show that the length of the focal chord for the parabola $y^2 = 4cx$ is $4c(c > 0)$.

60. Show that the polar equations

$$r = \frac{p}{1 - \cos\theta} \quad \text{and} \quad r = \frac{-p}{1 + \cos\theta}$$

represent the same graph.

61. Show that the vertex is the point on a parabola that is closest to the focus.

62. Show that the tangents to a parabola at the two ends of the focal chord intersect on the directrix.

63. Find the area of the triangle formed by the focal chord and the two tangent lines at the end of the focal chord of the parabola $x^2 = 4cy$.

64. Suppose a circle intersects the parabola $x^2 = 4cy$ in four distinct points (x_1, y_1), (x_2, y_2), (x_3, y_3), and (x_4, y_4). Show that

$$x_1 + x_2 + x_3 + x_4 = 0.$$

65. **Reflection property of the parabola**. Assume that a parabola is given by the equation

$$y = \frac{x^2}{4c}$$

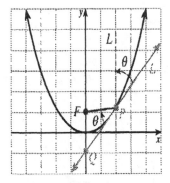

Figure 6.16   Reflection property

Use Figure 6.16 to prove the reflection property of the parabola by carrying out the indicated steps.

a. Find an equation for the tangent line T to the parabola at $P(x_0, y_0)$.

b. Find the coordinates of the point Q where T crosses the y-axis.

c. If F is the focus of the parabola, show that $|\overline{FP}| = |\overline{FQ}|$. Conclude that $\triangle QFP$ is isosceles.

d. Let L be a line parallel to the y-axis. Show that the angle between L and T equals $\theta = \angle FPQ$.

CHAPTER 7
Conic Sections: The Ellipse and the Hyperbola

7.1 ELLIPSES

In this chapter, we consider two more conic sections: the *ellipse* and the *hyperbola*.

ELLIPSE

> An **ellipse** is the set of all points in the plane, the sum of whose distances from two fixed points is constant.

The fixed points are called the **foci** (plural of **focus**). To see what an ellipse looks like, we will use the special type of graph paper shown in Figure 7.1a, where F_1 and F_2 are the foci.

Let the constant distance be 12. Plot all the points in the plane so that the sum of their distances from the foci is 12. If a point is 8 units from F_1, for example, then it is 4 units from F_2, and you can plot the points P_1 and P_2. The completed graph of this ellipse is shown in Figure 7.1b.

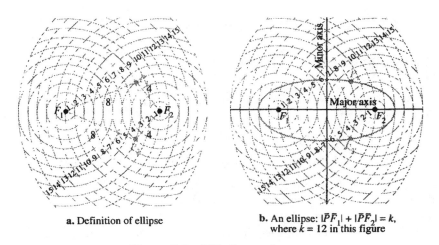

a. Definition of ellipse

b. An ellipse: $|\overline{PF_1}| + |\overline{PF_2}| = k$, where $k = 12$ in this figure

Figure 7.1   Elliptic graph paper

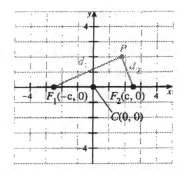

Figure 7.2 Developing the equation of an ellipse by using the definition

The line passing through F_1 and F_2 is called the **major axis**. The **center** is the midpoint of the segment $\overline{F_1F_2}$. The **semimajor axis** is the distance from the center to a point of intersection of the ellipse with its major axis. The line passing through the center and perpendicular to the major axis is called the **minor axis**. The **semiminor axis** is the distance from the center to a point of intersection of the minor axis with the ellipse. The ellipse is symmetric with respect to the major and minor axes. The intercepts on the major axis are called the **vertices** of the ellipse.

To find the equation of an ellipse, first consider a special case where the center is at the origin. Let the distance from the center to a focus be the positive number c; that is, let $F_1(-c, 0)$ and $F_2(c, 0)$ be the foci, and let the constant sum of distances be $2a$ (that is, $d_1 + d_2 = 2a$), as shown in Figure 7.2.

If $P(x, y)$ is any point on the ellipse, then, by definition,

$$|\overline{PF_1}| + |\overline{PF_2}| = 2a$$

$$\sqrt{(x + c)^2 + (y - 0)^2} + \sqrt{(x - c)^2 + (y - 0)^2} = 2a$$

Simplifying (the details are not shown), we obtain

$$\frac{x^2}{a^2} + \frac{y^2}{a^2 - c^2} = 1$$

Let $b^2 = a^2 - c^2$ to obtain $\dfrac{x^2}{a^2} + \dfrac{y^2}{b^2} = 1$. The graph of this equation is shown in Figure 7.3. Notice that the foci are on the major axis and that the intercepts on the minor axis are $(0, b)$ and $(0, -b)$. Notice also that $a > c$ and $a > b$.

A similar derivation applies to the ellipse in standard position with foci on the y-axis.

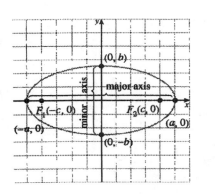 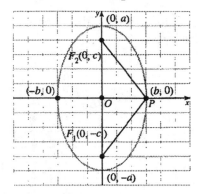

Figure 7.3   Standard-form ellipses

STANDARD-FORM EQUATIONS FOR ELLIPSES

Orientation	Equation	Foci	Constant	Center
Horizontal	$\dfrac{x^2}{a^2} + \dfrac{y^2}{b^2} = 1$	$(-c, 0), (c, 0)$	$2a$	$(0, 0)$
Vertical	$\dfrac{y^2}{a^2} + \dfrac{x^2}{b^2} = 1$	$(0, c), (0, -c)$	$2a$	$(0, 0)$

where $b^2 = a^2 - c^2$ or $c^2 = a^2 - b^2$ with $a > b > 0$

To sketch an ellipse, plot the center, the intercepts $\pm a$ on the major axis, and the intercepts $\pm b$ on the minor axis. Write the equation in standard form, so that there is a 1 on the right and coefficients of the square terms in the numerator are also 1. The center is $(0, 0)$; plot the intercepts on the x- and y-axes. For the x-intercepts, plot $\pm$ the square root of the number under the x^2 term; for the y-intercepts, plot $\pm$ the square root of the number under the y^2 term. Finally, draw the ellipse, using these intercepts. The longer axis is called the major axis; if this axis is horizontal, then the ellipse is horizontal, and if the major axis is vertical, then the ellipse is vertical.

EXAMPLE 7.1   Graphing an ellipse centered at the origin

Sketch $9x^2 + 4y^2 = 36$. Find the foci.

Solution   First, rewrite the equation in standard form by dividing both sides by 36:

$$\frac{x^2}{4} + \frac{y^2}{9} = 1$$

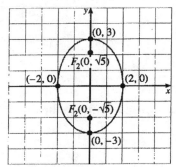

Figure 7.4   Graph of $9x^2 + 4y^2 = 36$

Because $a^2 = 9$, and $b^2 = 4$, the foci are found by calculating c: $c^2 = a^2 - b^2 = 9 - 4 = 5$. Thus, the foci are $(0, -\sqrt{5})$, $(0, \sqrt{5})$. The graph is shown in Figure 7.4.   □

EXAMPLE 7.2   Parameterize the equation of an ellipse

Graph $2x^2 + 5y^2 = 10$ by using a parameterization.

Solution   One way to parameterize an ellipse is to recall the identity $\cos^2 \theta + \sin^2 \theta = 1$. We begin by dividing both sides of the given equation by 10:

$$2x^2 + 5y^2 = 10$$

$$\frac{2x^2}{10} + \frac{5y^2}{10} = 1$$

$$\frac{x^2}{5} + \frac{y^2}{2} = 1$$

$$\left(\frac{x}{\sqrt{5}}\right)^2 + \left(\frac{y}{\sqrt{2}}\right)^2 = 1$$

We know that if $\cos \theta = \dfrac{x}{\sqrt{5}}$ and $\sin \theta = \dfrac{y}{\sqrt{2}}$, then $\cos^2 \theta + \sin^2 \theta = 1$. There are, of course, other choices we could make, but this observation leads us to let $x = \sqrt{5} \cos \theta$ and $y = \sqrt{2} \sin \theta$. You can set up a table of values or use a calculator to obtain the graph shown in

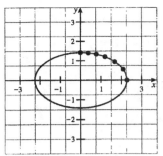

Figure 7.5   Graph of $x = \sqrt{5}\cos\theta$, $y = \sqrt{2}\sin\theta$

Figure 7.5. If you use a table of values, you need only consider values of θ between 0 and $\dfrac{\pi}{2}$, because we know that the ellipse is symmetric with respect to both the major and minor axes: □

The parameterization we obtained for the ellipse in Example 7.2 is not unique. For example, $x = \sqrt{5}\sin\theta$, $y = \sqrt{2}\cos\theta$ is the same ellipse, but if you sketch these parametric equations, you will note that even though the ellipse is the same, the orientation has reversed.

EXAMPLE 7.3   Finding the equation of a given ellipse

Find an equation for the ellipse with foci $(-1, 0)$ and $(1, 0)$ and vertices $(-2, 0)$ and $(2, 0)$.

Solution   By inspection, the center of the ellipse is $(0, 0)$ and the distance to a vertex is 2, so $a = 2$; the distance to a focus is 1, so $c = 1$. We find that $b^2 = a^2 - c^2 = 3$. An equation is

$$\frac{x^2}{4} + \frac{y^2}{3} = 1 \qquad\qquad □$$

If an ellipse is not in standard position, but its axes are parallel to the coordinate axes, complete the square to determine the translation. Here is an example of this procedure.

EXAMPLE 7.4   Graphing an ellipse by competing the square

Sketch the graph of the equation $9x^2 + 4y^2 - 18x + 16y - 11 = 0$.

Solution   Complete the square in both x and y:

$$9x^2 + 4y^2 - 18x + 16y - 11 = 0$$
$$9(x^2 - 2x) + 4(y^2 + 4y) = 11$$

$$9(x^2 - 2x + 1^2) + 4(y^2 + 4y\boxed{+2^2}) = 11 + 9 \cdot 1\boxed{+4.4}$$

$$9(x - 1)^2 + 4(y + 2)^2 = 36$$

$$\frac{(x - 1)^2}{4} + \frac{(y + 2)^2}{9} = 1$$

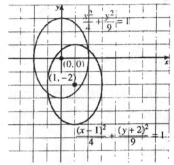

Figure 7.6   Graph of $9x^2 + 4y^2 - 18x + 16y - 11 = 0$

Thus, the graph may be obtained by translating the graph of the ellipse $\frac{x^2}{4} + \frac{y^2}{9} = 1$ by 1 unit to the right and 2 units down. This process is shown in Figure 7.6. First, plot the center $(h, k) = (1, -2)$, and then count out from that point a distance $a = \pm3$ (the vertices) on the major axis and label those vertices. Finally, count out from the center the distance $b = \pm2$ on the minor axis. Using those four points on the ellipse, you can sketch the graph.   □

7.2   Hyperbolas

The last of the conic sections to be considered has a definition similar to that of the ellipse.

HYPERBOLA

> A **hyperbola** is the set of all points in the plane such that, for each point on the hyperbola, the difference of its distances from two fixed points is constant.

The fixed points are called the **foci**. A hyperbola with foci at F_1 and F_2, where the given constant distance is 8, is shown in Figure 7.7.

The line passing through the foci is called the **transverse axis**. The **center** is the midpoint of the segment connecting the foci. The line

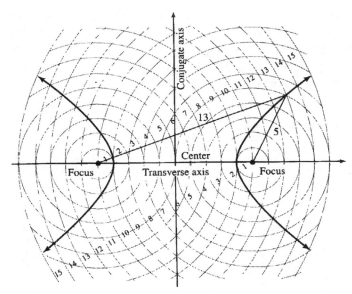

Figure 7.7   Graph of a hyperbola from the definition

passing through the center and perpendicular to the transverse axis is called the **conjugate axis**. The transverse axis intersects the hyperbola at points called the **vertices**, and the conjugate axis does not intersect the hyperbola. The hyperbola is symmetric with respect to both the transverse and conjugate axes.

If you use the definition, you can derive the equation for a hyperbola with foci at $(-c, 0)$ and $(c, 0)$ and constant difference $2a$ (both c and a are positive). If (x, y) is any point on the curve, then

$$\left| \sqrt{(x + c)^2 + (y - 0)^2} - \sqrt{(x - c)^2 + (y - 0)^2} \right| = 2a$$

The procedure for simplifying this expression is left as a problem. After several steps, you should obtain

$$\frac{x^2}{a^2} - \frac{y^2}{c^2 - a^2} = 1$$

If $b^2 = c^2 - a^2$, then

$$\frac{x^2}{a^2} - \frac{y^2}{b^2} = 1$$

which is the standard-form equation. Notice that $c^2 = a^2 - b^2$ for the ellipse and that $c^2 = a^2 + b^2$ for the hyperbola. For the ellipse it is necessary that $a^2 > b^2$, but for the hyperbola, there is no restriction on the relative sizes of a and b (but c is still less than a for the hyperbola).

Repeat the argument for a hyperbola with foci $F_1(0, c)$ and $F_2(0, -c)$, and you will obtain the other standard-form equation for a hyperbola with a vertical transverse axis.

STANDARD-FORM EQUATIONS FOR HYPERBOLAS

	Orientation	Foci	Constant	Center
Horizontal:	$\dfrac{x^2}{a^2} - \dfrac{y^2}{b^2} = 1$	$(-c, 0), (c, 0)$	$2a$	$(0, 0)$
Vertical:	$\dfrac{y^2}{a^2} - \dfrac{x^2}{b^2} = 1$	$(0, c), (0, -c)$	$2a$	$(0, 0)$

where $b^2 = c^2 - a^2$ or $c^2 = a^2 + b^2$

As with the other conics, we shall sketch a hyperbola by deducing some properties of the curve by inspection of the equation. The vertices are located $\pm a$ units from the center. The number $2a$ is the **length of the transverse axis**. The hyperbola does not intersect the conjugate axis, but if you plot the points located $\pm b$ units from the center, you determine a segment on the conjugate axis with length $2b$ called the **length of the conjugate axis**. The endpoints of this segment are useful in determining the shape of the hyperbola.

EXAMPLE 7.5   Sketching a hyperbola in standard form

Sketch $\dfrac{x^2}{4} - \dfrac{y^2}{9} = 1$.

Solution   The center of the hyperbola is $(0, 0)$; $a = 2$ and $b = 3$. Plot the vertices at $x = \pm 2$, as shown in the margin. From the form of the equation, we see that the transverse axis is along the x-axis and the conjugate axis is along the y-axis. Plot the length of the conjugate axis by plotting ± 3 units from the origin. We call these points the **pseudovertices**, because the curve does not actually pass through them.

Next, form a rectangle by drawing lines through the vertices and pseudovertices parallel to the axes of the hyperbola. This rectangle is called the **central rectangle**. The diagonal lines passing through the corners of the central rectangle are **oblique asymptotes** of the hyperbola, as shown in Figure 7.8; they aid in sketching the curve.

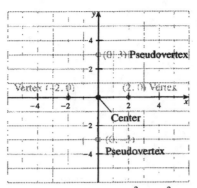

Figure 7.8   Graph of $\dfrac{x^2}{4} - \dfrac{y^2}{9} = 1$

For the general hyperbola given by the equation

$$\frac{x^2}{a^2} - \frac{y^2}{b^2} = 1$$

the equations of the oblique asymptotes described are found by replacing the constant term 1 by 0 and then factoring and solving:

$$y = \frac{b}{a}x \text{ and } y = -\frac{b}{a}x$$

To justify this result, you are asked in Problem 57 to show that the branches of the hyperbola approach $y = \pm\dfrac{b}{a}x$ as $|x| \to \infty$.

EXAMPLE 7.6   Completing the square to sketch a hyperbola

Sketch $16x^2 - 9y^2 - 128x - 18y + 103 = 0$.

Solution   Complete the square in both x and y:
→ *Watch the signs on the second pair of parentheses.*

$$16x^2 - 9y^2 - 128x - 18y + 103 = 0$$

$$16(x^2 - 8x) - 9(y^2 + 2y) = -103$$

$$16(x^2 - 8x + 4^2) - 9(y^2 + 2y + 1^2) = -103 + 16 \cdot 4^2 - 9 \cdot 1^2$$

$$16(x - 4)^2 - 9(y + 1)^2 = 144$$

$$\frac{(x-4)^2}{9} - \frac{(y+1)^2}{16} = 1$$

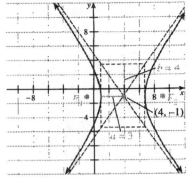

Figure 7.9   Sketch of $16x^2 - 9y^2 - 128x - 18y + 103 = 0$

The graph is shown in Figure 7.9.   □

We conclude our discussion of hyperbolas by considering an example in which information about the graph is given and we are asked to find the equation of the hyperbola.

EXAMPLE 7.7   Equation of a hyperbola, given information about the graph

Find the set of points such that, for any point, the difference of its distances from $(6, 2)$ and $(6, -5)$ is always 3.

Solution   From the definition, we see that the set of points is a hyperbola with center $(6, -\frac{3}{2})$ and $c = \frac{7}{2}$. Also, $2a = 3$, so $a = \frac{3}{2}$. Because $c^2 = a^2 + b^2$, we have

$$\frac{49}{4} = \frac{9}{4} + b^2 \text{ so that } b^2 = 10$$

The desired equation is

$$\frac{(y + \frac{3}{2})^2}{\frac{9}{4}} - \frac{(x-6)^2}{10} = 1 \text{ or } \frac{4(y+\frac{3}{2})^2}{9} - \frac{(x-6)^2}{10} = 1 \quad □$$

7.3   ECCENTRICITY AND POLAR COORDINATES

We defined the parabola as the set of all points P equidistant from a given point F (the focus) and a given line L (the directrix). In other words, for a parabola,

$$\frac{\text{DISTANCE FROM P TO F}}{\text{DISTANCE FROM P TO L}} = 1$$

This form of the definition of a parabola is part of the following characterization of conic sections:

ECCENTRICITY

Let F be a point in the plane, and let L be a line in the same plane. Then the set of all points P in the plane that satisfy

$$\frac{\text{DISTANCE FROM P TO F}}{\text{DISTANCE FROM P TO L}} = \epsilon$$

is a conic section, and ϵ is a fixed number for each conic, called the **eccentricity** of the conic. The conic is
- an *ellipse* if $\epsilon < 1$;
- a *parabola* if $\epsilon = 1$;
- a *hyperbola* if $\epsilon > 1$.

These criteria for a conic are illustrated in Figure 7.10.

Next, we shall examine polar characterizations for the ellipse and the hyperbola that involve the eccentricity ϵ. Consider an ellipse with one focus F at the origin of a polar coordinate plane. Assume that the corresponding directrix L is the vertical line $x = p$, or, in polar-form, $\cos \theta = p (p > 0)$, and that the ellipse has eccentricity ϵ. Then, if $P(r, \theta)$ is a polar-form point on the ellipse, we have

$$\epsilon = \frac{\text{DISTANCE FROM P TO F}}{\text{DISTANCE FROM P TO L}} = \frac{r}{p - r \cos \theta}$$

This relationship is shown in Figure 7.11.

Solving for r, we find that the ellipse has the polar equation

$$r = \frac{\epsilon p}{1 + \epsilon \cos \theta} \qquad \text{Because } 0 \leq \epsilon < 1, \epsilon \cos \theta \neq -1.$$

Similarly, if the directrix is $x = -p$, the equation is $r = \dfrac{\epsilon p}{1 - \epsilon \cos \theta}$, and if the directrix is $y = p$ or $y = -p$, the corresponding equations

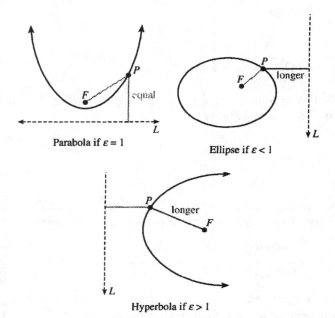

Figure 7.10   Eccentricity characterization of a conic section

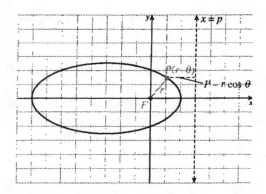

Figure 7.11   Polar representation of an ellipse

are, respectively,

$$r = \frac{\epsilon p}{1 + \epsilon \sin \theta} \quad \text{and} \quad r = \frac{\epsilon p}{1 - \epsilon \sin \theta}$$

These four possibilities are summarized in Figure 7.12.

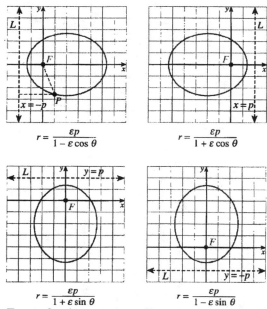

$$r = \frac{\varepsilon p}{1 - \varepsilon \cos \theta} \qquad\qquad r = \frac{\varepsilon p}{1 + \varepsilon \cos \theta}$$

$$r = \frac{\varepsilon p}{1 + \varepsilon \sin \theta} \qquad\qquad r = \frac{\varepsilon p}{1 - \varepsilon \sin \theta}$$

Figure 7.12   Forms for the equation of an ellipse ($\epsilon < 1$) in standard polar form

EXAMPLE 7.8   Describing the graph of an equation in polar form

Discuss the graph of the polar-form equation $r = \dfrac{2}{2 - \cos \theta}$.

Solution   We begin by writing the equation in standard form: $r = \dfrac{1}{1 - \frac{1}{2}\cos\theta}$.

This form involves a cosine and has $\epsilon = \frac{1}{2} < 1$, so by comparing it with the forms in Figure 7.12, we see that the graph must be a horizontal ellipse. The form also tells us that $\epsilon p = 1$, so $p = 2$ and the directrix is $x = -2$. The focus F_1 closer to the directrix is at the pole, and the vertices occur where $\theta = 0$ and $\theta = \pi$. For $\theta = 0$, we obtain $r = 2$, and for $\theta = \pi$, $r = \frac{2}{3}$, so the vertices are the polar points $V_1(\frac{2}{3}, \pi)$ and $V_2(2, 0)$. Since the focus $F_1(0, 0)$ is $\frac{2}{3}$ units to the left of $V_1(2, 0)$, F_2 is the polar point $(\frac{4}{3}, 0)$. The center of the ellipse is midway between the foci, at $(\frac{2}{3}, 0)$, so the minor axis is the vertical line passing through this point. The minor axis is the line $x = \frac{2}{3}$, or, in polar form,

$$r\cos\theta = \frac{2}{3} \quad \text{or} \quad r = \frac{\frac{2}{3}}{\cos\theta}$$

To find the endpoints of the minor axis, we need to solve simultaneously the equations for the axis with the equation of the ellipse; that is, we need to solve the set of equations

$$\frac{2}{2 - \cos\theta} = \frac{\frac{2}{3}}{\cos\theta}$$

$$2\cos\theta = \frac{2}{3}(2 - \cos\theta)$$

$$\cos\theta = \frac{1}{2}$$

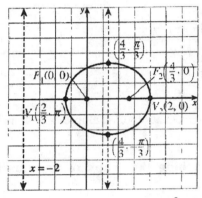

Figure 7.13   Graph of $r = \dfrac{2}{2 - \cos\theta}$

we obtain $\theta = \frac{\pi}{3}$ and $\frac{5\pi}{3}$. Then, solving for r, we get $r = \frac{4}{3}$, which gives the vertices $(\frac{4}{3}, \frac{\pi}{3})$ and $(\frac{4}{3}, \frac{5\pi}{3})$. The graph is shown in Figure 7.13. $\square$

Formulas for hyperbolas in polar coordinates are obtained in essentially the same way as polar formulas for ellipses. The four different cases that can occur for hyperbolas in standard form are summarized in Figure 7.14.

EXAMPLE 7.9   Describing the graph of a hyperbola in polar form

Discuss the graph of the polar equation $r = \dfrac{5}{3 + 4\sin\theta}$.

Solution   The standard form of the equation is $r = \dfrac{\frac{5}{3}}{1 + \frac{4}{3}\sin\theta}$. The form tells us that the eccentricity is $\epsilon = \frac{4}{3}$, and because $\epsilon > 1$, the

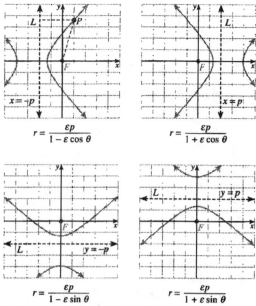

$$r = \frac{\varepsilon p}{1 - \varepsilon \cos \theta} \qquad\qquad r = \frac{\varepsilon p}{1 + \varepsilon \cos \theta}$$

$$r = \frac{\varepsilon p}{1 - \varepsilon \sin \theta} \qquad\qquad r = \frac{\varepsilon p}{1 + \varepsilon \sin \theta}$$

Figure 7.14 Forms for the equation of a hyperbola ($\epsilon > 1$) in standard polar form

graph is a hyperbola. We also see that the transverse axis is the y-axis and that because $\epsilon p = \frac{5}{3}$ we have $p = \frac{5}{4}$. Thus, the graph has one focus F_1 at the pole and directrix $y = p = \frac{5}{4}$.

The corresponding vertex occurs when $\theta = \frac{\pi}{2}$:

$$r = \frac{5}{3 + 4\sin\frac{\pi}{2}} = \frac{5}{7}$$

So the polar coordinates of this vertex V_1 are $(\frac{5}{7}, \frac{\pi}{2})$. The opposite vertex occurs where $\theta = \frac{3\pi}{2}$ and

$$r = \frac{5}{3 + 4\sin\frac{3\pi}{2}} = -5$$

So the point is $V_2(-5, \frac{3\pi}{2})$. Because the vertex V_1 is located $\frac{5}{7}$ units above $F_1(0, 0)$, we find that the other focus F_2, is located 5 units above the vertex V_1. Thus, F_2 is the polar point $(\frac{40}{7}, \frac{\pi}{2})$. The graph is shown in Figure 7.15. $\qquad\qquad\qquad\qquad\qquad\qquad\qquad\square$

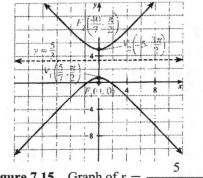

Figure 7.15 Graph of $r = \dfrac{5}{3 + 4\cos\theta}$

7.4 Geometric Properties

Like the parabola, the ellipse has some useful reflection properties. Let P be any point on an ellipse with foci F_1 and F_2, and let T be the line tangent to the ellipse at P, as shown in Figure 7.16.

Then the line segments $\overline{F_1 P}$ and $\overline{F_2 P}$ (called the **focal radii**) make equal angles with the tangent line T at P. The reflection property of an ellipse has the following physical interpretation:

REFLECTION PROPERTY OF AN ELLIPSE

> An elliptic mirror has the property that waves emanating from one focus are reflected toward the other focus.

The "whispering room" phenomenon found in many science museums and in famous buildings such as the old U.S. Capitol in Washington, DC, is an application of this principle. Two people

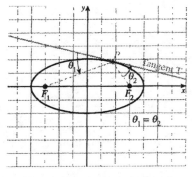

Figure 7.16 Reflection property of an ellipse

stand at each focus of an elliptic dome. If one person whispers, the other will clearly hear what is said, but anyone *not* near a focus will hear nothing. This is especially impressive if the foci are far apart.

The elliptic reflection principle is also used in a procedure for disintegrating kidney stones. A patient is placed in a tub of water with the shape of an ellipsoid (a three-dimensional elliptic figure) in such a way that the kidney stone is at one focus of the ellipsoid. A pulse generated at the other focus is then concentrated on the kidney stone.

There is also a useful reflection property of hyperbolas. Suppose an aircraft has crashed somewhere in the desert. A device in the wreckage emits a "beep" at regular intervals. Two observers, located at listening posts a known distance apart time the beeps. It turns out that the difference in time between the two listening posts multiplied by the velocity of sound gives the value $2a$ for a hyperbola on which the airplane is located. A third listening post will determine two more hyperbolas in a similar fashion, and the airplane must be at the intersection of these hyperbolas. (See Figure 7.17 and Problem 52.)

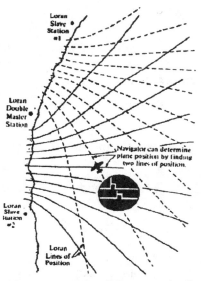

Figure 7.17 LORAN measures the differences in the time of arrival of signals from two sets of stations. The plane's position at the intersection lines is charted on a special map based on a hyperbolic coordinate system.

7.5   Problem Set 7

For each equation in Problems 1–20, sketch each curve.

1. $\dfrac{x^2}{4} + \dfrac{y^2}{16} = 1$ 2. $\dfrac{x^2}{16} + \dfrac{y^2}{4} = 1$

3. $\dfrac{x^2}{25} - \dfrac{y^2}{9} = 1$ 4. $\dfrac{x^2}{9} - \dfrac{y^2}{4} = 1$

5. $y^2 - x^2 = 1$ 6. $x^2 - y^2 = 8$

7. $(x - 1)^2 + 4y^2 = 64$ 8. $2x^2 + 3y^2 = 12$

9. $x^2 - 2y^2 + 2 = 0$ 10. $5x^2 - 3y^2 + 15 = 0$

11. $\dfrac{(x-1)^2}{4} + \dfrac{(y+3)^2}{16} = 1$ 12. $\dfrac{(x-1)^2}{16} + \dfrac{(y+3)^2}{4} = 1$

13. $4(x-3)^2 - 9(y+1)^2 = 36$

14. $9(x+1)^2 - 4(y-3)^2 = 36$

15. $4x^2 - 9y^2 - 8x + 54y - 41 = 0$

16. $x^2 - 4y^2 + 2x + 8y - 7 = 0$

17. $4x^2 + y^2 + 8x - 2y + 4 = 0$

18. $x^2 + 4y^2 + 2x - 8y + 4 = 0$

19. $9x^2 + 4y^2 - 8y = 32$

20. $4x^2 + 9y^2 - 8x = 32$

Find the standard-form equation for Problems 21–34.

21. an ellipse with vertices at (0, 8) and (0, 2) and $c = \sqrt{5}$.

22. an ellipse centered at the origin with focus at (0, 3); semimajor axis with length 4.

23. an ellipse centered at the origin with focus at (−2, 0); minor axis with length 4.

24. a hyperbola with foci at (0, 3) and (0, −3) and one vertex at (0, −2).

25. a hyperbola with foci at ($\sqrt{2}$, 0) and (−$\sqrt{2}$, 0) and one vertex at (1, 0).

26. a hyperbola with vertices at (5, 0) and (−5, 0) and one focus at (−7, 0).

27. a conic with major axis −4 ≤ x ≤ 4 and minor axis −3 ≤ y ≤ 3.

28. a conic with transverse axis $-3 \leq x \leq 3$ and conjugate axis $-4 \leq y \leq 4$.

29. an ellipse with center at $(2, 1)$, semiminor axis with length 3, and vertices at $(2, 6)$ and $(2, -4)$.

30. a conic with foci at $(-1, 0)$ and $(1, 0)$ with major axis with length 12.

31. a conic with foci at $(0, 6)$ and $(0, -6)$ with transverse axis with length 4.

32. the set of points such that for any point, the sum of its distances from $(4, -3)$ and $(-4, -3)$ is 12.

33. the set of points such that, for any point, the difference of its distances from $(4, -3)$ and $(-4, -3)$ is 6.

34. a hyperbola with vertices $(3, 0)$, $(-3, 0)$ and asymptotes $y = 3x$ and $y = -3x$.

Sketch the graph of each polar-form equation in Problems 35–38.

35. $r = \dfrac{4}{6 + \cos \theta}$ **36.** $r = \dfrac{4}{2 + 3 \cos \theta}$

37. $r = \dfrac{5}{1 - 2 \sin \theta}$ **38.** $r = \dfrac{-3}{2 - \sin \theta}$

39. Find an equation for the tangent line to the ellipse $5x^2 + 4y^2 = 56$ at the point $(-2, 3)$.

40. Find an equation of an ellipse that is tangent to the coordinate axes and to the line $y = 6$. Is there only one such ellipse?

41. Find two points on the ellipse $\dfrac{x^2}{4} + y^2 = 1$ where the tangent line also passes through the point $(0, -2)$.

42. Find the smallest distance from the point $(2, 0)$ to the ellipse $3x^2 + 2y^2 + 6x - 3 = 0$.

43. Find an equation for the hyperbola with vertices $(3, -1)$, $(-1, -1)$, and asymptotes $y = \dfrac{9}{4}x - \dfrac{13}{4}$ and $y = -\dfrac{9}{4}x + \dfrac{5}{4}$.

44. Find an equation for the hyperbola with vertices $(9, 0)$, $(-9, 0)$ and whose asymptotes are perpendicular to each other.

45. Find an equation for a hyperbola in standard position that contains the points $\left(3, \dfrac{\sqrt{5}}{2}\right)$ and $(-2, 0)$.

46. Show that $x = x_0 + a \cosh t$, and $y = y_0 + b \sinh t$ are parametric equations for one branch of a hyperbola. Find a Cartesian equation for this hyperbola. *Note*: This is the reason $\sinh t$ and $\cosh t$ are called ''hyperbolic functions.'' (See Section 7.8 of the text.)

47. Show that the equations $x = x_0 + a \sinh t$ and $y = y_0 + b \cosh t$ are parametric equations for one branch of a hyperbola. (See Section 7.8 of the text.)

48. An **equilateral hyperbola** is a hyperbola with an equation of the general form $y^2 - x^2 = a^2$. Show that a hyperbola is equilateral if and only if its asymptotes are perpendicular to each other.

49. The orbit of a planet is an ellipse whose major axis and minor axis are, respectively, 100 million and 81 million miles long. Find an equation for the ellipse. How far apart are its foci?

50. The orbit of the earth around the sun is elliptical, with the sun at one focus. The semimajor axis of this orbit is 9.3×10^7 mi, and the eccentricity is about 0.017. Determine the greatest and least distance of the earth from the sun (correct to two significant digits). *Hint*: Use polar coordinates.

51. Consider a person A who fires a rifle at a distant gong B. Assuming that the ground is flat, where must you stand to hear the sound of the gun and the sound of the gong simultaneously? *Hint*: To answer this question, let x be the distance that sound travels in the length of time it takes the bullet to travel from the gun to the gong. Show that the person who hears the sounds simultaneously must stand on a branch of a hyperbola (the one nearest the target), so that the difference of the distances from A to B is x.

52. Three LORAN stations are located at $(4, 0)$, $(0, 0)$, and $(4, \frac{\pi}{4})$ in a polar coordinate system. Radio signals are sent out from all

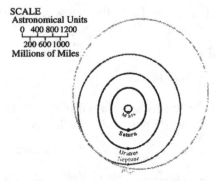

Figure 7.18 Planetary orbits (Problem 50)

three stations simultaneously. An airplane receiving the signals notes that the signals from the second and third stations arrive $\frac{2}{c}$ seconds later than the signal from the first, where c is the velocity of a radio signal. What is the location (in polar coordinates) of the airplane?

53. Derive the equation of the ellipse with foci $F_1(-c, 0)$ and $F_2(c, 0)$ for $c > 0$ and constant distance $2a$.

54. Derive the equation of the hyperbola with foci $F_1(-c, 0)$ and $F_2(c, 0)$ for $c > 0$ and constant distance $2a$.

55. Find conditions on the coefficients of the equation

$$Ax^2 + Cy^2 + Dx + Ey + F = 0$$

with $AC > 0$ that guarantee that the graph of the equation is
a. a line.
b. an ellipse.
c. a circle.
d. a hyperbola.
e. no graph.

56. a. Show that the tangent line to the ellipse

$$\frac{x^2}{a^2} + \frac{y^2}{b^2} = 1$$

at the point (x_0, y_0) has the equation

$$\frac{x_0 x}{a^2} + \frac{y_0 y}{b^2} = 1$$

b. Use part **a** to show that a tangent line to a vertex of an ellipse in standard form is either vertical or horizontal.

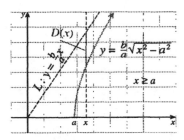

Figure 7.19   Problem 57

57. Prove that the lines $y = \dfrac{b}{a}x$ and $y = -\dfrac{b}{a}x$ are asymptotes of the hyperbola $\dfrac{x^2}{a^2} - \dfrac{y^2}{b^2} = 1$. *Hint*: Show that the vertical distance $D(x)$ between $y = \dfrac{b}{a}\sqrt{x^2 - a^2}$ and the line $y = \dfrac{b}{a}x$ tends to zero as $x \to \infty$, as shown in Figure 7.19.

CHAPTER 8
Curve Sketching

When sketching a curve, we first check to see whether it is a type of curve we recognize (a line, a conic, a trigonometric function, or something else). If it is not a curve we recognize, we ultimately sketch it by plotting some points; but *before* we plot points, we find out as much about the curve as we can. To do this, we check (1) symmetry, (2) extent, (3) asymptotes, and (4) intercepts.

[sMH] *Curve sketching is a major topic in Chapter 4 of the text. In particular, Section 4.7 and Table 4.1 use many of the techniques discussed in this chapter.*

8.1 Symmetry

One of the most valuable tools in curve sketching is symmetry. This section deals with recognizing when a curve is symmetric by performing a simple test on its equation. In general, two points are symmetric with respect to a line if that line is the perpendicular bisector of the line segment containing the two points. In this book, we will check for symmetry with respect to the coordinate axes and the origin. (See Figure 8.1.)

Figure 8.2 shows an example of a curve that is symmetric with respect to the x-axis: Whenever (x, y) is on the curve, so is $(x, -y)$. This gives us a simple algebraic test: *If the equation remains unchanged when y is replaced by $-y$, then the curve is symmetric with respect to the x-axis*, because (x, y) and $(x, -y)$ must both satisfy the equation.

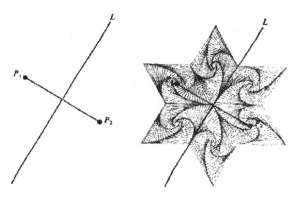

Figure 8.1 (a) Points P_1 and P_2 are symmetric with respect to L. (b) The star is symmetric with respect to L.

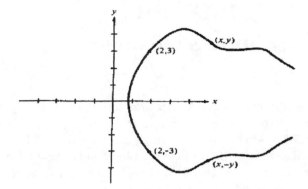

Figure 8.2   Symmetry with respect to the *x*-axis

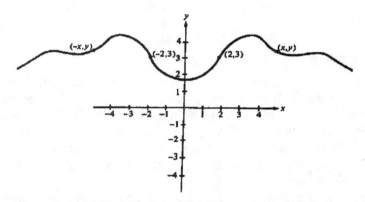

Figure 8.3   Symmetry with respect to the *y*-axis

Similarly, Figure 8.3 shows a curve that is symmetric with respect to the *y*-axis: Whenever (x, y) is on the curve, so is $(-x, y)$. This means that *if the equation is unchanged when x is replaced by −x, then the curve is symmetric with respect to the y-axis.*

Finally, Figure 8.4 shows a curve that is symmetric with respect to the origin: Whenever (x, y) is on the curve, so is $(-x, -y)$. This means that *if the equation is unchanged when x and y are replaced by −x and −y, respectively, then the curve is symmetric with respect to the origin.*

SYMMETRY

A curve is symmetric with respect to
the *x*-axis if the equation remains unchanged when y is replaced by $-y$;
the *y*-axis if the equation remains unchanged when x is replaced by $-x$;
the origin if the equation remains unchanged when x and y are simultaneously replaced by $-x$ and $-y$, respectively. Also, the curve is symmetric with respect to the origin if it is symmetric with respect to both the *x*- and *y*-axes.

EXAMPLE 8.1   Symmetry of a quadratic function

Check the symmetry of $x^2 + 2xy^2 + y^2 = 4$.

Solution   This curve is symmetric with respect to the *x*-axis, since

$$x^2 + 2x(-y)^2 + (-y)^2 = 4$$

is the same as the original equation. The curve is not symmetric with respect to the *y*-axis or the origin.   □

EXAMPLE 8.2   Symmetry with a trigonometric function

Check the symmetry of $y = \cos x$.

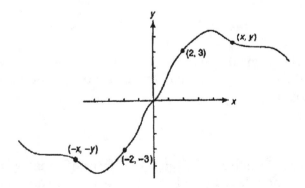

Figure 8.4   Symmetry with respect to the origin

Solution   This curve is symmetric with respect to the *y*-axis, since

$$y = \cos(-x)$$

is the same as the original equation. The curve is not symmetric with respect to the *x*-axis or the origin.   □

EXAMPLE 8.3   Symmetry of a third-degree equation

Check the symmetry of $x^3 + 2xy^2 + 4x^2y + 3y = 0$.

Solution   This curve is symmetric with respect to the origin, since

$$(-x)^3 + 2(-x)(-y)^2 + 4(-x)^2(-y) + 3(-y) = 0$$

is the same as the original equation if we multiply both sides by -1. The curve is not symmetric with respect to the *x*- or *y*-axis.   □

EXAMPLE 8.4   Symmetry of a fourth-degree equation

Check the symmetry of $x^2 + 5x^2y^2 = 5$.

Solution   This curve is symmetric with respect to the *x*-axis, since

$$x^2 + 5x^2(-y)^2 = 5$$

is the same as the original equation. The curve is also symmetric with respect to the *y*-axis, since

$$(-x)^2 + 5(-x)^2y^2 = 5$$

is the same as the original equation. If a curve is symmetric with respect to both the *x*- and *y*-axis, then it must also be symmetric with respect to the origin.   □

8.2   Extent

By *extent*, we mean the domain and range of a curve. If certain values of one or the other variable cause division by zero or imaginary values, those values must be excluded.

PROCEDURE FOR FINDING THE EXTENT

The domain is the set of all possible replacements for x. To find the domain:

a. Solve for y (if possible).
b. The domain is the set of all real values for x except those which

   i.   lead to division by zero; or
   ii. cause a negative number under a square root (or some other even-indexed root).

The range is the set of all possible replacements for y. To find the range:

a. Solve for x (if possible).
b. The range is the set of all real values for y except those which

   i.   lead to division by zero; or
   ii. cause a negative number under a square root (or some other even-indexed root).

EXAMPLE 8.5   Extent of a rational function

Find the domain and range of $y = \dfrac{4}{x}$.

Solution   The domain is the set of all real numbers *except* zero, since that value causes division by zero. In such a case, we write "all reals, $x \neq 0$." For the range, solve for x:

$$x = \frac{4}{y}$$

The range is also the set of all real numbers, $y \neq 0$.   □

EXAMPLE 8.6   Extent of a rational function

Find the domain of $y = \dfrac{(x-3)(x-2)(x-4)}{(x+2)(x-4)}$.

Solution   The domain is the set of all real numbers, $x \neq -2$ and $x \neq 4$.   □

EXAMPLE 8.7   Extent of a radical function

Find the domain and range of $y = \sqrt{\dfrac{x}{x-1}}$.

Solution   For the domain,

$$x \neq 1 \qquad \text{\textit{Exclude values that lead to division by zero.}}$$
$$\frac{x}{x-1} \geq 0 \qquad \text{\textit{Numbers under a square root must be non-negative.}}$$

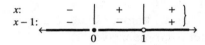

Domain: $(-\infty, 0] \cup (1, \infty)$
For the range, we solve for x:

$$y^2 = \frac{x}{x-1}$$

$$y^2(x-1) = x$$

$$y^2 x - y^2 = x$$

$$y^2 x - x = y^2$$

$$(y^2 - 1)x = y^2$$

$$x = \frac{y^2}{y^2 - 1}$$

We must exclude values that lead to division by zero:

$$y^2 - 1 \neq 0$$

$$y \neq 1, -1$$

But y cannot be negative, since y is a square root, which is nonnegative. Therefore, the range is the set of all non-negative real numbers except $y = 1$.   □

8.3 Asymptotes

An asymptote is a line such that, as a point P on the curve moves farther away from the origin, the distance between P and the asymptote tends toward zero. In this section, we are concerned with finding horizontal, vertical, and oblique asymptotes. The key to finding horizontal and vertical asymptotes is to find values that cause division by zero.

VERTICAL ASYMPTOTES

For easy reference, here are the examples of Section 8.2.

Example 8.1: $y = \dfrac{4}{x}$

Example 8.2: $y = \dfrac{(x-3)(x-2)(x-4)}{(x+2)(x-4)}$

Example 8.3: $y = \sqrt{\dfrac{x}{x-1}}$

Solve the equation for $y = \dfrac{P(x)}{D(x)}$, where the fraction is reduced. If r is a value for which $D(r) = 0$, then $x = r$ is a vertical asymptote. In Example 8.1 of Section 8.2, there is a vertical asymptote at $x = 0$, and in Example 8.2 of Section 8.2, there are vertical asymptotes at $x = -2$. The value $x = 4$ is a deleted point and not an asymptote. In Example 8.3, the vertical asymptote has equation $x = 1$.

HORIZONTAL ASYMPTOTES

Solve the equation for $x = \dfrac{Q(y)}{S(y)}$ if possible. If r is a value for which $S(r) = 0$, then $y = r$ is a horizontal asymptote. In Example 8.1 of Section 8.2, it is easy to solve for x to find a horizontal asymptote $x = 0$. Sometimes it is not convenient (or possible) to solve an equation for x, as you can see by looking at Examples 8.2 and 8.3 of Section 8.2.

Using calculus, one can show that if

$$y = \frac{P(x)}{D(x)}$$

where $P(x)$ and $D(x)$ are polynomial functions of x with no common factors (i.e., where the rational expression is reduced), the asymptotes depend on the degrees of P and D. Suppose that $P(x)$ has degree M with leading coefficient p and that $D(x)$ has degree N with leading coefficient d. The asymptotes can then be found according to the rules given in the next box.

OBLIQUE ASYMPTOTES

Notice that we included oblique (slanted) asymptotes in the box. A curve will have an oblique asymptote whenever the degree of the numerator is one more than the degree of the denominator. Once again, consider Example 8.2 of Section 8.2:

$$y = \frac{x^2 - 5x + 6}{x + 2}, x \neq 4$$

Notice that $M > N$, so there is no horizontal asymptote, but $M = 2$ and $N = 1$, so the degree of the numerator is one more than the degree of the denominator. Divide to find

$$y = x - 7 + \frac{20}{x + 2}$$

Disregard the remainder term to find the oblique asymptote, namely, $y = x - 7$.

PROCEDURE FOR FINDING ASYMPTOTES

Vertical asymptotes: $x = r$, where r is a value that causes division by zero when the equation is solved for y and is reduced.

Horizontal asymptotes: $y = r$, where r is a value that causes division by zero when the equation is solved for x and is reduced. Sometimes it is not possible (or convenient) to solve for x. If the equation is solved for y and is reduced, then

$y = 0$ is a horizontal asymptote if $M < N$

$y = \dfrac{p}{d}$ is a horizontal asymptote if $M = N$

no horizontal asymptote exists if $M > N$

oblique asymptotes: Solve the equation for y and reduce; then

$y = mx + b$ is an oblique asymptote if $M = N + 1$

where $mx + b$ is the quotient (disregard the remainder) obtained when $P(x)$ is divided by $D(x)$.

EXAMPLE 8.8   Asymptotes of a rational function

Find the vertical, horizontal, and oblique asymptotes of

$$y = \frac{6x^2 - x - 1}{4x^2 - 4x + 1}$$

Solution   First, make sure that the rational function is reduced:

$$y = \frac{6x^2 - x - 1}{4x^2 - 4x + 1}$$

$$= \frac{(3x + 1)(2x - 1)}{(2x - 1)^2}$$

$$= \frac{3x + 1}{2x - 1}$$

Vertical asymptote: can be found when $2x - 1 = 0$; $x = \frac{1}{2}$ is the equation of a vertical asymptote.

Horizontal asymptote: $y = \frac{3}{2}$, which is found by looking at the leading coefficients of the reduced form.

Oblique asymptotes: do not exist for this curve, since the degree of the numerator is not one more than the degree of the denominator. □

EXAMPLE 8.9   Asymptotes for a rational function

Find the vertical, horizontal, and oblique asymptotes for

$$y = \frac{3x^3 - 2x^2 - 4x + 6}{x^2 - 3}$$

Solution   If you use long division

$$\begin{array}{r} 3x - 2 \\ x^2 - 3 \overline{)3x^3 - 2x^2 - 4x + 6} \\ \underline{3x^3 \qquad\; - 9x} \\ -2x^2 + 5x + 6 \\ \underline{-2x^2 \qquad + 6} \\ 5x \end{array}$$

Since there is a remainder, the rational expression is reduced.

Vertical asymptotes: can be found when $x^2 - 3 = 0$; $x = \pm\sqrt{3}$.

Horizontal asymptotes: none, since the degree of the numerator is larger than the degree of the denominator.

Oblique asymptotes: exist when the degree of the numerator is one more than the degree of the denominator. Carry out the long division as shown, and disregard the remainder; the oblique asymptote is

$$y = 3x - 2 \qquad \qquad \square$$

It is possible that a curve crosses its oblique asymptotes. For Example 8.9, you could find the point of intersection by solving

$$3x - 2 = \frac{3x^3 - 2x^2 - 4x + 6}{x^2 - 3}$$

$$(x^2 - 3)(3x - 2) = 3x^3 - 2x^2 - 4x + 6$$

$$0 = 5x$$

$$0 = x$$

The point where the curve crosses its asymptote is $(0, -2)$.

8.4   Intercepts

The intercepts are the places where the curve crosses the coordinate axes. When finding the intercepts, we are really plotting points on the curve, but these are generally the easiest points to find.

PROCEDURE FOR FINDING INTERCEPTS

x-intercepts: set $y = 0$ and solve for x (if possible)

y-intercepts: set $x = 0$ and solve for y (if possible)

EXAMPLE 8.10   Curve sketching

Sketch the curve $x^2(y - 2) = 2$, given the following information:

Symmetry: with respect to the y-axis

Domain: $x \neq 0$

Range: $y > 2$

Asymptotes: $x = 0$, $y = 2$

Intercepts: none

Solution   Because we have symmetry with respect to the y-axis, we focus our attention on Quadrants I and II, since the symmetry will give us the curve in Quadrants III and IV. We draw the asymptotes and limit our attention to the domain and range. It is customary to darken the parts of the plane that are **not** included in the domain or range, as shown by the shaded portion of Figure 8.5(a). Since there are no intercepts, we plot the following points:

$$x = 1; \text{ then } 1(y - 2) = 2, \text{ so } y = 4$$

$$x = 2; \text{ then } 4(y - 2) = 2, \text{ so } y = \frac{5}{2}$$

Using the fact that $x = 0$ and $y = 2$ are asymptotes, we sketch the part of the curve in the first quadrant, as shown in Figure 8.5(b). By symmetry, we then sketch the rest of the curve, as shown in Figure 8.6. □

EXAMPLE 8.11   Sketching a rational function

Sketch $x^2 = \dfrac{1 + y^2}{1 - y^2}$.

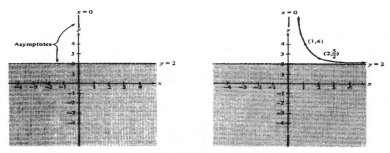

Figure 8.5   Preliminary sketch

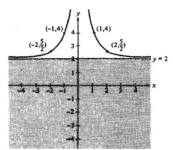

Figure 8.6   Graph of $x^2(y - 2) = 2$

Solution

Symmetry: The curve is symmetric with respect to the x-axis, since

$$x^2 = \frac{1 + (-y)^2}{1 - (-y)^2}$$

is the same as the original equation; the curve is also symmetric with respect to the y-axis and the origin.

Extent: **domain:** Solve for y.

$$x^2 = \frac{1 + y^2}{1 - y^2}$$

$$x^2 - x^2 y^2 = 1 + y^2$$

$$x^2 - 1 = y^2 + x^2 y^2$$

$$x^2 - 1 = (1 + x^2) y^2$$

$$y^2 = \frac{x^2 - 1}{x^2 + 1}$$

$$y = \pm \sqrt{\frac{x^2 - 1}{x^2 + 1}}$$

We must now rule out values of x that cause division by zero, as well as negative values under the square root radical. Solve

$$\frac{x^2 - 1}{x^2 + 1} \geq 0$$

The solution for this inequality gives the domain:

$$x \leq -1 \text{ or } x \geq 1$$

range: Solve for x:

$$x = \pm \sqrt{\frac{1 + y^2}{1 - y^2}}$$

We need to find the y-values that cause division by zero or negative values under the square root radical. First, solve

$$1 - y^2 = 0$$

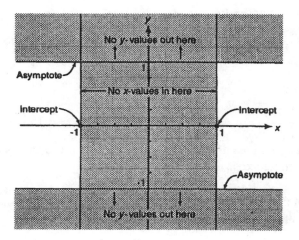

FIGURE 8.7

to find $y = \pm 1$. These are *excluded values*. Next, solve

$$\frac{1 + y^2}{1 - y^2} \geq 0, \qquad y \neq \pm 1$$

to find the range: $-1 < y < 1$

Use the information about extent to darken (shade) the portions of the plane that *cannot* contain the graph. The shaded graph is shown in Figure 8.7.

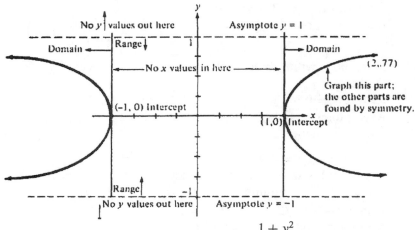

Figure 8.8   Graph of $x^2 = \dfrac{1 + y^2}{1 - y^2}$

Asymptotes: vertical:

$$y = \pm\frac{\sqrt{x^2-1}}{\sqrt{x^2+1}} \qquad \textit{No division by zero, so there are no vertical}$$

asymptotes.

horizontal:

$$x = \pm\frac{\sqrt{1+y^2}}{\sqrt{1-y^2}} \qquad \textit{Division by zero when } y = \pm1.$$

Horizontal asymptotes are $y = 1$, $y = -1$; draw these as dashed lines on the coordinate axes.

Intercepts: ***x*-intercepts**: if $y = 0$, then $x = \pm1$; so the x-intercepts are at $(1, 0)$ and $(-1, 0)$.

***y*-intercepts**: if $x = 0$, then $y = \pm\sqrt{-1}$; so there are no y-intercepts.

Plot points: Plot one or more relevant points, and make use of the information you just obtained to sketch the curve, as shown in Figure 8.8.   □

8.5   PROBLEM SET 8

In Problems 1–4, use the given information and plot some points to sketch the curve.

1. $x^2y = 4$
      Symmetry: with respect to the y-axis
      Domain: $x \neq 0$
      Range: $y > 0$
      Asymptotes: $x = 0$; $y = 0$
      Intercepts: none

2. $xy^2 - y^2 - 1 = 0$
      Symmetry: with respect to the x-axis
      Domain: $x > 1$
      Range: $y \neq 0$
      Asymptotes: $x = 1$; $y = 0$
      Intercepts: none

3. $x^2y - 4x + 2y = 0$
      Symmetry: with respect to the origin
      Domain: all real numbers
      Range: $(-\sqrt{2}, \sqrt{2})$
      Asymptotes: $y = 0$
      Intercept: $(0, 0)$

4. $x^2y^2 - 4xy^2 + 3y^2 - 4 = 0$
Symmetry: with respect to the x-axis
Domain: $(-\infty, 1) \cup (3, \infty)$
Range: $y \neq 0$
Asymptotes: $x = 1; x = 3; y = 0$
Intercepts: $(0, \frac{2}{3}\sqrt{3})$, $(0, -\frac{2}{3}\sqrt{3})$

Find the symmetry, extent, asymptotes, and intercepts for the curves whose equations are given in problems 5–20.

5. $xy = 2$ **6.** $xy = 6$

7. $y = \dfrac{x+1}{x}$ **8.** $y = \dfrac{x+1}{x+2}$

9. $y = \dfrac{2x^2 + x - 10}{x+2}$ **10.** $y = \dfrac{3x^2 + 5x - 2}{x+2}$

11. $y = \dfrac{2x^3 - 3x^2 - 2x}{2x+1}$ **12.** $y = \dfrac{x^3 + 6x^2 + 15x + 14}{x+2}$

13. $9x^2 + 4y^2 - 36 = 0$ **14.** $6x^2 - 2y^2 + 10 = 0$
15. $13x^2 - 10xy + 13y^2 - 72 = 0$ **16.** $y^2x - 2y^2 + 2 = 0$
17. $x^2y - 4xy + 3y - 4 = 0$ **18.** $x^3 - y^2 - 4y = 0$
19. $x^4 - x^2y^2 - 4x^2 + y^2 = 0$ **20.** $2y^2 - xy^2 + x - 1 = 0$

Graph the curves in Problems 21–36. Note that these curves are the same curves that are given in Problems 5–20.

21. $xy = 2$ **22.** $xy = 6$

23. $y = \dfrac{x+1}{x}$ **24.** $y = \dfrac{x+1}{x+2}$

25. $y = \dfrac{2x^2 + x - 10}{x+2}$ **26.** $y = \dfrac{3x^2 + 5x - 2}{x+2}$

27. $y = \dfrac{2x^3 - 3x^2 - 2x}{2x+1}$ **28.** $y = \dfrac{x^3 + 6x^2 + 15x + 14}{x+2}$

29. $9x^2 + 4y^2 - 36 = 0$ **30.** $6x^2 - 2y^2 + 10 = 0$
31. $13x^2 - 10xy + 13y^2 - 72 = 0$ **32.** $y^2x - 2y^2 + 2 = 0$
33. $x^2y - 4xy + 3y - 4 = 0$ **34.** $x^3 - y^2 - 4y = 0$
35. $x^4 - x^2y^2 - 4x^2 + y^2 = 0$ **36.** $2y^2 - xy^2 + x - 1 = 0$

37. Graph $f(x) = 1 + 2x + \dfrac{18}{x}$.   **38.** Graph $f(x) = \dfrac{1}{x^2 + 3}$.

39. Graph $y = \dfrac{x^2 - x - 2}{x - 3}$.   **40.** Graph $y = \dfrac{x^3 + 1}{x^3 - 8}$.

CHAPTER 9
Catalog of Special Curves

Boldface curves are fundamental and are listed in Table 1.3 of the text. For some of these curves, we give the area enclosed (A) and the arc length s. Rectangular curves can be translated to (h, k) by replacing x by $x' - h$ and y by $y' - k$. Polar-form curves can be rotated through an angle α by replacing $\theta = \theta' - \alpha$. The particular values for the constants used for each graph are shown in parentheses.

Absolute-value function

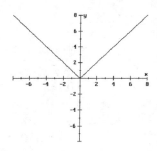

$$y = a|x| \quad (a = 1)$$

Archimedean spiral (see spiral of Archimedes)

Arccosecant, arccosine, arccotangent, arcsecant, arcsine, and arctangent functions (see inverse functions)

Astroid

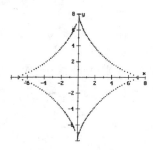

$$x^{2/3} + y^{2/3} = a^{2/3} \quad (a = 8)$$
$$A = \tfrac{3}{8}\pi a^2 \qquad s = 6a$$

This curve is described by a point P on a circle of radius $a/4$ as it rolls on the inside of a circle of radius a.

Bifolium

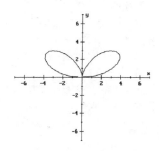

$$(x^2 + y^2)^2 = ax^2 y \text{ or}$$

$$r = a \sin\theta \cos^2\theta$$
$$(a = 12)$$

Cardioid (this is also a special case of an epicycloid)

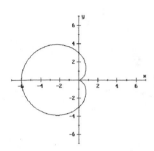

Cissoid of Diocles

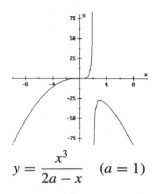

$$y = \frac{x^3}{2a - x} \quad (a = 1)$$

$$r = a(1 - \cos\theta) \quad (a = 3)$$

$$A = \tfrac{3}{2}\pi a^2 \qquad s = 8a$$

This is the curve described by a point P of a circle of radius a as it rolls on the outside of a fixed circle of radius a. This curve is also a special case of a limacon.

Cassinian curves (see ovals of Cassini)

Catenary (see hyperbolic cosine)

Circle

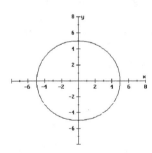

$$x^2 + y^2 = r^2 \quad (r = 5)$$
$$A = \pi r^2 \qquad s = 2\pi r$$

This is a curve described by a point P such that $|OP| = |RS|$. The cissoid of Diocles is used in the problem of *duplication of a cube* (i.e., finding the side of a cube that is twice the volume of a given cube).

Cochleoid (or Ouija™ board curve)

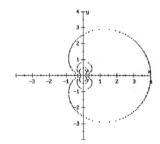

$$\tan = \left(\frac{ay}{x^2 + y^2}\right) = \frac{y}{x} \quad (a = 4)$$

Conic section (see circle, ellipse, hyperbola, and parabola)

Cosecant function

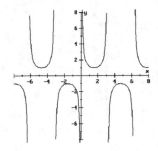

$$y = a \csc bx \quad (a = b = 1)$$

Cosine function

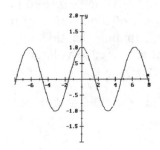

$$y = a \cos bx \quad (a = b = 1)$$

Cotangent function

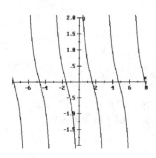

$$y = a \cot bx \quad (a = b = 1)$$

Cube-root function

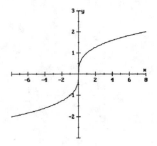

$$y = a^3 \sqrt{x} \quad (a = 1)$$

Cubical parabola

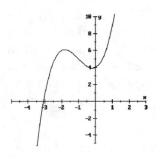

$$y = ax^3 + bx^2 + cx + d$$

$$(a = 1, b = 3, c = 1, d = 4)$$

Cubic function

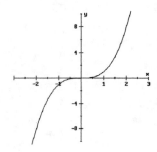

$$y = ax^3 \quad (a = 1)$$

Curate cycloid (see trochoid)

Cycloid

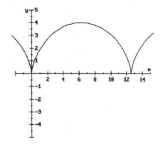

$$\begin{cases} x = a\theta - b\sin\theta \\ y = a - b\cos\theta \quad (a = b = 2) \end{cases}$$

$$x = a\cos^{-1}\left(\frac{a-y}{a}\right)$$

$$\mp\sqrt{2ay - y^2}$$

For one arch, $A = 3\pi a^2$, $s = 8a$

Deltoid

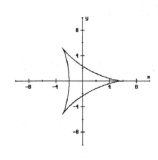

$$\begin{cases} x = 2a\cos\phi + a\cos 2\phi \\ y = 2a\sin\phi - a\sin 2\phi \end{cases}$$

$$(a = 2)$$

Ellipse

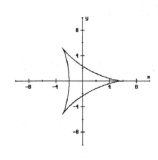

$$\frac{x^2}{a^2} + \frac{y^2}{b^2} = 1 \quad (a = 2, a = 3)$$

$$A = \pi ab \qquad s \approx 2\pi\sqrt{\frac{a^2 + b^2}{2}}$$

Epicycloid

$$\begin{cases} x = (a+b)\cos\theta \\ \quad -b\cos\left(\frac{a+b}{b}\right)\theta \\ y = (a+b)\sin\theta \\ \quad -b\sin\left(\frac{a+b}{b}\right)\theta \end{cases}$$

$$(a = 2, b = 1)$$

This is the curve described by a point P on a circle of radius b as it rolls on the outside of a circle of radius a.

Evolute of an ellipse

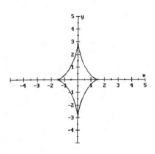

$$(az)^{2/3} + (by)^{2/3} = (a^2 - b^2)^{2/3}$$
$$(a = 2, b = 1)$$

$$\begin{cases} x = \dfrac{a^2 - b^2}{a} \cos^3 \theta \\ y = \dfrac{a^2 - b^2}{b} \sin^3 \theta \end{cases}$$

Exponential curve

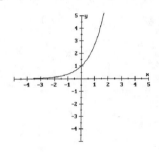

$$y = e^{ax} \quad (a = 1)$$

Folium of Descartes

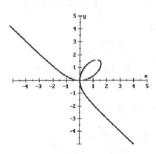

$$x^3 + y^3 = 3axy \quad (a = 1)$$

$$A = \tfrac{3}{2}a^2$$

Four-leaved rose

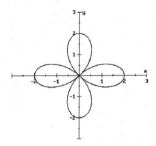

$$r = a \cos 2\theta \quad (a = 2)$$

Gamma function

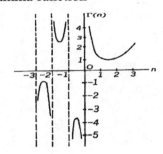

$$\Gamma(n) = \int_0^\infty x^{n-1} e^{-x} \, dx \ (n > 0)$$

Hyperbola

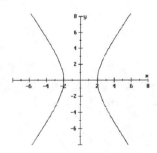

$$\frac{x^2}{a^2} - \frac{y^2}{b^2} = 1 \quad (a = 2, b = 3)$$

Hyperbolic cosecant

Hyperbolic secant

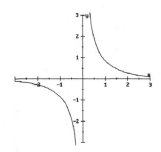

$y = \operatorname{csch} x$

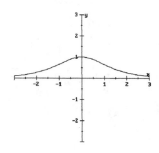

$y = \operatorname{sech} x$

Hyperbolic cosine (catenary)

Hyperbolic sine

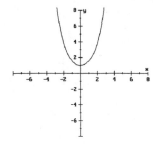

$y = \cosh x$

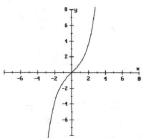

$y = \sinh x$

Hyperbolic cotangent

Hyperbolic tangent

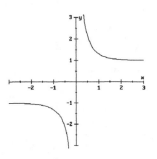

$y = \coth x$

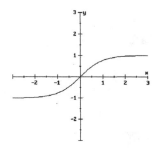

$y = \tanh x$

Hypocycloid

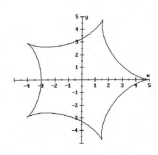

$$x = (a - b)\cos\phi$$
$$+ b\cos\left(\frac{a-b}{b}\right)\phi$$
$$y = (a - b)\sin\phi$$
$$- b\sin\left(\frac{a-b}{b}\right)\phi$$

This curve is described by a point P on a circle of radius b as it rolls on the inside of a circle of radius a.

Hypocycloid with four cusps (see astroid)
Hypocycloid with three cusps (see deltoid)

Identity function

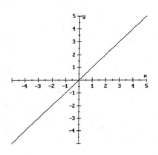

$$y = x$$

Inverse cosecant

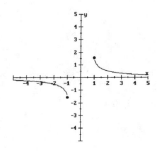

$$y = \csc^{-1}x$$

Inverse cosine

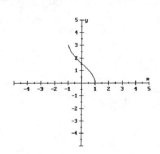

$$y = \cos^{-1}x$$

Inverse cotangent

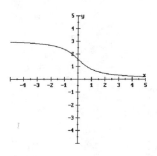

$$y = \cot^{-1}x$$

Inverse secant

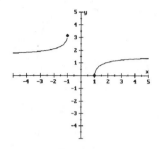

$$y = \sec^{-1}x$$

Inverse sine

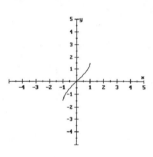

$$y = \sin^{-1}x$$

Inverse tangent

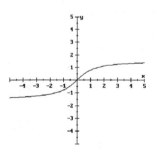

$$y = \tan^{-1}x$$

Involute of a circle

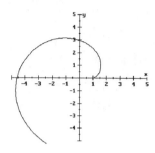

$$\begin{cases} x = a(\cos\theta + \theta\sin\theta) \\ y = a(\sin\theta - \theta\cos\theta) \ (a = 1) \end{cases}$$

Lemniscate (or lemniscate of Bernoulli)

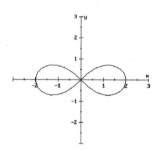

$$(x^2 + y^2)^2 = a^2(x^2 - y^2) \ (a = 2)$$
or $r^2 = a^2 \cos 2\theta$

Limaçon of Pascal

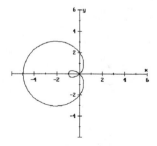

$$r = b - a\cos\theta \quad (a = 3, b = 2)$$

Lituus

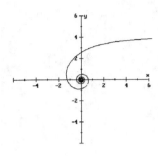

$$r^2\theta = a^2 \quad (a = 2)$$

Logarithmix curve

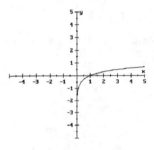

$$y = \log_a x \quad (a = 10)$$

Ouija™ board curve (see cochleoid)

Ovals of Cassini

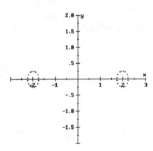

$$b > k \quad (b = 2, k = 1)$$

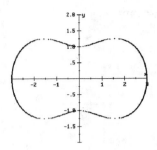

$$b < k \quad (b = 2, k = 5)$$
$$(x^2 + y^2 + b^2)^2 - 4b^2x^2 = k^2$$

These curves are sections of a torus on planes parallel to the axis of the torus.

Parabola (standard quadratic)

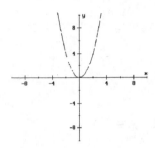

$$y = ax^2 \quad (a = 1)$$

Probability curve

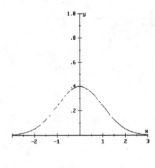

$$y = \frac{1}{\sqrt{2\pi}} e^{-x^2/2}$$

Prolate cycloid (see trochoid)

Quadratrix of Hippias

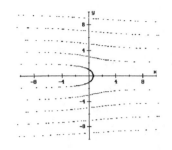

$$y = ax \tan \frac{\pi b y}{2} \quad (a = b = 1)$$

Reciprocal function

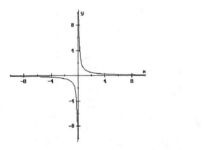

$$y = \frac{a}{x} \quad (a = 1)$$

Reciprocal-squared function

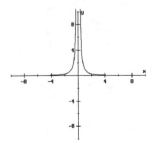

$$y = \frac{a}{x^2} \quad (a = 1)$$

Rose curves (indexed under number of leaves)

Secant function

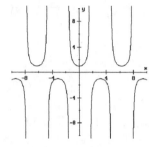

$$y = a \sec bx \quad (a = b = 1)$$

Semicubical parabola

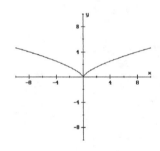

$$y = ax^{2/3} \quad (a = 1)$$

Serpentine curve

$$(a^2 + x^2)y = abx \quad (a = b = 1)$$

Sine function

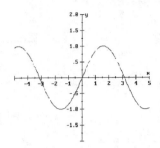

$$y = a \sin bx \quad (a = b = 1)$$

Sinusoid curve (general sine function) $y = a \sin(bx + c)$

Spiral of Archimedes

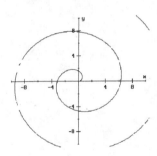

$$r = a\theta \quad (a = 1)$$

Spiral, hyperbolic

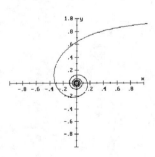

$$r\theta = a \quad (a = 1)$$

Spiral, logarithmic

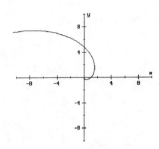

$$r = e^{a\theta} \text{ or } \ln r = a\theta \quad (a = 1)$$

Spiral, parabolic

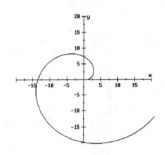

$$(r - a)^2 = 4ak\theta \quad (a = k = 1)$$

Square-root function

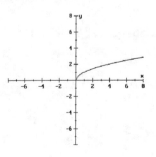

$$y = a\sqrt{x} \quad (a = 1)$$

Strophoid

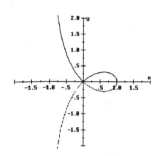

$$y^2 = x^2 \frac{a - x}{a + x} \quad (a = 1)$$

Tangent function

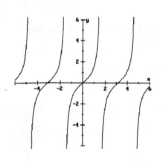

$$y = a \tan bx \quad (a = b = 1)$$

Three-leaved rose

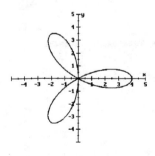

$$r = a \cos 3\theta \quad (a = 4)$$

Tractrix

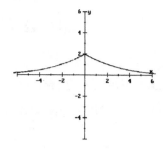

$$x = a(\ln \cot \tfrac{1}{2}\phi - \cos \phi)$$
$$y = a \sin \phi \quad (a = 2)$$

Trechoid

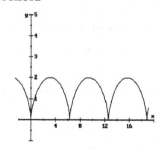

$$x = a\phi - b \sin \phi$$
$$y = a - b \cos \phi \quad (a = b = 1)$$

Two-leaved rose (see lemniscate)

Witch of Agnesi

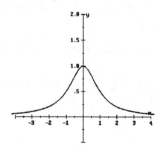

$$y = \frac{a^3}{x^2 + a^2} \quad (a = 1)$$
$$\text{or} \quad \begin{cases} x = a \cot \theta \\ y = a \sin^2 \theta \end{cases}$$

CHAPTER 10
Limit Formulas

10.1 Definition of Limit

LIMIT OF A FUNCTION (INFORMAL DEFINITION)

The notation

$$\lim_{x \to c} f(x) = L$$

is read "the limit of $f(x)$ as x approaches c is L" and means that the functional values $f(x)$ can be made arbitrarily close to L by choosing x sufficiently close to c.

LIMIT OF A FUNCTION (FORMAL DEFINITION)

The limit statement

$$\lim_{x \to c} f(x) = L$$

means that for each $\epsilon > 0$, there corresponds a number $\delta > 0$ with the property that

$$|f(x) - L| < \epsilon \text{ whenever } 0 < |x - c| < \delta$$

A FUNCTION DIVERGES TO INFINITY (INFORMAL DEFINITION)

A function f that increases or decreases without bound as x approaches c is said to **diverge to infinity** (∞) at c. We indicate this behavior by writing

(continued)

$$\lim_{x \to c} f(x) = +\infty$$

if x increases without bound and by

$$\lim_{x \to c} f(x) = -\infty$$

if x decreases without bound.

INFINITE LIMIT (FORMAL DEFINITION)

We write $\lim_{x \to c} f(x) = +\infty$ if, for any number $N > 0$ (no matter how large), it is possible to find a number $\delta > 0$ such that $f(x) > N$ whenever $0 < |x - c| < \delta$.

LIMITS INVOLVING INFINITY

The limit statement $\lim_{x \to +\infty} f(x) = L$ means that for any number $\epsilon > 0$, there exists a number N_1 such that

$$|f(x) - L| < \epsilon \text{ whenever } x > N_1$$

for x in the domain of f. Similarly $\lim_{x \to -\infty} f(x) = M$ means that for any $\epsilon > 0$, there exists a number N_2 such that

$$|f(x) - M| < \epsilon \text{ whenever } x < N_2$$

LIMIT OF A FUNCTION OF TWO VARIABLES (INFORMAL DEFINITION)

The notation

$$\lim_{(x, y) \to (x_0, y_0)} f(x, y) = L$$

(continued)

means that the functional values $f(x, y)$ can be made arbitrarily close to L by choosing the point (x, y) close to the point (x_0, y_0).

LIMIT OF A FUNCTION OF TWO VARIABLES (FORMAL DEFINITION)

Suppose the point $P_0(x_0, y_0)$ has the property that every disk centered at P_0 contains at least one point in the domain of f other than P_0 itself. Then the number L is the **limit of f at P** if, for every $\epsilon > 0$, there exists a $\delta > 0$ such that

$$|f(x, y) - L| < \epsilon \text{ whenever } 0 < \sqrt{(x - x_0)^2 + (y - y_0)^2} < \delta$$

In this case, we write

$$\lim_{(x,y)\to(x_0,y_0)} f(x, y) = L$$

10.2   Rules of Limits

BASIC RULES

For any real numbers a and c, suppose the functions f and g both have limits at $x = c$. Suppose also that both $\lim_{x\to+\infty} f(x)$ and $\lim_{x\to-\infty} f(x)$ exist.

Limit of a constant	$\lim_{x\to c} k = k$ for any constant k
Limit of x	$\lim_{x\to c} x = c$
Scalar rule	$\lim_{x\to c}[af(x)] = a \lim_{x\to c} f(x)$
Sum rule	$\lim_{x\to c}[f(x) + g(x)] = \lim_{x\to c} f(x) + \lim_{x\to c} g(x)$
Difference rule	$\lim_{x\to c}[f(x) - g(x)] = \lim_{x\to c} f(x) - \lim_{x\to c} g(x)$
Linearity rule	$\lim_{x\to+\infty}[af(x) + bg(x)] = a \lim_{x\to+\infty} f(x) + b \lim_{x\to+\infty} g(x)$

Product rules

$$\lim_{x\to c}[f(x)g(x)] = [\lim_{x\to c} f(x)][\lim_{x\to c} g(x)]$$

$$\lim_{x\to +\infty}[f(x)g(x)] =$$
$$[\lim_{x\to +\infty} f(x)][\lim_{x\to +\infty} g(x)]$$

Quotient rules

$$\lim_{x\to c} \frac{f(x)}{g(x)} = \frac{\lim_{x\to c} f(x)}{\lim_{x\to c} g(x)} \text{ if } \lim_{x\to c} g(x) \neq 0$$

$$\lim_{x\to +\infty} \frac{f(x)}{g(x)} =$$
$$\frac{\lim_{x\to +\infty} f(x)}{\lim_{x\to +\infty} g(x)} \text{ if } \lim_{x\to +\infty} g(x) \neq 0$$

Power rules

$$\lim_{x\to c}[f(x)]^n = \left[\lim_{x\to c} f(x)\right]^n \ n \text{ is a}$$
rational number

$$\lim_{x\to +\infty}[f(x)]^n = [\lim_{x\to +\infty} f(x)]^n$$

Limit limitation theorem

Suppose $\lim_{x\to c} f(x)$ exists and $f(x) \geq 0$ throughout an open interval containing the number c, except possibly at c itself. Then $\lim_{x\to c} f(x) \geq 0$.

The squeeze rule

If $g(x) \leq f(x) \leq h(x)$ for all x in an open interval containing c (except possibly at c itself) and if

$$\lim_{x\to c} g(x) = \lim_{x\to c} h(x) = L$$

then $\lim_{x\to c} f(x) = L$.

Limits to infinity

$$\lim_{x\to +\infty} \frac{A}{x^n} = 0 \text{ and } \lim_{x\to -\infty} \frac{A}{x^n} = 0$$

Infinite-limit theorem

If $\lim_{x\to c} f(x) = +\infty$ and $\lim_{x\to c} g(x) = A$, then

$$\lim_{x\to c}[f(x)g(x)] = +\infty \text{ and } \lim_{x\to c} \frac{f(x)}{g(x)} = +\infty \text{ if } A > 0$$

$$\lim_{x\to c}[f(x)g(x)] = -\infty \text{ and } \lim_{x\to c} \frac{f(x)}{g(x)} = -\infty \text{ if } A < 0$$

l'Hôpital's rule

Let f and g be differentiable functions on an open interval containing c (except possibly at c itself).

If $\lim_{x\to c} \frac{f(x)}{g(x)}$ produces an indeterminate form $\frac{0}{0}$ or $\frac{\infty}{\infty}$, then

$$\lim_{x \to c} \frac{f(x)}{g(x)} = \lim_{x \to c} \frac{f'(x)}{g'(x)}$$

provided that the limit on the right side exists.

TRIGONOMETRIC LIMITS

$$\lim_{x \to c} \cos x = \cos c \qquad \lim_{x \to c} \sec x = \sec c$$

$$\lim_{x \to c} \sin x = \sin c \qquad \lim_{x \to c} \csc x = \csc c$$

$$\lim_{x \to c} \tan x = \tan c \qquad \lim_{x \to c} \cot x = \cot c$$

$$\lim_{x \to 0} \frac{\sin x}{x} = 1 \quad \lim_{x \to 0} \frac{\sin ax}{x} = a \quad \lim_{x \to 0} \frac{\tan x}{x} = 1 \quad \lim_{x \to 0} \frac{1 - \cos x}{x} = 0$$

MISCELLANEOUS LIMITS

$$\lim_{n \to +\infty} \left(1 + \frac{1}{n}\right)^n = e \qquad \lim_{n \to 0} (1 + n)^{1/n} = e$$

$$\lim_{n \to +\infty} \left(1 + \frac{k}{n}\right)^n = e^k \qquad \lim_{n \to +\infty} p \left(1 + \frac{1}{n}\right)^{nt} = pe^t$$

$$\lim_{n \to +\infty} n^{1/n} = 1$$

10.3 Limits of a Function of Two Variables

BASIC FORMULAS AND RULES FOR LIMITS OF A FUNCTION OF TWO VARIABLES

Suppose $\lim\limits_{(x, y) \to (x_0, y_0)} f(x, y)$ and $\lim\limits_{(x, y) \to (x_0, y_0)} g(x, y)$ both exist, with $\lim\limits_{(x, y) \to (x_0, y_0)} f(x, y) = L$ and $\lim\limits_{(x, y) \to (x_0, y_0)} g(x, y) = M$. Then the following rules obtain:

Scalar rule

$$\lim_{(x, y) \to (x_0, y_0)} [af(x, y)]$$

$$= a \lim_{(x, y) \to (x_0, y_0)} f(x, y) = aL$$

Sum rule

$$\lim_{(x, y) \to (x_0, y_0)} [f + g](x, y)$$

$$= \left[\lim_{(x, y) \to (x_0, y_0)} f(x, y) \right] + \left[\lim_{(x, y) \to (x_0, y_0)} g(x, y) \right]$$

$$= L + M$$

Product rule $\displaystyle\lim_{(x,y)\to(x_0,y_0)}[fg](x,y)$

$$= \left[\lim_{(x,y)\to(x_0,y_0)} f(x,y)\right]\left[\lim_{(x,y)\to(x_0,y_0)} g(x,y)\right]$$

$$= LM$$

Quotient rule $\displaystyle\lim_{(x,y)\to(x_0,y_0)}\left[\frac{f}{g}\right](x,y) = \frac{\displaystyle\lim_{(x,y)\to(x_0,y_0)} f(x,y)}{\displaystyle\lim_{(x,y)\to(x_0,y_0)} g(x,y)} = \frac{L}{M}$$

if $M \neq 0$

Substitution rule

If $f(x,y)$ is a polynomial or a rational function, limits may be found by substituting for x and y (excluding values that cause division by zero).

CHAPTER 11
Differentiation Formulas

11.1   Definition of Derivative

DERIVATIVE

The **derivative** of f at x is given by

$$f'(x) = \lim_{\Delta x \to 0} \frac{f(x + \Delta x) - f(x)}{\Delta x}$$

provided that this limit exists.

EXAMPLE 11.1   Derivative using the definition

Differentiate $f(t) = \sqrt{t}$.

Solution

$$f(t) = \lim_{\Delta t \to 0} \frac{f(t + \Delta t) - f(t)}{\Delta t}$$

$$= \lim_{\Delta t \to 0} \frac{\sqrt{t + \Delta t} - \sqrt{t}}{\Delta t}$$

$$= \lim_{\Delta t \to 0} \frac{\sqrt{t + \Delta t} - \sqrt{t}}{\Delta t} \left(\frac{\sqrt{t + \Delta t} + \sqrt{t}}{\sqrt{t + \Delta t} + \sqrt{t}} \right)$$

Rationalize the numerator

$$= \lim_{\Delta t \to 0} \frac{(t + \Delta t) - t}{\Delta t(\sqrt{t + \Delta t} + \sqrt{t})}$$

$$= \lim_{\Delta t \to 0} \frac{1}{\sqrt{t + \Delta t} + \sqrt{t}}$$

$$= \frac{1}{2\sqrt{t}} \qquad\qquad\qquad \textit{for } t > 0 \qquad \square$$

PARTIAL DERIVATIVE OF A FUNCTION OF TWO VARIABLES

If $z = f(x, y)$, then the **first partial derivative** of f with respect to x and y are the functions f_x and f_y, respectively, defined by

$$f_x(x, y) = \lim_{\Delta x \to 0} \frac{f(x + \Delta x, y) - f(x, y)}{\Delta x}$$

$$f_y(x, y) = \lim_{\Delta y \to 0} \frac{f(x, y + \Delta y) - f(x, y)}{\Delta y}$$

provided that the limits exist.

DIRECTIONAL DERIVATIVE

Let $f(x, y)$ be a function defined on a disk centered at the point $P_0(x_0, y_0)$, and let $\boldsymbol{u} = u_1\boldsymbol{i} + u_2\boldsymbol{j}$ be a unit vector. Then the **directional derivative** of f at P_0 in the direction of $\boldsymbol{u}$ is given by

$$D_{\boldsymbol{u}}f(x_0, y_0) = \lim_{h \to 0} \frac{f(x_0 + hu_1, y_0 + hu_2) - f(x_0, y_0)}{h}$$

provided that the limit exists.

11.2 Procedural Rules of Differentiation

If f and g are differentiable functions of x, u is a differentiable function of x, and a, b, and c are any real numbers, then the functions cf, $f + g$, fg, and f/g (for $g(x) \neq 0$) are also differentiable, and their derivatives satisfy the following formulas:

	Rule	*Derivative*
1.	**Constant-multiple rule**	$(cf)' = cf'$
2.	**Sum rule**	$(f + g)' = f' + g'$
3.	**Difference rule**	$(f - g)' = f' - g'$
4.	**Linearity rule**	$(af + bg)' = af' + bg'$
5.	**Product rule**	$(fg)' = fg' + f'g$

6. Quotient rule

$$\left(\frac{f}{g}\right)' = \frac{gf' - fg'}{g^2}$$

7. Chain rule

$$\frac{dy}{dx} = \frac{dy}{du}\frac{du}{dx}$$

11.3   Differentiation Rules

EXTENDED-POWER RULE

8. $\dfrac{d}{dx}u^n = nu^{n-1}\dfrac{du}{dx}$

TRIGONOMETRIC FUNCTIONS

9. $\dfrac{d}{dx}\cos u = -\sin u\dfrac{du}{dx}$ **10.** $\dfrac{d}{dx}\sin u = \cos u\dfrac{du}{dx}$

11. $\dfrac{d}{dx}\tan u = \sec^2 u\dfrac{du}{dx}$ **12.** $\dfrac{d}{dx}\cot u = -\csc^2 u\dfrac{du}{dx}$

13. $\dfrac{d}{dx}\sec u = \sec u\tan u\dfrac{du}{dx}$ **14.** $\dfrac{d}{dx}\csc u = -\csc u\cot u\dfrac{du}{dx}$

INVERSE TRIGONOMETRIC FUNCTIONS

15. $\dfrac{d}{dx}\cos^{-1}u = \dfrac{-1}{\sqrt{1-u^2}}\dfrac{du}{dx}$

16. $\dfrac{d}{dx}\sin^{-1}u = \dfrac{1}{\sqrt{1-u^2}}\dfrac{du}{dx}$

17. $\dfrac{d}{dx}\tan^{-1}u = \dfrac{1}{1+u^2}\dfrac{du}{dx}$

18. $\dfrac{d}{dx}\cot^{-1}u = \dfrac{-1}{1+u^2}\dfrac{du}{dx}$

19. $\dfrac{d}{dx}\sec^{-1}u = \dfrac{1}{|u|\sqrt{u^2-1}}\dfrac{du}{dx}$

20. $\dfrac{d}{dx}\csc^{-1}u = \dfrac{-1}{|u|\sqrt{u^2-1}}\dfrac{du}{dx}$

EXPONENTIAL AND LOGARITHMIC FUNCTIONS

21. $\dfrac{d}{dx}\ln|u| = \dfrac{1}{u}\dfrac{du}{dx}$ **22.** $\dfrac{d}{dx}\log_b|u| = \dfrac{\log_b e}{u}\dfrac{du}{dx}$

$$= \dfrac{1}{u\ln b}\dfrac{du}{dx}$$

23. $\dfrac{d}{dx}e^u = e^u\dfrac{du}{dx}$ **24.** $\dfrac{d}{dx}b^u = b^u\ln b\dfrac{du}{dx}$

HYPERBOLIC FUNCTIONS

25. $\dfrac{d}{dx}\cosh u = \sinh u \dfrac{du}{dx}$ **26.** $\dfrac{d}{dx}\sinh u = \cosh u \dfrac{du}{dx}$

27. $\dfrac{d}{dx}\tanh u = \operatorname{sech}^2 u \dfrac{du}{dx}$ **28.** $\dfrac{d}{dx}\coth u = -\operatorname{csch}^2 u \dfrac{du}{dx}$

29. $\dfrac{d}{dx}\operatorname{sech} u = -\operatorname{sech} u \tanh u \dfrac{du}{dx}$

30. $\dfrac{d}{dx}\operatorname{csch} u = -\operatorname{csch} u \coth u \dfrac{du}{dx}$

INVERSE HYPERBOLIC FUNCTIONS

31. $\dfrac{d}{dx}\sinh^{-1} u = \dfrac{1}{\sqrt{u^2 + 1}}\dfrac{du}{dx}$

32. $\dfrac{d}{dx}\cosh^{-1} u = \dfrac{1}{\sqrt{u^2 - 1}}\dfrac{du}{dx}$

33. $\dfrac{d}{dx}\tanh^{-1} u = \dfrac{1}{1 - u^2}\dfrac{du}{dx}$
$$|u| < 1$$

34. $\dfrac{d}{dx}\coth^{-1} u = \dfrac{1}{1 - u^2}\dfrac{du}{dx}$
$$|u| > 1$$

35. $\dfrac{d}{dx}\operatorname{sech}^{-1} u = \dfrac{-1}{u\sqrt{1 - u^2}}\dfrac{du}{dx}$ "

36. $\dfrac{d}{dx}\operatorname{csch}^{-1} u = \dfrac{-1}{|u|\sqrt{1 + u^2}}\dfrac{du}{dx}$

11.4   Functions of Two Variables

Chain Rule for One Independent Variable
Let $f(x, y)$ be a differentiable function of x and y, and let $x = x(t)$ and $y = y(t)$ be differentiable functions of t. Then $z = f(x, y)$ is a differentiable function of t, and

$$\frac{dz}{dt} = \frac{\partial z}{\partial x}\frac{dx}{dt} + \frac{\partial z}{\partial y}\frac{dy}{dt}$$

The Chain Rule for Two Independent Variables
Suppose that $z = f(x, y)$ is differentiable at (x, y) and that the partial derivatives of $x = x(u, v)$ and $y = y(u, v)$ exist at (u, v). Then the composite function $z = f[x(u, v), y(u, v)]$ is differentiable at (u, v), with

$$\frac{\partial z}{\partial u} = \frac{\partial z}{\partial x}\frac{\partial x}{\partial u} + \frac{\partial z}{\partial y}\frac{\partial y}{\partial u}$$

and

$$\frac{\partial z}{\partial v} = \frac{\partial z}{\partial x}\frac{\partial x}{\partial v} + \frac{\partial z}{\partial y}\frac{\partial y}{\partial v}$$

GRADIENT

Let $f(x, y)$ have partial derivatives $f_x(x, y)$ and $f_y(x, y)$. Then the **gradient** of f, denoted by ∇f, is given by

$$\nabla f(x, y) = f_x(x, y)\mathbf{i} + f_y(x, y)\mathbf{j}$$

Basic properties of the gradient
assuming the existence of the following gradients:

constant rule $\nabla c = \mathbf{0}$ for any constant c
linearity rule $\nabla(af + bg) = a\nabla f + b\nabla g$ for constants a and b
product rule $\nabla(fg) = f(\nabla g) + g(\nabla f)$
quotient rule $\nabla\left(\dfrac{f}{g}\right) = \dfrac{g(\nabla f) - f(\nabla g)}{g^2}$, $g \neq 0$
power rule $\nabla(f^n) = nf^{n-1}\nabla f$

CHAPTER 12
Integration Formulas

12.1   Definition of Integral

DEFINITE INTEGRAL

If f is defined on the closed interval $[a, b]$, we say that f is **integrable** on $[a, b]$ if

$$I = \lim_{|P| \to 0} \sum_{k=1}^{n} f(x_k^*) \Delta x_k$$

exists. This limit, if it exists, is called the **definite integral** of f from a to b. The definite integral is denoted by

$$I = \int_a^b f(x)\, dx$$

EXAMPLE 12.1   Evaluating a definite integral by using the definition

Evaluate $\displaystyle\int_{-2}^{1} 4x\, dx$

Solution   The integral exists, since $f(x) = 4x$ is continuous on $[-2, 1]$. Because the integral can be computed by any partition whose norm approaches zero, we shall simplify matters by choosing a partition in which the points are evenly spaced. Specifically, we divide the interval $[-2, 1]$ into n subintervals, each of width

$$\Delta x = \frac{1 - (-2)}{n} = \frac{3}{n}$$

For each k, we choose the representative of the kth subinterval to be the right endpoint of the subinterval; that is,

$$x_k^* = -2 + k \Delta x = -2 + k\left(\frac{3}{n}\right)$$

Finally, we form the Riemann sum

$$\int_{-2}^{1} 4x\,dx$$

$$= \lim_{|P| \to 0} \sum_{k=1}^{n} f(x_k^*)\Delta x_k = \lim_{n \to +\infty} \sum_{k=1}^{n} 4\left(-2 + \frac{3k}{n}\right)\left(\frac{3}{n}\right)$$

$$n \to +\infty \text{ as } |P| \to 0$$

$$= \lim_{n \to +\infty} \frac{12}{n^2} \sum_{k=1}^{n}(-2n + 3k) = \lim_{n \to +\infty} \frac{12}{n^2}\left(\sum_{k=1}^{n}(-2n) + \sum_{k=1}^{n} 3k\right)$$

$$= \lim_{n \to +\infty} \frac{12}{n^2}\left((-2n)n + 3\left[\frac{n(n+1)}{2}\right]\right)$$

$$= \lim_{n \to +\infty} \frac{12}{n^2}\left(\frac{-4n^2 + 3n^2 + 3n}{2}\right)$$

$$= \lim_{n \to +\infty} \frac{-6n^2 + 18n}{n^2} = -6 \qquad \square$$

INDEFINITE INTEGRAL

If $\dfrac{dy}{dx} = f(x)$, then y is the function whose derivative is $f(x)$. y is called the **antiderivative** of $f(x)$ or the **indefinite integral** of $f(x)$ and is denoted by

$$\int f(x)\,dx$$

DOUBLE INTEGRAL

If f is defined on a closed, bounded region R in the xy-plane, then the **double integral of f over R** is defined by

$$\iint\limits_{R} f(x, y)\,dA = \lim_{|P| \to 0} \sum_{k=1}^{n} f(x_k^*, y_k^*)\Delta A_k$$

provided that the limit exists. If it does, then we say that f is **integrable** over R.

TRIPLE INTEGRAL

If f is a continuous function defined over a bounded solid region S, then the **triple integral of f over S** is defined to be the limit

$$\iiint\limits_{S} f(x, y, z)\,dV = \lim_{|P|\to 0} \sum_{k=1}^{n} f(x_k^*, y_k^*, z_k^*)\Delta V_k$$

provided that this limit exists.

12.2   Procedural Rules for Integration

In what follows, u, v, and w are functions of x, and a, b, p, q, and n are any constants, restricted if indicated. Since the derivative of a constant is zero, all indefinite integrals differ by an arbitrary constant. In the formulas that follow, all constants of integration are omitted, but implied. It is assumed in all cases that division by zero is excluded.

Properties of integrals

Name of Rule	*Integral*
Constant multiple	$\displaystyle \int c f(u)\,du = c \int f(u)\,du$
Sum rule	$\displaystyle \int [f(u) + g(u)]\,du = \int f(u)\,du + \int g(u)\,du$
Difference rule	$\displaystyle \int [f(u) - g(u)]\,du = \int f(u)\,du - \int g(u)\,du$
Linearity rule	$\displaystyle \int [af(u) + bg(u)]\,du$
	$\displaystyle = a \int f(u)\,du + b \int g(u)\,du$
By parts	$\displaystyle \int u\,dv = uv - \int v\,du$

Properties of double integrals   Assume that all the given integrals exist.

Linearity rule   For constants a and b,

$$\iint\limits_{D} [af(x, y) + bg(x, y)]\,dA = a \iint\limits_{D} f(x, y)\,dA + b \iint\limits_{D} g(x, y)\,dA$$

$$\iiint_S [af(x, y, z) + bg(x, y, z)] \, dV$$

$$= a \iiint_S f(x, y, z) \, dV + b \iiint_S g(x, y, z) \, dV$$

Dominance rules If $f(x, y) \geq g(x, y)$ throughout a region D, then

$$\iint_D f(x, y) \, dA \geq \iint_D g(x, y) \, dA$$

If $f(x, y, z) \geq g(x, y, z)$ on S, then

$$\iiint_S f(x, y, z) \, dV \geq \iiint_S g(x, y, z) \, dV$$

Subdivision rules

If the region of integration, D, can be subdivided into two subregions D_1 and D_2, then

$$\iint_D f(x, y) \, dA = \iiint_{D_1} f(x, y) \, dA + \iiint_{D_2} f(x, y) \, dA$$

If the solid region of integration, S, can be subdivided into two solid subregions S_1 and S_2, then

$$\iiint_S f(x, y, z) \, dV = \iiint_{S_1} f(x, y, z) \, dV + \iiint_{S_2} f(x, y, z) \, dV$$

12.3   Integration Rules

BASIC FORMULAS

1. Constant rule

$$\int 0 \, du = c$$

2. Power rule

$$\int u^n \, du = \frac{u^{n+1}}{n+1}; n \neq -1$$

$$\int u^n \, du = \ln |u|; n = -1$$

3. Exponential rule

$$\int e^u \, du = e^u$$

4. Logarithmic rule

$$\int \ln |u| \, du = u \ln |u| - u$$

Trigonometric rules

5. $\displaystyle\int \sin u \, du = -\cos u$

6. $\displaystyle\int \cos u \, du = \sin u$

7. $\displaystyle\int \tan u \, du = -\ln |\cos u|$

8. $\displaystyle\int \cot u \, du = \ln |\sin u|$

9. $\displaystyle\int \sec u \, du = \ln |\sec u + \tan u|$

10. $\displaystyle\int \csc u \, du = -\ln |\csc u + \cot u|$

11. $\displaystyle\int \sec^2 u \, du = \tan u$

12. $\displaystyle\int \csc^2 u \, du = -\cot u$

13. $\displaystyle\int \sec u \tan u \, du = \sec u$

14. $\displaystyle\int \csc u \cot u \, du = -\csc u$

Exponential rule (base b)

15. $\displaystyle\int b^u \, du = \frac{b^u}{\ln b} b > 0, b \neq 1$

Hyperbolic rules

16. $\displaystyle\int \cosh u \, du = \sinh u$

17. $\displaystyle\int \sinh u \, du = \cosh u$

18. $\displaystyle\int \tanh u \, du = \ln \cosh u$

19. $\displaystyle\int \coth u \, du = \ln |\sinh u|$

20. $\displaystyle\int \text{sech} \, u \, du = 2 \tan^{-1} e^u$

21. $\displaystyle\int \text{csch} \, u \, du = \ln \left| \tanh \frac{u}{2} \right|$

Inverse rules

22. $\displaystyle\int \frac{du}{\sqrt{a^2 - u^2}} = \sin^{-1} \frac{u}{a}$

23. $\displaystyle\int \frac{du}{\sqrt{u^2 - a^2}} = \cosh^{-1} \frac{u}{a}$

24. $\displaystyle\int \frac{du}{a^2 + u^2} = \frac{1}{a} \tan^{-1} \frac{u}{a}$

25. $\displaystyle\int \frac{du}{a^2 - u^2} = \begin{cases} \dfrac{1}{a} \tanh^{-1} \dfrac{u}{a}, & \text{if } \left| \dfrac{u}{a} \right| < 1 \\ \dfrac{1}{a} \coth^{-1} \dfrac{u}{a}, & \text{if } \left| \dfrac{u}{a} \right| > 1 \end{cases}$

26. $\displaystyle\int \frac{du}{u\sqrt{u^2 - a^2}} = \frac{1}{a} \sec^{-1} \left| \frac{u}{a} \right|$

27. $\displaystyle\int \frac{du}{u\sqrt{a^2 - u^2}} = -\frac{1}{a}\ln\left|\frac{a + \sqrt{a^2 - u^2}}{u}\right| = -\frac{1}{a}\operatorname{sech}^{-1}\left|\frac{u}{a}\right|$,

28. $\displaystyle\int \frac{du}{\sqrt{a^2 + u^2}} = \ln(u + \sqrt{a^2 + u^2}) = \sinh^{-1}\frac{u}{a}$

29. $\displaystyle\int \frac{du}{u\sqrt{a^2 + u^2}} = -\frac{1}{a}\ln\left|\frac{\sqrt{a^2 + u^2} + a}{u}\right| = -\frac{1}{a}\operatorname{csch}^{-1}\left|\frac{u}{a}\right|$

Commonly used reduction formulas (from the table of integrals):

Cosine-squared integration formula (317)

$$\int \cos^2 u\, du = \tfrac{1}{2}u + \tfrac{1}{4}\sin 2u$$

Sine-squared integration formula (348)

$$\int \sin^2 u\, du = \tfrac{1}{2}u - \tfrac{1}{4}\sin 2u$$

Secant integration formula (428)

$$\int \sec^n u\, du = \frac{\sec^{n-2} u \tan u}{n-1} + \frac{n-2}{n-1}\int \sec^{n-2} u\, du, \; n \neq 1$$

Tangent reduction formula (406)

$$\int \tan^n u\, du = \frac{\tan^{n-1} u}{n-1} - \int \tan^{n-2} u\, du$$

12.4   Integral Table

INTEGRALS INVOLVING $au + b$

30. $\displaystyle\int (au + b)^n\, du = \frac{(au + b)^{n+1}}{(n + 1)a}$

31. $\displaystyle\int u(au + b)^n\, du = \frac{(au + b)^{n+2}}{(n + 2)a^2} - \frac{b(au + b)^{n+1}}{(n + 1)a^2}$

32. $\displaystyle\int u^2(au + b)^n\, du = \frac{(au + b)^{n+3}}{(n + 3)a^3} - \frac{2b(au + b)^{n+2}}{(n + 2)a^3}$

$$+ \frac{b^2(au + b)^{n+1}}{(n + 1)a^3}$$

33. $\displaystyle\int u^m(au+b)^n\,du$

$$= \begin{cases} \dfrac{u^{m+1}(au+b)^n}{m+n+1} + \dfrac{nb}{m+n+1}\displaystyle\int u^m(au+b)^{n-1}\,du \\[2ex] \dfrac{u^m(au+b)^{n+1}}{(m+n+1)a} - \dfrac{mb}{(m+n+1)a}\displaystyle\int u^{m-1}(au+b)^n\,du \\[2ex] \dfrac{-u^{m+1}(au+b)^{n+1}}{(n+1)b} + \dfrac{m+n+2}{(n+1)b}\displaystyle\int u^m(au+b)^{n+1}\,du \end{cases}$$

34. $\displaystyle\int \frac{du}{au+b} = \frac{1}{a}\ln|au+b|$

35. $\displaystyle\int \frac{u\,du}{au+b} = \frac{u}{a} - \frac{b}{a^2}\ln|au+b|$

36. $\displaystyle\int \frac{u^2\,du}{au+b} = \frac{(au+b)^2}{2a^3} - \frac{2b(au+b)}{a^3} + \frac{b^2}{a^3}\ln|au+b|$

37. $\displaystyle\int \frac{u^3\,du}{au+b} = \frac{(au+b)^3}{3a^4} - \frac{3b(au+b)^2}{2a^4}$

$$+ \frac{3b^2(au+b)}{a^4} - \frac{b^3}{a^4}\ln|au+b|$$

38. $\displaystyle\int \frac{du}{u(au+b)} = \frac{1}{b}\ln\left|\frac{u}{au+b}\right|$

39. $\displaystyle\int \frac{du}{u^2(au+b)} = -\frac{1}{bu} + \frac{a}{b^2}\ln\left|\frac{au+b}{u}\right|$

40. $\displaystyle\int \frac{du}{u^3(au+b)} = \frac{2au-b}{2b^2u^2} + \frac{a^2}{b^3}\ln\left|\frac{u}{au+b}\right|$

41. $\displaystyle\int \frac{du}{(au+b)^2} = \frac{-1}{a(au+b)}$

42. $\displaystyle\int \frac{u\,du}{(au+b)^2} = \frac{b}{a^2(au+b)} + \frac{1}{a^2}\ln|au+b|$

43. $\displaystyle\int \frac{u^2\,du}{(au+b)^2} = \frac{au+b}{a^3} - \frac{b^2}{a^3(au+b)} - \frac{2b}{a^3}\ln|au+b|$

44. $\displaystyle\int \frac{u^3\,du}{(au+b)^2} = \frac{(au+b)^2}{2a^4} - \frac{3b(au+b)}{a^4}$

$$+ \frac{b^3}{a^4(au+b)} + \frac{3b^2}{a^4}\ln|au+b|$$

45. $\displaystyle\int \frac{du}{u(au+b)^2} = \frac{1}{b(au+b)} + \frac{1}{b^2}\ln\left|\frac{u}{au+b}\right|$

46. $\displaystyle\int \frac{du}{u^2(au+b)^2} = \frac{-a}{b^2(au+b)} + \frac{1}{b^2u} + \frac{2a}{b^3}\ln\left|\frac{au+b}{u}\right|$

47. $\displaystyle\int \frac{du}{u^3(au+b)^2} = -\frac{(au+b)^2}{2b^4u^2} + \frac{3a(au+b)}{b^4u}$

$$- \frac{a^3u}{b^4(au+b)} - \frac{3a^2}{b^4}\ln\left|\frac{au+b}{u}\right|$$

48. $\displaystyle\int \frac{du}{(au+b)^3} = \frac{-1}{2a(au+b)^2}$

49. $\displaystyle\int \frac{u\,du}{(au+b)^3} = \frac{-1}{a^2(au+b)} + \frac{b}{2a^2(au+b)^2}$

50. $\displaystyle\int \frac{u^2\,du}{(au+b)^3} = \frac{2b}{a^3(au+b)} - \frac{b^2}{2a^3(au+b)^2} + \frac{1}{a^3}\ln|au+b|$

51. $\displaystyle\int \frac{u^3\,du}{(au+b)^3} = \frac{u}{a^3} - \frac{3b^2}{a^4(au+b)}$

$$+ \frac{b^3}{2a^4(au+b)^2} - \frac{3b}{a^4}\ln|au+b|$$

52. $\displaystyle\int \frac{du}{u(au+b)^3} = \frac{a^2u^2}{2b^3(au+b)^2} - \frac{2au}{b^3(au+b)} - \frac{1}{b^3}\ln\left|\frac{au+b}{u}\right|$

53. $\displaystyle\int \frac{du}{u^2(au+b)^3} = \frac{-a}{2b^2(au+b)^2} - \frac{2a}{b^3(au+b)}$

$$- \frac{1}{b^3u} + \frac{3a}{b^4}\ln\left|\frac{au+b}{u}\right|$$

54. $\displaystyle\int \frac{du}{u^3(au+b)^3} = \frac{a^4u^2}{2b^5(au+b)^2} - \frac{4a^3u}{b^5(au+b)}$

$$- \frac{(au+b)^2}{2b^5u^2} - \frac{6a^2}{b^5}\ln\left|\frac{au+b}{u}\right|$$

INTEGRALS INVOLVING $u^2 + a^2$

55. $\displaystyle\int \frac{du}{u^2 + a^2} = \frac{1}{a}\tan^{-1}\frac{u}{a}$

56. $\displaystyle\int \frac{u\,du}{u^2 + a^2} = \frac{1}{2}\ln(u^2 + a^2)$

57. $\displaystyle\int \frac{u^2\,du}{u^2 + a^2} = u - a\tan^{-1}\frac{u}{a}$

58. $\displaystyle\int \frac{u^3\,du}{u^2 + a^2} = \frac{u^2}{2} - \frac{a^2}{2}\ln(u^2 + a^2)$

59. $\displaystyle\int \frac{du}{u(u^2 + a^2)} = \frac{1}{2a^2}\ln\left(\frac{u^2}{u^2 + a^2}\right)$

60. $\displaystyle\int \frac{du}{u^2(u^2 + a^2)} = -\frac{1}{a^2 u} - \frac{1}{a^3}\tan^{-1}\frac{u}{a}$

61. $\displaystyle\int \frac{du}{u^3(u^2 + a^2)} = -\frac{1}{2a^2 u^2} - \frac{1}{2a^4}\ln\left(\frac{u^2}{u^2 + a^2}\right)$

62. $\displaystyle\int \frac{du}{(u^2 + a^2)^2} = \frac{u}{2a^2(u^2 + a^2)} + \frac{1}{2a^3}\tan^{-1}\frac{u}{a}$

63. $\displaystyle\int \frac{u\,du}{(u^2 + a^2)^2} = \frac{-1}{2(u^2 + a^2)}$

64. $\displaystyle\int \frac{u^2\,du}{(u^2 + a^2)^2} = \frac{-u}{2(u^2 + a^2)} + \frac{1}{2a^3}\tan^{-1}\frac{u}{a}$

65. $\displaystyle\int \frac{u^3\,du}{(u^2 + a^2)^2} = \frac{a^2}{2(u^2 + a^2)} + \frac{1}{2}\ln(u^2 + a^2)$

66. $\displaystyle\int \frac{du}{u(u^2 + a^2)^2} = \frac{1}{2a^2(u^2 + a^2)} + \frac{1}{2a^4}\ln\left(\frac{u^2}{u^2 + a^2}\right)$

67. $\displaystyle\int \frac{du}{u^2(u^2 + a^2)^2} = -\frac{1}{a^4 y} - \frac{u}{2a^4(u^2 + a^2)} - \frac{3}{2a^5}\tan^{-1}\frac{u}{a}$

68. $\displaystyle\int \frac{du}{u^3(u^2 + a^2)^2} = \frac{1}{2a^4 u^2} - \frac{1}{2a^4(u^2 + a^2)}$
$$- \frac{1}{a^6}\ln\left(\frac{u^2}{u^2 + a^2}\right)$$

69. $\displaystyle\int \frac{du}{(u^2 + a^2)^n} = \frac{u}{2(n-1)a^2(u^2 + a^2)^{n-1}}$
$$+ \frac{2n-3}{(2n-2)a^2}\int \frac{du}{(u^2 + a^2)^{n-1}}$$

70. $\displaystyle\int \frac{u\,du}{(u^2 + a^2)^n} = \frac{-1}{2(n-1)(u^2 + a^2)^{n-1}}$

71. $\displaystyle\int \frac{du}{u(u^2+a^2)^n} = \frac{1}{2(n-1)a^2(u^2+a^2)^{n-1}}$

$$+ \frac{1}{a^2}\int \frac{du}{u(u^2+a^2)^{n-1}}$$

72. $\displaystyle\int \frac{u^m\,du}{(u^2+a^2)^n} = \int \frac{u^{m-2}\,du}{(u^2+a^2)^{n-1}} - a^2\int \frac{u^{m-2}\,du}{(u^2+a^2)^n}$

73. $\displaystyle\int \frac{du}{u^m(u^2+a^2)^n} = \frac{1}{a^2}\int \frac{du}{u^m(u^2+a^2)^{n-1}}$

$$- \frac{1}{a^2}\int \frac{du}{u^{m-2}(u^2+a^2)^n}$$

INTEGRALS INVOLVING $u^2 - a^2, u^2 > a^2$

74. $\displaystyle\int \frac{du}{u^2-a^2} = \frac{1}{2a}\ln\left|\frac{u-a}{u+a}\right| \text{ or } -\frac{1}{a}\coth^{-1}\frac{u}{a}$

75. $\displaystyle\int \frac{u\,du}{u^2-a^2} = \frac{1}{2}\ln|u^2-a^2|$

76. $\displaystyle\int \frac{u^2\,du}{u^2-a^2} = u + \frac{a}{2}\ln\left|\frac{u-a}{u+a}\right|$

77. $\displaystyle\int \frac{u^3\,du}{u^2-a^2} = \frac{u^2}{2} + \frac{a^2}{2}\ln|u^2-a^2|$

78. $\displaystyle\int \frac{du}{u(u^2-a^2)} = \frac{1}{2a^2}\ln\left|\frac{u^2-a^2}{u^2}\right|$

79. $\displaystyle\int \frac{du}{u^2(u^2-a^2)} = \frac{1}{a^2u} + \frac{1}{2a^3}\ln\left|\frac{u-a}{u+a}\right|$

80. $\displaystyle\int \frac{du}{u^3(u^2-a^2)} = \frac{1}{2a^2u^2} - \frac{1}{2a^4}\ln\left|\frac{u^2}{u^2-a^2}\right|$

81. $\displaystyle\int \frac{du}{(u^2-a^2)^2} = \frac{-u}{2a^2(u^2-a^2)} - \frac{1}{4a^3}\ln\left|\frac{u-a}{u+a}\right|$

82. $\displaystyle\int \frac{u\,du}{(u^2-a^2)^2} = \frac{-1}{2(u^2-a^2)}$

83. $\displaystyle\int \frac{u^2\,du}{(u^2-a^2)^2} = \frac{-u}{2(u^2-a^2)} + \frac{1}{4a}\ln\left|\frac{u-a}{u+a}\right|$

84. $\displaystyle\int \frac{u^3\,du}{(u^2-a^2)^2} = \frac{-a^2}{2(u^2-a^2)} + \frac{1}{2}\ln|u^2-a^2|$

85. $\displaystyle\int \frac{du}{u(u^2-a^2)^2} = \frac{-1}{2a^2(u^2-a^2)} + \frac{1}{2a}\ln\left|\frac{u^2}{u^2-a^2}\right|$

86. $\displaystyle\int \frac{du}{u^2(u^2-a^2)^2} = -\frac{1}{a^4u} - \frac{u}{2a^4(u^2-a^2)} - \frac{3}{4a^5}\ln\left|\frac{u-a}{u+a}\right|$

87. $\displaystyle\int \frac{du}{u^3(u^2-a^2)^2} = -\frac{1}{2a^4u^2} - \frac{1}{2a^4(u^2-a^2)} + \frac{1}{a^6}\ln\left|\frac{u^2}{u^2-a^2}\right|$

88. $\displaystyle\int \frac{du}{(u^2-a^2)^n} = \frac{-u}{2(n-1)a^2(u^2-a^2)^{n-1}}$

$$- \frac{2n-3}{(2n-2)a^2}\int \frac{du}{(u^2-a^2)^{n-1}}$$

89. $\displaystyle\int \frac{u\,du}{(u^2-a^2)^n} = \frac{-1}{2(n-1)(u^2-a^2)^{n-1}}$

90. $\displaystyle\int \frac{du}{u(u^2-a^2)^n} = \frac{-1}{2(n-1)a^2(u^2-a^2)^{n-1}}$

$$- \frac{1}{a^2}\int \frac{du}{u(u^2-a^2)^{n-1}}$$

91. $\displaystyle\int \frac{u^m\,du}{(u^2-a^2)^n} = \int \frac{u^{m-2}\,du}{(u^2-a^2)^{n-1}} + a^2\int \frac{u^{m-2}\,du}{(u^2-a^2)^n}$

92. $\displaystyle\int \frac{du}{u^m(u^2-a^2)^n} = \frac{1}{a^2}\int \frac{du}{u^{m-2}(u^2-a^2)^n}$

$$- \frac{1}{a^2}\int \frac{du}{u^m(u^2-a^2)^{n-1}}$$

INTEGRALS INVOLVING $a^2-u^2, u^2 < a^2$

93. $\displaystyle\int \frac{du}{a^2-u^2} = \frac{1}{2a}\ln\left|\frac{a+u}{a-u}\right|$ or $\frac{1}{a}\tanh^{-1}\frac{u}{a}$

94. $\displaystyle\int \frac{u\,du}{a^2-u^2} = -\frac{1}{2}\ln|a^2-u^2|$

95. $\displaystyle\int \frac{u^2\,du}{a^2-u^2} = -u + \frac{a}{2}\ln\left|\frac{a+u}{a-u}\right|$

96. $\displaystyle\int \frac{u^3\,du}{a^2-u^2} = -\frac{u^2}{2} - \frac{a^2}{2}\ln|a^2-u^2|$

97. $\displaystyle\int \frac{du}{u(a^2-u^2)} = \frac{1}{2a^2}\ln\left|\frac{u^2}{a^2-u^2}\right|$

98. $\displaystyle\int \frac{du}{u^2(a^2-u^2)} = -\frac{1}{a^2u} + \frac{1}{2a^3}\ln\left|\frac{a+u}{a-u}\right|$

99. $\displaystyle\int \frac{du}{u^3(a^2-u^2)} = -\frac{1}{2a^2u^2} + \frac{1}{2a^4}\ln\left|\frac{u^2}{a^2-u^2}\right|$

100. $\displaystyle\int \frac{du}{(a^2 - u^2)^2} = \frac{u}{2a^2(a^2 - u^2)} + \frac{1}{4a^3} \ln\left|\frac{a+u}{a-u}\right|$

101. $\displaystyle\int \frac{u\,du}{(a^2 - u^2)^2} = \frac{1}{2(a^2 - u^2)}$

102. $\displaystyle\int \frac{u^2\,du}{(a^2 - u^2)^2} = \frac{u}{2(a^2 - u^2)} - \frac{1}{4a} \ln\left|\frac{a+u}{a-u}\right|$

103. $\displaystyle\int \frac{u^3\,du}{(a^2 - u^2)^2} = \frac{a^2}{2(a^2 - u^2)} + \frac{1}{2} \ln|a^2 - u^2|$

104. $\displaystyle\int \frac{du}{u(a^2 - u^2)^2} = \frac{1}{2a^2(a^2 - u^2)} + \frac{1}{2a^4} \ln\left|\frac{u^2}{a^2 - u^2}\right|$

105. $\displaystyle\int \frac{du}{u^2(a^2 - u^2)^2} = \frac{-1}{a^4 u} + \frac{u}{2a^4(a^2 - u^2)} + \frac{3}{4a^5} \ln\left|\frac{a+u}{a-u}\right|$

106. $\displaystyle\int \frac{du}{u^3(a^2 - u^2)^2} = \frac{-1}{2a^4 u^2} + \frac{1}{2a^4(a^2 - u^2)} + \frac{1}{a^6} \ln\left|\frac{u^2}{a^2 - u^2}\right|$

107. $\displaystyle\int \frac{du}{(a^2 - u^2)^n} = \frac{u}{2(n - 1)a^2(a^2 - u^2)^{n-1}}$

$$+ \frac{2n - 3}{(2n - 2)a^2} \int \frac{du}{(a^2 - u^2)^{n-1}}$$

108. $\displaystyle\int \frac{u\,du}{(a^2 - u^2)^n} = \frac{1}{2(n - 1)(a^2 - u^2)^{n-1}}$

109. $\displaystyle\int \frac{du}{u(a^2 - u^2)^n} = \frac{1}{2(n - 1)a^2(a^2 - u^2)^{n-1}}$

$$+ \frac{1}{a^2} \int \frac{du}{u(a^2 - u^2)^{n-1}}$$

110. $\displaystyle\int \frac{u^m\,du}{(a^2 - u^2)^n} = a^2 \int \frac{u^{m-2}\,du}{(a^2 - u^2)^n} - \int \frac{u^{m-2}\,du}{(a^2 - u^2)^{n-1}}$

111. $\displaystyle\int \frac{du}{u^m(a^2 - u^2)^n} = \frac{1}{a^2} \int \frac{du}{u^m(a^2 - u^2)^{n-1}}$

$$+ \frac{1}{a^2} \int \frac{du}{u^{m-2}(a^2 - u^2)^n}$$

INTEGRALS INVOLVING $au + b$ AND $pu + q$

112. $\displaystyle\int \frac{du}{(au + b)(pu + q)} = \frac{1}{bp - aq} \ln\left|\frac{pu + q}{au + b}\right|$

113. $\displaystyle\int \frac{u\,du}{(au + b)(pu + q)}$

$$= \frac{1}{bp - aq} \left\{ \frac{b}{a} \ln|au + b| - \frac{q}{p} \ln|pu + q| \right\}$$

114. $\displaystyle\int \frac{du}{(au+b)^2(pu+q)}$

$$= \frac{1}{bp-aq}\left\{\frac{1}{au+b} + \frac{p}{bp-aq}\ln\left|\frac{pu+q}{au+b}\right|\right\}$$

115. $\displaystyle\int \frac{u\,du}{(au+b)^2(pu+q)}$

$$= \frac{1}{bp-aq}\left\{\frac{q}{bp-aq}\ln\left|\frac{au+b}{pu+q}\right| - \frac{b}{a(au+b)}\right\}$$

116. $\displaystyle\int \frac{u^2\,du}{(au+b)^2(pu+q)} = \frac{b^2}{(bp-aq)a^2(au+b)}$

$$+\frac{1}{(bp-aq)^2}\left\{\frac{q^2}{p}\ln|pu+q| + \frac{b(bp-2aq)}{a^2}\ln|au+b|\right\}$$

117. $\displaystyle\int \frac{du}{(au+b)^m(pu+q)^n}$

$$= \frac{-1}{(n-1)(bp-aq)}\left\{\frac{1}{(au+b)^{m-1}(pu+q)^{n-1}}\right.$$

$$\left. +a(m+n-2)\int \frac{du}{(au+b)^m(pu+q)^{n-1}}\right\}$$

118. $\displaystyle\int \frac{au+b}{pu+q}\,du = \frac{au}{p} + \frac{bp-aq}{p^2}\ln|pu+q|$

119. $\displaystyle\int \frac{(au+b)^m}{(pu+q)^n}\,du$

$$= \begin{cases} \dfrac{-1}{(n-1)(bp-aq)}\left\{\dfrac{(au+b)^{m+1}}{(pu+q)^{n-1}}\right. \\[2mm] \left. +(n-m-2)a\displaystyle\int \dfrac{(au+b)^m}{(pu+q)^{n-1}}\,du\right\} \\[4mm] \dfrac{-1}{(n-m-1)p}\left\{\dfrac{(au+b)^m}{(pu+q)^{n-1}}\right. \\[2mm] \left. +m(bp-aq)\displaystyle\int \dfrac{(au+b)^{m-1}}{(pu+q)^n}\,du\right\} \\[4mm] \dfrac{-1}{(n-1)p}\left\{\dfrac{(au+b)^m}{(pu+q)^{n-1}} - ma\displaystyle\int \dfrac{(au+b)^{m-1}}{(pu+q)^{n-1}}\,du\right\} \end{cases}$$

INTEGRALS INVOLVING $au^2 + bu + c$

120. $$\int \frac{du}{au^2 + bu + c} = \begin{cases} \dfrac{2}{\sqrt{4ac - b^2}} \tan^{-1} \dfrac{2au + b}{\sqrt{4ac - b^2}} \\[4mm] \dfrac{1}{\sqrt{b^2 - 4ac}} \ln \left| \dfrac{2au + b - \sqrt{b^2 - 4ac}}{2au + b + \sqrt{b^2 - 4ac}} \right| \end{cases}$$

121. $$\int \frac{u\,du}{au^2 + bu + c} = \frac{1}{2a} \ln |au^2 + bu + c|$$
$$- \frac{b}{2a} \int \frac{du}{au^2 + bu + c}$$

122. $$\int \frac{u^2\,du}{au^2 + bu + c} = \frac{u}{a} - \frac{b}{2a^2} \ln |au^2 + bu + c|$$
$$+ \frac{b^2 - 2ac}{2a^2} \int \frac{du}{au^2 + bu + c}$$

123. $$\int \frac{u^m\,du}{au^2 + bu + c} = \frac{u^{m-1}}{(m-1)a} - \frac{c}{a} \int \frac{u^{m-2}\,du}{au^2 + bu + c}$$
$$- \frac{b}{a} \int \frac{u^{m-1}\,du}{au^2 + bu + c}$$

124. $$\int \frac{du}{u(au^2 + bu + c)} = \frac{1}{2c} \ln \left| \frac{u^2}{au^2 + bu + c} \right|$$
$$- \frac{b}{2c} \int \frac{du}{au^2 + bu + c}$$

125. $$\int \frac{du}{u^2(au^2 + bu + c)} = \frac{b}{2c^2} \ln \left| \frac{au^2 + bu + c}{u^2} \right|$$
$$- \frac{1}{cu} + \frac{b^2 - 2ac}{2c^2} \int \frac{du}{au^2 + bu + c}$$

126. $$\int \frac{du}{u^n(au^2 + bu + c)}$$
$$= -\frac{1}{(n-1)cu^{n-1}} - \frac{b}{c} \int \frac{du}{u^{n-1}(au^2 + bu + c)}$$
$$- \frac{a}{c} \int \frac{du}{u^{n-2}(au^2 + bu + c)}$$

127. $$\int \frac{du}{(au^2 + bu + c)} = \frac{2au + b}{(4ac - b^2)(au^2 + bu + c)}$$
$$+ \frac{2a}{4ac - b^2} \int \frac{du}{au^2 + bu + c}$$

128. $$\int \frac{u\,du}{(au^2+bu+c)^2} = -\frac{bu+2c}{(4ac-b^2)(au^2+bu+c)}$$
$$-\frac{b}{4ac-b^2}\int \frac{du}{au^2+bu+c}$$

129. $$\int \frac{u^2\,du}{(au^2+bu+c)^2} = \frac{(b^2-2ac)u+bc}{a(4ac-b^2)(au^2+bu+c)}$$
$$+\frac{2c}{4ac-b^2}\int \frac{du}{au^2+bu+c}$$

130. $$\int \frac{u^m\,du}{(au^2+bu+c)^n} = \frac{-u^{m-1}}{(2n-m-1)a(au^2+bu+c)^{n-1}}$$
$$+\frac{(m-1)c}{(2n-m-1)a}\int \frac{u^{m-2}\,du}{(au^2+bu+c)^n}$$
$$-\frac{(n-m)b}{(2n-m-1)a}\int \frac{u^{m-1}\,du}{(au^2+bu+c)^n}$$

131. $$\int \frac{u^{2n-1}\,du}{(au^2+bu+c)^n} = -\frac{1}{a}\int \frac{u^{2n-3}\,du}{(au^2+bu+c)^{n-1}}$$
$$-\frac{c}{a}\int \frac{u^{2n-3}\,du}{(au^2+bu+c)^n}$$
$$-\frac{b}{a}\int \frac{u^{2n-2}\,du}{(au^2+bu+c)^n}$$

132. $$\int \frac{du}{u(au^2+bu+c)^2} = \frac{1}{2c(au^2+bu+c)}$$
$$-\frac{b}{2c}\int \frac{du}{(au^2+bu+c)^2}$$
$$+\frac{1}{c}\int \frac{du}{u(au^2+bu+c)}$$

133. $$\int \frac{du}{u^2(au^2+bu+c)^2} = -\frac{1}{cu(au^2+bu+c)}$$
$$-\frac{3a}{c}\int \frac{du}{(au^2+bu+c)^2}$$
$$-\frac{2b}{c}\int \frac{du}{u(au^2+bu+c)^2}$$

134.
$$\int \frac{du}{u^m(au^2 + bu + c)^n} = -\frac{1}{(m-1)cu^{m-1}(au^2+bu+c)^{n-1}}$$
$$-\frac{(m+2n-3)a}{(m-1)c}\int \frac{du}{u^{m-2}(au^2+bu+c)^n}$$
$$-\frac{(m+n-2)b}{(m-1)c}\int \frac{du}{u^{m-1}(au^2+bu+c)^n}$$

INTEGRALS INVOLVING $\sqrt{au+b}$

135.
$$\int \frac{du}{\sqrt{au+b}} = \frac{2\sqrt{au+b}}{a}$$

136.
$$\int \frac{u\,du}{\sqrt{au+b}} = \frac{2(au-2b)}{3a^2}\sqrt{au+b}$$

137.
$$\int \frac{u^2\,du}{\sqrt{au+b}} = \frac{2(3a^2u^2-4abu+8b^2)}{15a^3}\sqrt{au+b}$$

138.
$$\int \frac{du}{u\sqrt{au+b}} = \begin{cases} \dfrac{1}{\sqrt{b}}\ln\left|\dfrac{\sqrt{au+b}-\sqrt{b}}{\sqrt{au+b}+\sqrt{b}}\right| \\ \dfrac{2}{\sqrt{-b}}\tan^{-1}\sqrt{\dfrac{au+b}{-b}} \end{cases}$$

139.
$$\int \frac{du}{u^2\sqrt{au+b}} = -\frac{\sqrt{au+b}}{bu} - \frac{a}{2b}\int \frac{du}{u\sqrt{au+b}}$$

140.
$$\int \sqrt{au+b}\,du = \frac{2\sqrt{(au+b)^3}}{3a}$$

141.
$$\int u\sqrt{au+b}\,du = \frac{2(3au-2b)}{15a^2}\sqrt{(au+b)^3}$$

142.
$$\int u^2\sqrt{au+b}\,du = \frac{2(15a^2u^2-12abu+8b^2)}{105a^3}\sqrt{(au+b)^3}$$

143.
$$\int \frac{\sqrt{au+b}}{u}\,du = 2\sqrt{au+b} + b\int \frac{du}{u\sqrt{au+b}}$$

144.
$$\int \frac{\sqrt{au+b}}{u^2}\,du = -\frac{\sqrt{au+b}}{u} + \frac{a}{2}\int \frac{du}{u\sqrt{au+b}}$$

145.
$$\int \frac{u^m}{\sqrt{au+b}}\,du = \frac{2u^m\sqrt{au+b}}{(2m+1)a} - \frac{2mb}{(2m+1)a}\int \frac{u^{m-1}}{\sqrt{au+b}}\,du$$

146.
$$\int \frac{du}{u^m\sqrt{au+b}} = -\frac{\sqrt{au+b}}{(m-1)bu^{m-1}}$$
$$-\frac{(2m-3)a}{(2m-2)b}\int \frac{du}{u^{m-1}\sqrt{au+b}}$$

147. $\int u^m \sqrt{au + b}\, du = \dfrac{2u^m}{(2m + 3)a}(au + b)^{3/2}$

$$- \dfrac{2mb}{(2m + 3)a} \int u^{m-1}\sqrt{au + b}\, du$$

148. $\int \dfrac{\sqrt{au + b}}{u^m}\, du = -\dfrac{\sqrt{au + b}}{(m - 1)u^{m-1}}$

$$+ \dfrac{a}{2(m - 1)} \int \dfrac{du}{u^{m-1}\sqrt{au + b}}$$

149. $\int \dfrac{\sqrt{au + b}}{u^m}\, du = \dfrac{-(au + b)^{3/2}}{(m - 1)bu^{m-1}}$

$$- \dfrac{(2m - 5)a}{(2m - 2)b} \int \dfrac{\sqrt{au + b}}{u^{m-1}}\, du$$

150. $\int (au + b)^{m/2}\, du = \dfrac{2(au + b)^{(m+2)/2}}{a(m + 2)}$

151. $\int u(au + b)^{m/2}\, du = \dfrac{2(au + b)^{(m+4)/2}}{a^2(m + 4)} - \dfrac{2b(au + b)^{(m+2)/2}}{a^2(m + 2)}$

152. $\int u^2(au + b)^{m/2}\, du = \dfrac{2(au + b)^{(m+6)/2}}{a^3(m + 6)} - \dfrac{4b(au + b)^{(m+4)/2}}{a^3(m + 4)}$

$$+ \dfrac{2b^2(au + b)^{(m+2)/2}}{a^3(m + 2)}$$

153. $\int \dfrac{(au + b)^{m/2}}{u}\, du = \dfrac{2(au + b)^{m/2}}{m} + b\int \dfrac{(au + b)^{(m-2)/2}}{u}\, du$

154. $\int \dfrac{(au + b)^{m/2}}{u^2}\, du = \dfrac{(au + b)^{(m+2)/2}}{bu}$

$$+ \dfrac{ma}{2b} \int \dfrac{(au + b)^{m/2}}{u}\, du$$

155. $\int \dfrac{du}{u(au + b)^{m/2}} = \dfrac{2}{(m - 2)b(au + b)^{(m-2)/2}}$

$$+ \dfrac{1}{b} \int \dfrac{du}{u(au + b)^{(m-2)/2}}$$

INTEGRALS INVOLVING $\sqrt{au + b}$ AND $pu + q$

156. $\int \dfrac{pu + q}{\sqrt{au + b}}\, du = \dfrac{2(apu + 3aq - 2bp)}{3a^2}\sqrt{au + b}$

157. $\displaystyle\int \frac{du}{(pu+q)\sqrt{au+b}}$

$$= \begin{cases} \dfrac{1}{\sqrt{bp-aq}\sqrt{p}} \ln \left| \dfrac{\sqrt{p(au+b)} - \sqrt{bp-aq}}{\sqrt{p(au+b)} + \sqrt{bp-aq}} \right| \\[4ex] \dfrac{2}{\sqrt{aq-bp}\sqrt{p}} \tan^{-1} \sqrt{\dfrac{p(au+b)}{aq-bp}} \end{cases}$$

158. $\displaystyle\int \frac{\sqrt{au+b}}{pu+q}\, du$

$$= \begin{cases} \dfrac{2\sqrt{au+b}}{p} + \dfrac{\sqrt{bp-aq}}{p\sqrt{p}} \ln \left| \dfrac{\sqrt{p(au+b)} - \sqrt{bp-aq}}{\sqrt{p(au+b)} + \sqrt{bp-aq}} \right| \\[4ex] \dfrac{2\sqrt{au+b}}{p} - \dfrac{2\sqrt{aq-bp}}{p\sqrt{p}} \tan^{-1} \sqrt{\dfrac{p(au+b)}{aq-bp}} \end{cases}$$

159. $\displaystyle\int (pu+q)^n \sqrt{au+b}\, du = \frac{2(pu+q)^{n+1}\sqrt{au+b}}{(2n+3)p}$

$$+ \frac{bp-aq}{(2n+3)p} \int \frac{(pu+q)^n}{\sqrt{au+b}}\, du$$

160. $\displaystyle\int \frac{du}{(pu+q)^n \sqrt{au+b}}$

$$= \frac{\sqrt{au+b}}{(n-1)(aq-bp)(pu+q)^{n-1}}$$

$$+ \frac{(2n-3)a}{2(n-1)(aq-bp)} \int \frac{du}{(pu+q)^{n-1}\sqrt{au+b}}$$

161. $\displaystyle\int \frac{(pu+q)^n}{\sqrt{au+b}}\, du = \frac{2(pu+q)^n \sqrt{au+b}}{(2n+1)a}$

$$+ \frac{2n(aq-bp)}{(2n+1)a} \int \frac{(pu+q)^{n-1}\, du}{\sqrt{au+b}}$$

162. $\displaystyle\int \frac{\sqrt{au+b}}{(pu+q)^n}\, du = \frac{-\sqrt{au+b}}{(n-1)p(pu+q)^{n-1}}$

$$+ \frac{a}{2(n-1)p} \int \frac{du}{(pu+q)^{n-1}\sqrt{au+b}}$$

INTEGRALS INVOLVING $\sqrt{au+b}$ AND $\sqrt{pu+q}$

163. $\displaystyle\int \frac{du}{\sqrt{(au+b)(pu+q)}}$

$$= \begin{cases} \dfrac{2}{\sqrt{ap}}\ln|\sqrt{a(pu+q)}+\sqrt{p(au+b)}| \\[2ex] \dfrac{2}{\sqrt{-ap}}\tan^{-1}\sqrt{\dfrac{-p(au+b)}{a(pu+q)}} \end{cases}$$

164. $\displaystyle\int \frac{du}{\sqrt{(au+b)(pu+q)}} = \frac{\sqrt{(au+b)(pu+q)}}{ap}$

$$-\frac{bp+aq}{2ap}\int \frac{du}{\sqrt{(au+b)(pu+q)}}$$

165. $\displaystyle\int \sqrt{(au+b)(pu+q)}\,du$

$$= \frac{2apu+bp+aq}{4ap}\sqrt{(au+b)(pu+q)}$$

$$-\frac{(bp-aq)^2}{8ap}\int \frac{du}{\sqrt{(au+b)(pu+q)}}$$

166. $\displaystyle\int \sqrt{\frac{pu+q}{au+b}}\,du = \frac{\sqrt{(au+b)(pu+q)}}{a}$

$$+\frac{aq-bp}{2a}\int \frac{du}{\sqrt{(au+b)(pu+q)}}$$

167. $\displaystyle\int \frac{du}{(pu+q)\sqrt{(au+b)(pu+q)}} = \frac{2\sqrt{au+b}}{(aq-bp)\sqrt{pu+q}}$

INTEGRALS INVOLVING $\sqrt{u^2+a^2}$

168. $\displaystyle\int \sqrt{u^2+a^2}\,du = \frac{u\sqrt{u^2+a^2}}{2} + \frac{a^2}{2}\ln(u+\sqrt{u^2+a^2})$

169. $\displaystyle\int u\sqrt{u^2+a^2}\,du = \frac{(u^2+a^2)^{3/2}}{3}$

170. $\displaystyle\int u^2\sqrt{u^2+a^2}\,du = \frac{u(u^2+a^2)^{3/2}}{4} - \frac{a^2u\sqrt{u^2+a^2}}{8}$

$$-\frac{a^4}{8}\ln(u+\sqrt{u^2+a^2})$$

171. $\displaystyle\int u^3\sqrt{u^2+a^2}\,du = \frac{(u^2+a^2)^{5/2}}{5} - \frac{a^2(u^2+a^2)^{3/2}}{3}$

172. $\displaystyle\int \frac{du}{\sqrt{u^2+a^2}} = \ln(u + \sqrt{u^2+a^2}) \text{ or } \sinh^{-1}\frac{u}{a}$

173. $\displaystyle\int \frac{u\,du}{\sqrt{u^2+a^2}} = \sqrt{u^2+a^2}$

174. $\displaystyle\int \frac{u^2\,du}{\sqrt{u^2+a^2}} = \frac{u\sqrt{u^2+a^2}}{2} - \frac{a^2}{2}\ln(u + \sqrt{u^2+a^2})$

175. $\displaystyle\int \frac{u^3\,du}{\sqrt{u^2+a^2}} = \frac{(u^2+a^2)^{3/2}}{3} - a^2\sqrt{u^2+a^2}$

176. $\displaystyle\int \frac{du}{u\sqrt{u^2+a^2}} = -\frac{1}{a}\ln\left|\frac{a+\sqrt{u^2+a^2}}{u}\right|$

177. $\displaystyle\int \frac{du}{u^2\sqrt{u^2+a^2}} = -\frac{\sqrt{u^2+a^2}}{a^2u}$

178. $\displaystyle\int \frac{du}{u^3\sqrt{u^2+a^2}} = -\frac{\sqrt{u^2+a^2}}{2a^2u^2} + \frac{1}{2a^3}\ln\left|\frac{a+\sqrt{u^2+a^2}}{u}\right|$

179. $\displaystyle\int \frac{\sqrt{u^2+a^2}}{u}\,du = \sqrt{u^2+a^2} - a\ln\left|\frac{a+\sqrt{u^2+a^2}}{u}\right|$

180. $\displaystyle\int \frac{\sqrt{u^2+a^2}}{u^2}\,du = -\frac{\sqrt{u^2+a^2}}{u} + \ln(u + \sqrt{u^2+a^2})$

181. $\displaystyle\int \frac{\sqrt{u^2+a^2}}{u^3}\,du = -\frac{\sqrt{u^2+a^2}}{2u^2} - \frac{1}{2a}\ln\left|\frac{a+\sqrt{u^2+a^2}}{u}\right|$

182. $\displaystyle\int \frac{du}{(u^2+a^2)^{3/2}} = \frac{u}{a^2\sqrt{u^2+a^2}}$

183. $\displaystyle\int \frac{u\,du}{(u^2+a^2)^{3/2}} = \frac{-1}{\sqrt{u^2+a^2}}$

184. $\displaystyle\int \frac{u^2\,du}{(u^2+a^2)^{3/2}} = \frac{-u}{\sqrt{u^2+a^2}} + \ln\left|u + \sqrt{u^2+a^2}\right|$

185. $\displaystyle\int \frac{u^3\,du}{(u^2+a^2)^{3/2}} = \sqrt{u^2+a^2} + \frac{a^2}{\sqrt{u^2+a^2}}$

186. $\displaystyle\int \frac{du}{u(u^2+a^2)^{3/2}} = \frac{1}{a^2\sqrt{u^2+a^2}} - \frac{1}{a^3}\ln\left|\frac{a+\sqrt{u^2+a^2}}{u}\right|$

187. $\displaystyle\int \frac{du}{u^2(u^2+a^2)^{3/2}} = -\frac{\sqrt{u^2+a^2}}{a^4 u} - \frac{u}{a^4\sqrt{u^2+a^2}}$

188. $\displaystyle\int \frac{du}{u^3(u^2+a^2)^{3/2}} = \frac{-1}{2a^2 u^2\sqrt{u^2+a^2}} - \frac{3}{2a^4\sqrt{u^2+a^2}}$

$$+ \frac{3}{2a^5}\ln\left|\frac{a+\sqrt{u^2+a^2}}{u}\right|$$

189. $\displaystyle\int (u^2+a^2)^{3/2}\,du = \frac{u(u^2+a^2)^{3/2}}{4} + \frac{3a^2 u\sqrt{u^2+a^2}}{8}$

$$+ \frac{3}{8}a^4\ln\left|u+\sqrt{u^2+a^2}\right|$$

190. $\displaystyle\int u(u^2+a^2)^{3/2}\,du = \frac{(u^2+a^2)^{5/2}}{5}$

191. $\displaystyle\int u^2(u^2+a^2)^{3/2}\,du = \frac{u(u^2+a^2)^{5/2}}{6} - \frac{a^2 u(u^2+a^2)^{3/2}}{24}$

$$- \frac{a^4 u\sqrt{u^2+a^2}}{16}$$

$$- \frac{a^6}{16}\ln\left|u+\sqrt{u^2+a^2}\right|$$

192. $\displaystyle\int u^3(u^2+a^2)^{3/2}\,du = \frac{(u^2+a^2)^{7/2}}{7} - \frac{a^2(u^2+a^2)^{5/2}}{5}$

193. $\displaystyle\int \frac{(u^2+a^2)^{3/2}}{u}\,du = \frac{(u^2+a^2)^{3/2}}{3} + a^2\sqrt{u^2+a^2}$

$$- a^3\ln\left|\frac{a+\sqrt{u^2+a^2}}{u}\right|$$

194. $\displaystyle\int \frac{(u^2+a^2)^{3/2}}{u^2}\,du = -\frac{(u^2+a^2)^{3/2}}{u}$

$$+ \frac{3u\sqrt{u^2+a^2}}{2} + \frac{3}{2}a^2\ln(u^2+a^2)$$

195. $\displaystyle\int \frac{(u^2+a^2)^{3/2}}{u^3}\,du = -\frac{(u^2+a^2)^{3/2}}{2u^2} + \frac{3}{2}\sqrt{u^2+a^2}$

$$- \frac{3}{2}a\ln\left|\frac{a+\sqrt{u^2+a^2}}{u}\right|$$

INTEGRALS INVOLVING $\sqrt{u^2 - a^2}$

196. $\displaystyle\int \frac{du}{\sqrt{u^2 - a^2}} = \ln\left|u + \sqrt{u^2 - a^2}\right|$

197. $\displaystyle\int \frac{u\,du}{\sqrt{u^2 - a^2}} = \sqrt{u^2 - a^2}$

198. $\displaystyle\int \frac{u^2\,du}{\sqrt{u^2 - a^2}} = \frac{u\sqrt{u^2 - a^2}}{2} + \frac{a^2}{2}\ln\left|u + \sqrt{u^2 - a^2}\right|$

199. $\displaystyle\int \frac{u^3\,du}{\sqrt{u^2 - a^2}} = \frac{(u^2 - a^2)^{3/2}}{3} + a^2\sqrt{u^2 - a^2}$

200. $\displaystyle\int \frac{du}{u\sqrt{u^2 - a^2}} = \frac{1}{a}\sec^{-1}\left|\frac{u}{a}\right|$

201. $\displaystyle\int \frac{du}{u^2\sqrt{u^2 - a^2}} = \frac{\sqrt{u^2 - a^2}}{a^2 u}$

202. $\displaystyle\int \frac{du}{u^3\sqrt{u^2 - a^2}} = \frac{\sqrt{u^2 - a^2}}{2a^2 u^2} + \frac{1}{2a^3}\sec^{-1}\left|\frac{u}{a}\right|$

203. $\displaystyle\int \sqrt{u^2 - a^2}\,du = \frac{u\sqrt{u^2 - a^2}}{2} - \frac{a^2}{2}\ln\left|u + \sqrt{u^2 - a^2}\right|$

204. $\displaystyle\int u\sqrt{u^2 - a^2}\,du = \frac{(u^2 - a^2)^{3/2}}{3}$

205. $\displaystyle\int u^2\sqrt{u^2 - a^2}\,du = \frac{u(u^2 - a^2)^{3/2}}{4} + \frac{a^2 u\sqrt{u^2 - a^2}}{8}$
$$- \frac{a^4}{8}\ln\left|u + \sqrt{u^2 - a^2}\right|$$

206. $\displaystyle\int u^3\sqrt{u^2 - a^2}\,du = \frac{(u^2 - a^2)^{5/2}}{5} + \frac{a^2(u^2 - a^2)^{3/2}}{3}$

207. $\displaystyle\int \frac{\sqrt{u^2 - a^2}}{u}\,du = \sqrt{u^2 - a^2} - a\sec^{-1}\left|\frac{u}{a}\right|$

208. $\displaystyle\int \frac{\sqrt{u^2 - a^2}}{u^2}\,du = -\frac{\sqrt{u^2 - a^2}}{u} + \ln\left|u + \sqrt{u^2 - a^2}\right|$

209. $\displaystyle\int \frac{\sqrt{u^2 - a^2}}{u^3}\,du = -\frac{u^2 - a^2}{2u^2} + \frac{1}{2a}\sec^{-1}\left|\frac{u}{a}\right|$

210. $\displaystyle\int \frac{du}{(u^2 - a^2)^{3/2}} = -\frac{u}{a^2\sqrt{u^2 - a^2}}$

211. $\displaystyle\int \frac{u\,du}{(u^2 - a^2)^{3/2}} = \frac{-1}{\sqrt{u^2 - a^2}}$

212. $\displaystyle\int \frac{u^2\,du}{(u^2 - a^2)^{3/2}} = -\frac{u}{\sqrt{u^2 - a^2}} + \ln\left|u + \sqrt{u^2 - a^2}\right|$

213. $\displaystyle\int \frac{u^3 \, du}{(u^2 - a^2)^{3/2}} = \sqrt{u^2 - a^2} - \frac{a^2}{\sqrt{u^2 - a^2}}$

214. $\displaystyle\int \frac{du}{u(u^2 - a^2)^{3/2}} = \frac{-1}{a^2\sqrt{u^2 - a^2}} - \frac{1}{a^3}\sec^{-1}\left|\frac{u}{a}\right|$

215. $\displaystyle\int \frac{du}{u^2(u^2 - a^2)^{3/2}} = -\frac{\sqrt{u^2 - a^2}}{a^4 u} - \frac{u}{a^4\sqrt{u^2 - a^2}}$

216. $\displaystyle\int \frac{du}{u^3(u^2 - a^2)^{3/2}} = \frac{1}{2a^2 u^2\sqrt{u^2 - a^2}} - \frac{3}{2a^4\sqrt{u^2 - a^2}}$

$$- \frac{3}{2a^5}\sec^{-1}\left|\frac{u}{a}\right|$$

217. $\displaystyle\int (u^2 - a^2)^{3/2} \, du = \frac{u(u^2 - a^2)^{3/2}}{4} - \frac{3a^2 u\sqrt{u^2 - a^2}}{8}$

$$+ \frac{3}{8}a^4 \ln\left|u + \sqrt{u^2 - a^2}\right|$$

218. $\displaystyle\int u(u^2 - a^2)^{3/2} \, du = \frac{(u^2 + a^2)^{5/2}}{5}$

219. $\displaystyle\int u^2(u^2 - a^2)^{3/2} \, du = \frac{u(u^2 - a^2)^{5/2}}{6} + \frac{a^2 u(u^2 - a^2)^{3/2}}{24}$

$$- \frac{a^4 u\sqrt{u^2 - a^2}}{16}$$

$$+ \frac{a^6}{16} \ln\left|u + \sqrt{u^2 - a^2}\right|$$

220. $\displaystyle\int u^3(u^2 - a^2)^{3/2} \, du = \frac{(u^2 - a^2)^{7/2}}{7} + \frac{a^2(u^2 - a^2)^{5/2}}{5}$

221. $\displaystyle\int \frac{(u^2 - a^2)^{3/2}}{u} \, du = \frac{(u^2 - a^2)^{3/2}}{3} - a^2\sqrt{u^2 - a^2}$

$$+ a^3 \sec^{-1}\left|\frac{u}{a}\right|$$

222. $\displaystyle\int \frac{(u^2 - a^2)^{3/2}}{u^2} \, du = -\frac{(u^2 - a^2)^{3/2}}{u} + \frac{3u\sqrt{x^2 - a^2}}{2}$

$$- \frac{3}{2}a^2 \ln\left|u + \sqrt{u^2 - a^2}\right|$$

223. $\displaystyle \int \frac{(u^2 - a^2)^{3/2}}{u^3} \, du = -\frac{(u^2 - a^2)^{3/2}}{2u^2} + \frac{3\sqrt{x^2 - a^2}}{2}$

$$-\frac{3}{2} a \sec^{-1} \left| \frac{u}{a} \right|$$

INTEGRALS INVOLVING $\sqrt{a^2 - u^2}$

224. $\displaystyle \int \frac{du}{\sqrt{a^2 - u^2}} = \sin^{-1} \frac{u}{a}$

225. $\displaystyle \int \frac{u \, du}{\sqrt{a^2 - u^2}} = -\sqrt{a^2 - u^2}$

226. $\displaystyle \int \frac{u^2 \, du}{\sqrt{a^2 - u^2}} = -\frac{u\sqrt{a^2 - u^2}}{2} + \frac{a^2}{2} \sin^{-1} \frac{u}{a}$

227. $\displaystyle \int \frac{u^3 \, du}{\sqrt{a^2 - u^2}} = \frac{(a^2 - u^2)^{3/2}}{3} - a^2 \sqrt{a^2 - u^2}$

228. $\displaystyle \int \frac{du}{u\sqrt{a^2 - u^2}} = -\frac{1}{a} \ln \left| \frac{a + \sqrt{a^2 - u^2}}{u} \right| \text{ or } -\frac{1}{a} \operatorname{sech}^{-1} \left| \frac{u}{a} \right|$

229. $\displaystyle \int \frac{du}{u^2\sqrt{a^2 - u^2}} = -\frac{\sqrt{a^2 - u^2}}{a^2 u}$

230. $\displaystyle \int \frac{du}{u^3\sqrt{a^2 - u^2}} = -\frac{\sqrt{a^2 - u^2}}{2a^2 u^2} - \frac{1}{2a^3} \ln \left| \frac{a + \sqrt{a^2 - u^2}}{u} \right|$

231. $\displaystyle \int \sqrt{a^2 - u^2} \, du = \frac{u\sqrt{a^2 - u^2}}{2} + \frac{a^2}{2} \sin^{-1} \frac{u}{a}$

232. $\displaystyle \int u\sqrt{a^2 - u^2} \, du = -\frac{(a^2 - u^2)^{3/2}}{3}$

233. $\displaystyle \int u^2 \sqrt{a^2 - u^2} \, du = -\frac{u(a^2 - u^2)^{3/2}}{4} + \frac{a^2 u\sqrt{a^2 - u^2}}{8}$

$$+ \frac{a^4}{8} \sin^{-1} \frac{u}{a}$$

234. $\displaystyle \int u^3 \sqrt{a^2 - u^2} \, du = \frac{(a^2 - u^2)^{5/2}}{5} - \frac{a^2(a^2 - u^2)^{3/2}}{3}$

235. $\displaystyle \int \frac{\sqrt{a^2 - u^2}}{u} \, du = \sqrt{a^2 - u^2} - a \ln \left| \frac{a + \sqrt{a^2 - u^2}}{u} \right|$

236. $\displaystyle \int \frac{\sqrt{a^2 - u^2}}{u^2} \, du = -\frac{\sqrt{a^2 - u^2}}{u} - \sin^{-1} \frac{u}{a}$

237. $\displaystyle \int \frac{\sqrt{a^2 - u^2}}{u^3} \, du = -\frac{\sqrt{a^2 - u^2}}{2u^2} + \frac{1}{2a} \ln \left| \frac{a + \sqrt{a^2 - u^2}}{u} \right|$

238. $\displaystyle\int \frac{du}{(a^2 - u^2)^{3/2}} = \frac{u}{a^2\sqrt{a^2 - u^2}}$

239. $\displaystyle\int \frac{u\,du}{(a^2 - u^2)^{3/2}} = \frac{1}{\sqrt{a^2 - u^2}}$

240. $\displaystyle\int \frac{u^2\,du}{(a^2 - u^2)^{3/2}} = \frac{u}{\sqrt{a^2 - u^2}} - \sin^{-1}\frac{u}{a}$

241. $\displaystyle\int \frac{u^3\,du}{(a^2 - u^2)^{3/2}} = \sqrt{a^2 - u^2} + \frac{a^2}{\sqrt{a^2 - u^2}}$

242. $\displaystyle\int \frac{du}{u(a^2 - u^2)^{3/2}} = \frac{1}{a^2\sqrt{a^2 - u^2}} - \frac{1}{a^3}\ln\left|\frac{a + \sqrt{a^2 - u^2}}{u}\right|$

243. $\displaystyle\int \frac{du}{u^2(a^2 - u^2)^{3/2}} = -\frac{\sqrt{a^2 - u^2}}{a^4 u} + \frac{u}{a^4\sqrt{a^2 - u^2}}$

244. $\displaystyle\int \frac{du}{u^3(a^2 - u^2)^{3/2}} = \frac{-1}{2a^2 u^2\sqrt{a^2 - u^2}} + \frac{3}{2a^4\sqrt{a^2 - u^2}}$

$$- \frac{3}{2a^5}\ln\left|\frac{a + \sqrt{a^2 - u^2}}{u}\right|$$

245. $\displaystyle\int (a^2 - u^2)^{3/2}\,du = \frac{u(a^2 - u^2)^{3/2}}{4} + \frac{3a^2 u\sqrt{a^2 - u^2}}{8}$

$$+ \frac{3}{8}a^4 \sin^{-1}\frac{u}{a}$$

246. $\displaystyle\int u(a^2 - u^2)^{3/2}\,du = -\frac{(a^2 - u^2)^{5/2}}{5}$

247. $\displaystyle\int u^2(a^2 - u^2)^{3/2}\,du = -\frac{u(a^2 - u^2)^{5/2}}{6} + \frac{a^2 u(a^2 - u^2)^{3/2}}{24}$

$$+ \frac{a^4 u\sqrt{a^2 - u^2}}{16} + \frac{a^6}{16}\sin^{-1}\frac{u}{a}$$

248. $\displaystyle\int u^3(a^2 - u^2)^{3/2}\,du = \frac{(a^2 - u^2)^{7/2}}{7} - \frac{a^2(a^2 - u^2)^{5/2}}{5}$

249. $\displaystyle\int \frac{(a^2 - u^2)^{3/2}}{u}\,du = \frac{(a^2 - u^2)^{3/2}}{3} + a^2\sqrt{a^2 - u^2}$

$$- a^3 \ln\left|\frac{a + \sqrt{a^2 - u^2}}{u}\right|$$

250. $\displaystyle\int \frac{(a^2 - u^2)^{3/2}}{u^2}\, du = -\frac{(a^2 - u^2)^{3/2}}{u} - \frac{3u\sqrt{a^2 - x^2}}{2}$

$$-\frac{3}{2}a^2 \sin^{-1}\frac{u}{a}$$

251. $\displaystyle\int \frac{(a^2 - u^2)^{3/2}}{u^3}\, du = -\frac{(a^2 - u^2)^{3/2}}{2u^2} - \frac{3\sqrt{a^2 - x^2}}{2}$

$$+\frac{3}{2}a \ln\left|\frac{a + \sqrt{a^2 - u^2}}{u}\right|$$

INTEGRALS INVOLVING $\sqrt{au^2 + bu + c}$

252. $\displaystyle\int \sqrt{au^2 + bu + c}\, du$

$$= \frac{(2au + b)\sqrt{au^2 + bu + c}}{4a} + \frac{4ac - b^2}{8a}\int \frac{du}{\sqrt{au^2 + bu + c}}$$

253. $\displaystyle\int u\sqrt{au^2 + bu + c}\, du$

$$= \frac{(au^2 + bu + c)^{3/2}}{3a} - \frac{b(2ac + b)}{8a^2}\sqrt{au^2 + bx + c}$$

$$-\frac{b(4ac - b^2)}{16a^2}\int \frac{du}{\sqrt{au^2 + bu + c}}$$

254. $\displaystyle\int u^2\sqrt{au^2 + bu + c}\, du = \frac{6au - 5b}{24a^2}(au^2 + bx + c)^{3/2}$

$$+\frac{5b^2 - 4ac}{16a^2}\int \sqrt{au^2 + bu + c}\, du$$

255. $\displaystyle\int (au^2 + bu + c)^{n+1/2}\, du$

$$= \frac{(2au + b)(au^2 + bu + c)^{n+1/2}}{4a(n + 1)}$$

$$+\frac{(2n + 1)(4ac - b^2)}{8a(n + 1)}\int (au^2 + bu + c)^{n-1/2}\, du$$

256. $\displaystyle\int u(au^2 + bu + c)^{n+1/2}\, du = \frac{(au^2 + bu + c)^{n+3/2}}{a(2n + 3)}$

$$-\frac{b}{2a}\int (au^2 + bu + c)^{n+1/2}\, du$$

257. $\displaystyle\int \frac{du}{\sqrt{au^2 + bu + c}} = \begin{cases} \dfrac{1}{\sqrt{a}} \ln |2\sqrt{a}\sqrt{au^2 + bu + c} \\[2mm] \qquad\qquad\qquad +2au + b)| \\[3mm] -\dfrac{1}{\sqrt{-a}} \sin^{-1}\left(\dfrac{2au + b}{\sqrt{b^2 - 4ac}} \right) \\[3mm] \text{or } \dfrac{1}{\sqrt{a}} \sinh^{-1}\left(\dfrac{2au + b}{\sqrt{4ac - b^2}} \right) \end{cases}$

258. $\displaystyle\int \frac{u\,du}{\sqrt{au^2 + bu + c}} = \frac{\sqrt{au^2 + bu + c}}{a}$

$\displaystyle\qquad\qquad -\frac{b}{2a}\int \frac{du}{\sqrt{au^2 + bu + c}}$

259. $\displaystyle\int \frac{u^2\,du}{\sqrt{au^2 + bu + c}} = \frac{2au - 3b}{4a^2}\sqrt{au^2 + bu + c}$

$\displaystyle\qquad\qquad +\frac{3b^2 - 4ac}{8a^2}\int \frac{du}{\sqrt{au^2 + bu + c}}$

260. $\displaystyle\int \frac{du}{u\sqrt{au^2 + bu + c}}$

$= \begin{cases} -\dfrac{1}{\sqrt{c}} \ln \left| \dfrac{2\sqrt{c}\sqrt{au^2 + bu + c} + bu + 2c}{u} \right| \\[4mm] \dfrac{1}{\sqrt{-c}} \sin^{-1}\left(\dfrac{bu + 2c}{|u|\sqrt{b^2 - 4ac}} \right) \\[4mm] \text{or } -\dfrac{1}{\sqrt{c}} \sinh^{-1}\left(\dfrac{bu + 2c}{|u|\sqrt{4ac - b^2}} \right) \end{cases}$

261. $\displaystyle\int \frac{du}{u^2\sqrt{au^2 + bu + c}} = -\frac{\sqrt{au^2 + bu + c}}{cu}$

$\displaystyle\qquad\qquad -\frac{b}{2c}\int \frac{du}{u\sqrt{au^2 + bu + c}}$

262. $\displaystyle\int \frac{\sqrt{au^2 + bu + c}}{u}\,du$

$\displaystyle = \sqrt{au^2 + bu + c} + \frac{b}{2}\int \frac{du}{\sqrt{au^2 + bu + c}}$

$\displaystyle\qquad\qquad +c\int \frac{du}{u\sqrt{au^2 + bu + c}}$

263. $\displaystyle\int \frac{\sqrt{au^2 + bu + c}}{u^2}\, du =$

$$-\frac{\sqrt{au^2 + bu + c}}{u} + a\int \frac{du}{\sqrt{au^2 + bu + c}}$$

$$+\frac{b}{2}\int \frac{du}{u\sqrt{au^2 + bu + c}}$$

264. $\displaystyle\int \frac{du}{(au^2 + bu + c)^{3/2}} = \frac{2(2au + b)}{(4ac - b^2)\sqrt{au^2 + bu + c}}$

265. $\displaystyle\int \frac{u\,du}{(au^2 + bu + c)^{3/2}} = \frac{2(bu + 2c)}{(b^2 - 4ac)\sqrt{au^2 + bu + c}}$

266. $\displaystyle\int \frac{u^2\,du}{(au^2 + bu + c)^{3/2}} = \frac{(2b^2 - 4ac)\,u + 2bc}{a(4ac - b^2)\sqrt{au^2 + bu + c}}$

$$+\frac{1}{a}\int \frac{du}{\sqrt{au^2 + bu + c}}$$

267. $\displaystyle\int \frac{du}{u(au^2 + bu + c)^{3/2}}$

$$= \frac{1}{c\sqrt{au^2 + bu + c}} + \frac{1}{c}\int \frac{du}{u\sqrt{au^2 + bu + c}}$$

$$-\frac{b}{2c}\int \frac{du}{(au^2 + bu + c)^{3/2}}$$

268. $\displaystyle\int \frac{du}{u^2(au^2 + bu + c)^{3/2}} =$

$$-\frac{au^2 + 2bu + c}{c^2 u\sqrt{au^2 + bu + c}} + \frac{b^2 - 2ac}{2c^2}\int \frac{du}{(au^2 + bu + c)^{3/2}}$$

$$-\frac{3b}{2c^2}\int \frac{du}{u\sqrt{au^2 + bu + c}}$$

269. $\displaystyle\int \frac{du}{(au^2 + bu + c)^{n+1/2}} =$

$$\frac{2(2au + b)}{(2n - 1)(4ac - b^2)(au^2 + bu + c)^{n-1/2}}$$

$$+\frac{8a(n - 1)}{(2n - 1)(4ac - b^2)}\int \frac{du}{(au^2 + bu + c)^{n-1/2}}$$

270. $\displaystyle\int \frac{du}{u(au^2+bu+c)^{n+1/2}} = \frac{1}{(2n-1)c(au^2+bu+c)^{n-1/2}}$

$$+ \frac{1}{c}\int \frac{du}{u(au^2+bu+c)^{n-1/2}}$$

$$- \frac{b}{2c}\int \frac{du}{(au^2+bu+c)^{n+1/2}}$$

INTEGRALS INVOLVING $u^3 + a^3$

271. $\displaystyle\int \frac{du}{u^3+a^3} = \frac{1}{6a^2}\ln\left|\frac{(u+a)^2}{u^2-au+a^2}\right| + \frac{1}{a^2\sqrt{3}}\tan^{-1}\frac{2u-a}{a\sqrt{3}}$

272. $\displaystyle\int \frac{u\,du}{u^3+a^3} = \frac{1}{6a}\ln\left|\frac{u^2-au+a^2}{(u+a)^2}\right| + \frac{1}{a\sqrt{3}}\tan^{-1}\frac{2u-a}{a\sqrt{3}}$

273. $\displaystyle\int \frac{u^2\,du}{u^3+a^3} = \frac{1}{3}\ln|u^3+a^3|$

274. $\displaystyle\int \frac{du}{u(u^3+a^3)} = \frac{1}{3a^3}\ln\left|\frac{u^3}{u^3+a^3}\right|$

275. $\displaystyle\int \frac{du}{u^2(u^3+a^3)} = -\frac{1}{a^3u} - \frac{1}{6a^4}\ln\left|\frac{u^2-au+a^2}{(u+a)^2}\right|$

$$- \frac{1}{a^4\sqrt{3}}\tan^{-1}\frac{2u-a}{a\sqrt{3}}$$

276. $\displaystyle\int \frac{du}{(u^3+a^3)^2} = \frac{u}{3a^3(u^3+a^3)} + \frac{1}{9a^5}\ln\left|\frac{(u+a)^2}{u^2-au+a^2}\right|$

$$+ \frac{2}{3a^5\sqrt{3}}\tan^{-1}\frac{2u-a}{a\sqrt{3}}$$

277. $\displaystyle\int \frac{u\,du}{(u^3+a^3)^2} = \frac{u^2}{3a^3(u^3+a^3)} + \frac{1}{18a^4}\ln\left|\frac{u^2-au+a^2}{(u+a)^2}\right|$

$$+ \frac{1}{3a^4\sqrt{3}}\tan^{-1}\frac{2u-a}{a\sqrt{3}}$$

278. $\displaystyle\int \frac{u^2\,du}{(u^3+a^3)^2} = -\frac{1}{3(u^3+a^3)}$

279. $\displaystyle\int \frac{du}{u(u^3+a^3)^2} = \frac{1}{3a^3(u^3+a^3)} + \frac{1}{3a^6}\ln\left|\frac{u^3}{u^3+a^3}\right|$

280. $\displaystyle\int \frac{du}{u^2(u^3+a^3)^2} = -\frac{1}{a^6 u} - \frac{u^2}{3a^6(u^3+a^3)} - \frac{4}{3a^6}\int \frac{u\,du}{u^3+a^3}$

281. $\displaystyle\int \frac{u^m\,du}{u^3+a^3} = \frac{u^{m-2}}{m-2} - a^3\int \frac{u^{m-3}\,du}{u^3+a^3}$

282. $\displaystyle\int \frac{du}{u^n(u^3+a^3)} = \frac{-1}{a^3(n-1)u^{n-1}} - \frac{1}{a^3}\int \frac{du}{u^{n-3}(u^3+a^3)}$

INTEGRALS INVOLVING $u^4 \pm a^4$

283. $\displaystyle\int \frac{du}{u^4+a^4} = \frac{1}{4a^3\sqrt{2}}\ln\left|\frac{u^2+ax\sqrt{2}+a^2}{u^2-au\sqrt{2}+a^2}\right|$

$$-\frac{1}{2a^3\sqrt{2}}\tan^{-1}\frac{au\sqrt{2}}{u^2-a^2}$$

284. $\displaystyle\int \frac{u\,du}{u^4+a^4} = \frac{1}{2a^2}\tan^{-1}\frac{u^2}{a^2}$

285. $\displaystyle\int \frac{u^2\,du}{u^4+a^4} = \frac{1}{4a\sqrt{2}}\ln\left|\frac{u^2-ax\sqrt{2}+a^2}{u^2+au\sqrt{2}+a^2}\right|$

$$-\frac{1}{2a\sqrt{2}}\tan^{-1}\frac{au\sqrt{2}}{u^2-a^2}$$

286. $\displaystyle\int \frac{u^3\,du}{u^4+a^4} = \frac{1}{4}\ln(u^4+a^4)$

287. $\displaystyle\int \frac{du}{u(u^4+a^4)} = \frac{1}{4a^4}\ln\left(\frac{u^4}{u^4+a^4}\right)$

288. $\displaystyle\int \frac{du}{u^2(u^4+a^4)} = -\frac{1}{a^4 u} - \frac{1}{4a^5\sqrt{2}}\ln\left|\frac{u^2-ax\sqrt{2}+a^2}{u^2+au\sqrt{2}+a^2}\right|$

$$+\frac{1}{2a^5\sqrt{2}}\tan^{-1}\frac{au\sqrt{2}}{u^2-a^2}$$

289. $\displaystyle\int \frac{du}{u^3(u^4+a^4)} = -\frac{1}{2a^4 u^2} - \frac{1}{2a^6}\tan^{-1}\frac{u^2}{a^2}$

290. $\displaystyle\int \frac{du}{u^4-a^4} = \frac{1}{4a^3}\ln\left|\frac{u-a}{u+a}\right| - \frac{1}{2a^3}\tan^{-1}\frac{u}{a}$

291. $\displaystyle\int \frac{u\,du}{u^4-a^4} = \frac{1}{4a^2}\ln\left|\frac{u^2-a^2}{u^2+a^2}\right|$

292. $\displaystyle \int \frac{u^2\,du}{u^4 - a^4} = \frac{1}{4a} \ln \left| \frac{u-a}{u+a} \right| + \frac{1}{2a} \tan^{-1} \frac{u}{a}$

293. $\displaystyle \int \frac{u^3\,du}{u^4 - a^4} = \frac{1}{4} \ln |u^4 - a^4|$

294. $\displaystyle \int \frac{du}{u(u^4 - a^4)} = \frac{1}{4a^4} \ln \left| \frac{u^4 - a^4}{u^4} \right|$

295. $\displaystyle \int \frac{du}{u^2(u^4 - a^4)} = \frac{1}{a^4 u} + \frac{1}{4a^5} \ln \left| \frac{u-a}{u+a} \right| + \frac{1}{2a^5} \tan^{-1} \frac{u}{a}$

296. $\displaystyle \int \frac{du}{u^3(u^4 - a^4)} = \frac{1}{2a^4 u^2} + \frac{1}{4a^6} \ln \left| \frac{u^2 - a^2}{u^2 + a^2} \right|$

INTEGRALS INVOLVING $u^n \pm a^n$

297. $\displaystyle \int \frac{du}{u(u^n - a^n)} = \frac{1}{na^n} \ln \left| \frac{u^n}{u^n + a^n} \right|$

298. $\displaystyle \int \frac{u^{n-1}\,du}{u^n + a^n} = \frac{1}{n} \ln |u^n + a^n|$

299. $\displaystyle \int \frac{u^m\,du}{(u^n + a^n)^r} = \int \frac{u^{m-n}\,du}{(u^n + a^n)^{r-1}} - a^n \int \frac{u^{m-n}\,du}{(u^n + a^n)^r}$

300. $\displaystyle \int \frac{du}{u^m(u^n + a^n)^r} = \frac{1}{a^n} \int \frac{du}{u^m(u^n + a^n)^{r-1}}$

$\displaystyle \qquad\qquad - \frac{1}{a^n} \int \frac{du}{u^{m-n}(u^n + a^n)^r}$

301. $\displaystyle \int \frac{du}{u\sqrt{u^n + a^n}} = \frac{1}{n\sqrt{a^n}} \ln \left| \frac{\sqrt{u^n + a^n} - \sqrt{a^n}}{\sqrt{u^n + a^n} + \sqrt{a^n}} \right|$

302. $\displaystyle \int \frac{du}{u(u^n - a^n)} = \frac{1}{na^n} \ln \left| \frac{u^n - a^n}{u^n} \right|$

303. $\displaystyle \int \frac{u^{n-1}\,du}{u^n + a^n} = \frac{1}{n} \ln |u^n + a^n|$

304. $\displaystyle \int \frac{u^m\,du}{(u^n + a^n)^r} = a^n \int \frac{u^{m-n}\,du}{(u^n + a^n)^r} + \int \frac{u^{m-n}\,du}{(u^n + a^n)^{r-1}}$

305. $\displaystyle \int \frac{du}{u^m(u^n - a^n)^r} = \frac{1}{a^n} \int \frac{du}{u^{m-n}(u^n - a^n)^r}$

$\displaystyle \qquad\qquad - \frac{1}{a^n} \int \frac{du}{u^m(u^n - a^n)^{r-1}}$

306. $\displaystyle\int \frac{du}{u\sqrt{u^n - a^n}} = \frac{2}{n\sqrt{a^n}}\cos^{-1}\sqrt{\frac{a^n}{u^n}}$

307. $\displaystyle\int \frac{u^{p-1}\,du}{u^{2m} + a^{2m}}$

$$= \frac{1}{ma^{2m-p}}\sum_{k=0}^{m}\sin\frac{(2k-1)p\pi}{2m}\tan^{-1}\left(\frac{u + a\cos[(2k-1)\pi/2m]}{a\sin[(2k-2)\pi/2m]}\right)$$

$$- \frac{1}{2ma^{2m-p}}\sum_{k=0}^{m}\cos\frac{(2k-1)p\pi}{2m}\ln\left|u^2 + 2au\cos\frac{(2k-1)}{2m} + a^2\right|$$

where $0 < p \le 2m$.

308. $\displaystyle\int \frac{u^{p-1}\,du}{u^{2m} - a^{2m}}$

$$= \frac{1}{2ma^{2m-p}}\sum_{k=1}^{m-1}\cos\frac{kp\pi}{m}\left(u^2 - 2au\cos\frac{k\pi}{m} + a^2\right)$$

$$- \frac{1}{ma^{2m-p}}\sum_{k=1}^{m-1}\sin\frac{kp\pi}{m}\tan^{-1}\left(\frac{u - a\cos(k\pi/m)}{a\sin(k\pi/m)}\right)$$

where $0 < p \le 2m$.

309. $\displaystyle\int \frac{u^{p-1}\,du}{u^{2m+1} + a^{2m+1}}$

$$= \frac{2(-1)^{p-1}}{(2m+1)a^{2m-p+1}}\sum_{k=1}^{m}\sin\frac{2kp\pi}{2m+1}\tan^{-1}\left(\frac{u + a\cos[(2k\pi/(2m+1)]}{a\sin[2k\pi/(2m+1)]}\right)$$

$$- \frac{(-1)^{p-1}}{(2m+1)a^{2m-p+1}}\sum_{k=1}^{m}\cos\frac{2kp\pi}{2m+1}\ln\left|u^2 + 2au\cos\frac{2k\pi}{2m+1} + a^2\right|$$

$$+ \frac{(-1)^{p-1}\ln|u+a|}{(2m+1)a^{2m-p+1}}$$

where $0 < p \le 2m + 1$

310. $\displaystyle\int \frac{u^{p-1}\,du}{u^{2m+1} + a^{2m+1}}$

$$= \frac{-2}{(2m+1)a^{2m-p+1}} \sum_{k=1}^{m} \sin\frac{2kp\pi}{2m+1} \tan^{-1}\left(\frac{u - a\cos[2k\pi/(2m+1)]}{a\sin[2k\pi/(2m+1)]}\right)$$

$$+ \frac{1}{(2m+1)a^{2m-p+1}} \sum_{k=1}^{m} \cos\frac{2kp\pi}{2m+1} \ln\left|u^2 - 2au\cos\frac{2k\pi}{2m+1} + a^2\right|$$

$$+ \frac{\ln|u-a|}{(2m+1)a^{2m-p+1}} \text{ where } 0 < p \le 2m+1$$

INTEGRALS INVOLVING $\cos au$

311. $\displaystyle\int \cos au\,du = \frac{\sin au}{a}$

312. $\displaystyle\int u\cos au\,du = \frac{\cos au}{a^2} + \frac{u\sin au}{a}$

313. $\displaystyle\int u^2\cos au\,du = \frac{2u}{a^2}\cos au + \left(\frac{u^2}{a} - \frac{2}{a^3}\right)\sin au$

314. $\displaystyle\int u^3\cos au\,du = \left(\frac{3u^2}{a^2} - \frac{6}{a^4}\right)\cos au + \left(\frac{u^3}{a} - \frac{6u}{a^3}\right)\sin au$

315. $\displaystyle\int u^n\cos au\,du = \frac{u^n\sin au}{a} - \frac{n}{a}\int u^{n-1}\sin au\,du$

316. $\displaystyle\int u^n\cos au\,du = \frac{u^n\sin au}{a} + \frac{nu^{n-1}}{a^2}\cos au$

$$- \frac{n(n-1)}{a^2}\int u^{n-2}\cos au\,du$$

317. $\displaystyle\int \cos^2 au\,du = \frac{u}{2} + \frac{\sin 2au}{4a}$

318. $\displaystyle\int u\cos^2 au\,du = \frac{u^2}{4} + \frac{u\sin 2au}{4a} + \frac{\cos 2au}{8a^2}$

319. $\displaystyle\int \cos^3 au\,du = \frac{\sin au}{a} - \frac{\sin^3 au}{3a}$

320. $\displaystyle\int \cos^4 au\,du = \frac{3u}{8} + \frac{\sin 2au}{4a} + \frac{\sin 4au}{32a}$

321. $\displaystyle\int \cos^n au\, du = \frac{\cos^{n-1} au \sin au}{an} + \frac{n-1}{n} \int \cos^{n-2} au\, du$

322. $\displaystyle\int \frac{\cos au}{u}\, du = \ln|u| - \frac{(au)^2}{2\cdot 2!} + \frac{(au)^4}{4\cdot 4!} - \frac{(au)^6}{6\cdot 6!} + \cdots$

323. $\displaystyle\int \frac{\cos au}{u^2}\, du = -\frac{\cos au}{u} - a\int \frac{\sin au}{u}\, du$

324. $\displaystyle\int \frac{\cos au}{u^n}\, du = -\frac{\cos au}{(n-1)u^{n-1}} - \frac{a}{n-1}\int \frac{\sin au}{u^{n-1}}\, du$

325. $\displaystyle\int \frac{du}{\cos au} = \frac{1}{a}\ln|\sec au + \tan au| = \frac{1}{a}\ln\tan\left|\frac{\pi}{4} + \frac{au}{2}\right|$

326. $\displaystyle\int \frac{u\, du}{\cos au} = \frac{1}{a^2}\left\{ \frac{(au)^2}{2} + \frac{(au)^4}{8} + \frac{5(au)^6}{144} + \cdots \right.$

$$\left. + \frac{E_n (au)^{2n+2}}{(2n+2)(2n)!} + \cdots \right\}$$

327. $\displaystyle\int \frac{du}{\cos^2 au} = \frac{\tan au}{a}$

328. $\displaystyle\int \frac{du}{\cos^3 au} = \frac{\sin au}{2a\cos^2 au} + \frac{1}{2a}\ln\left|\tan\left(\frac{\pi}{4} + \frac{au}{2}\right)\right|$

329. $\displaystyle\int \frac{du}{\cos^n au} = \frac{\sin au}{a(n-1)\cos^{n-1} au} + \frac{n-2}{n-1}\int \frac{du}{\cos^{n-2} au}$

330. $\displaystyle\int \frac{u\, du}{\cos^n au} = \frac{u\sin au}{a(n-1)\cos^{n-1} au}$

$$- \frac{1}{a^2(n-1)(n-2)\cos^{n-2} au}$$

$$+ \frac{n-2}{n-1}\int \frac{u\, du}{\cos^{n-2} au}$$

331. $\displaystyle\int \cos au \cos bu\, du = \frac{\sin(a-b)u}{2(a-b)} + \frac{\sin(a+b)u}{2(a+b)}$

332. $\displaystyle\int \frac{du}{1-\cos au} = -\frac{1}{a}\cot\frac{au}{2}$

333. $\displaystyle\int \frac{u\, du}{1-\cos au} = -\frac{u}{a}\cot\frac{au}{2} + \frac{2}{a^2}\ln\left|\sin\frac{au}{2}\right|$

334. $\displaystyle\int \frac{du}{1+\cos au} = \frac{1}{a}\tan\frac{au}{2}$

335. $\displaystyle\int \frac{u\, du}{1+\cos au} = \frac{u}{a}\tan\frac{au}{2} + \frac{2}{a^2}\ln\left|\cos\frac{au}{2}\right|$

336. $\displaystyle\int \frac{du}{(1-\cos au)^2} = -\frac{1}{2a}\cot\frac{au}{2} - \frac{1}{6a}\cot^3\frac{au}{2}$

337. $\displaystyle\int \frac{du}{(1+\cos au)^2} = \frac{1}{2a}\tan\frac{au}{2} + \frac{1}{6a}\tan^3\frac{au}{2}$

338. $\displaystyle\int \frac{du}{p+q\cos au}$

$$= \begin{cases} \dfrac{2}{a\sqrt{p^2-q^2}}\tan^{-1}\sqrt{(p-q)/(p+q)}\tan\dfrac{1}{2}au \\[4mm] \dfrac{1}{a\sqrt{q^2-p^2}}\ln\left|\dfrac{\tan\dfrac{1}{2}au+\sqrt{(q+p)/(q-p)}}{\tan\dfrac{1}{2}au-\sqrt{(q+p)/(q-p)}}\right| \end{cases}$$

339. $\displaystyle\int \frac{du}{(p+q\cos au)^2} = \frac{q\sin au}{a(q^2-p^2)(p+q\cos au)}$

$$-\frac{p}{q^2-p^2}\int\frac{du}{p+q\cos au}$$

340. $\displaystyle\int \frac{du}{p^2+q^2\cos^2 au} = \frac{1}{ap\sqrt{p^2+q^2}}\tan^{-1}\frac{p\tan au}{\sqrt{p^2+q^2}}$

341. $\displaystyle\int \frac{du}{p^2-q^2\cos^2 au}$

$$= \begin{cases} \dfrac{1}{ap\sqrt{p^2-q^2}}\tan^{-1}\dfrac{p\tan au}{\sqrt{p^2-q^2}} \\[4mm] \dfrac{1}{2ap\sqrt{q^2-p^2}}\ln\left|\dfrac{p\tan au-\sqrt{q^2-p^2}}{p\tan au+\sqrt{q^2-p^2}}\right| \end{cases}$$

INTEGRALS INVOLVING $\sin au$

342. $\displaystyle\int \sin au\,du = -\frac{\cos au}{a}$

343. $\displaystyle\int u\sin au\,du = \frac{\sin au}{a^2} - \frac{u\cos au}{a}$

344. $\displaystyle\int u^2\sin au\,du = \frac{2u}{a^2}\sin au + \left(\frac{2}{a^3}-\frac{u^2}{a}\right)\cos au$

345. $\displaystyle\int u^3\sin au\,du = \left(\frac{3u^2}{a^2}-\frac{6}{a^4}\right)\sin au + \left(\frac{6u}{a^3}-\frac{u^3}{a}\right)\cos au$

346. $\displaystyle\int u^n\sin au\,du = -\frac{u^n\cos au}{a} + \frac{n}{a}\int u^{n-1}\cos au\,du$

347. $\displaystyle\int u^n \sin au\,du = -\frac{u^n \cos au}{a} + \frac{nu^{n-1}\sin au}{a^2}$

$$-\frac{n(n-1)}{a^2}\int u^{n-2}\sin au\,du$$

348. $\displaystyle\int \sin^2 au\,du = \frac{u}{2} - \frac{\sin 2au}{4a}$

349. $\displaystyle\int u\sin^2 au\,du = \frac{u^2}{4} - \frac{u\sin 2au}{4a} - \frac{\cos 2au}{8a^2}$

350. $\displaystyle\int \sin^3 au\,du = -\frac{\cos au}{a} + \frac{\cos^3 au}{3a}$

351. $\displaystyle\int \sin^4 au\,du = \frac{3u}{8} - \frac{\sin 2au}{4a} + \frac{\sin 4au}{32a}$

352. $\displaystyle\int \sin^n au\,du = -\frac{\sin^{n-1}au\cos au}{an} + \frac{n-1}{n}\int \sin^{n-2}au\,du$

353. $\displaystyle\int \frac{\sin au}{u}\,du = au - \frac{(au)^3}{3\cdot 3!} + \frac{(au)^5}{5\cdot 5!} - \cdots$

354. $\displaystyle\int \frac{\sin au}{u^2}\,du = -\frac{\sin au}{u} + a\int \frac{\cos au}{u}\,du$

355. $\displaystyle\int \frac{\sin au}{u^n}\,du = -\frac{\sin au}{(n-1)u^{n-1}} + \frac{a}{n-1}\int \frac{\cos au}{u^{n-1}}\,du$

356. $\displaystyle\int \frac{du}{\sin au} = \frac{1}{a}\ln|\csc au - \cot au| = \frac{1}{a}\ln\left|\tan\frac{au}{2}\right|$

357. $\displaystyle\int \frac{u\,du}{\sin au} = \frac{1}{a^2}\left\{au + \frac{(au)^3}{18} + \frac{7(au)^5}{1800} + \cdots\right.$

$$\left.+\frac{2(2^{2n-1}-1)B_n(au)^{2n+1}}{(2n+1)!} + \cdots\right\}$$

358. $\displaystyle\int \frac{du}{\sin^2 au} = -\frac{1}{a}\cot au$

359. $\displaystyle\int \frac{du}{\sin^3 au} = -\frac{\cos au}{2a\sin^2 au} + \frac{1}{2a}\ln\left|\tan\frac{au}{2}\right|$

360. $\displaystyle\int \frac{du}{\sin^n au} = \frac{-\cos au}{a(n-1)\sin^{n-1}au} + \frac{n-2}{n-1}\int \frac{du}{\sin^{n-2}au}$

361. $\displaystyle\int \frac{u\,du}{\sin^n au} = \frac{-u\cos au}{a(n-1)\sin^{n-1}au} + \frac{n-2}{n-1}\int \frac{du}{\sin^{n-2}au}$

362. $\displaystyle\int \sin pu \sin qu\,du = \frac{\sin(p-q)u}{2(p-q)} - \frac{\sin(p+q)u}{2(p+q)}$

363. $\displaystyle\int \frac{du}{1-\sin au} = \frac{1}{a}\tan\left(\frac{\pi}{4}+\frac{au}{2}\right)$

364. $\displaystyle\int \frac{u\,du}{1-\sin au} = \frac{u}{a}\tan\left(\frac{\pi}{4}+\frac{au}{2}\right) + \frac{2}{a^2}\ln\left|\sin\left(\frac{\pi}{4}-\frac{au}{2}\right)\right|$

365. $\displaystyle\int \frac{du}{1+\sin au} = -\frac{1}{a}\tan\left(\frac{\pi}{4}-\frac{au}{2}\right)$

366. $\displaystyle\int \frac{u\,du}{1+\sin au} = -\frac{u}{a}\tan\left(\frac{\pi}{4}-\frac{au}{2}\right) + \frac{2}{a^2}\ln\left|\sin\left(\frac{\pi}{4}+\frac{au}{2}\right)\right|$

367. $\displaystyle\int \frac{du}{(1-\sin au)^2} = \frac{1}{2a}\tan\left(\frac{\pi}{4}+\frac{au}{2}\right) + \frac{1}{6a}\tan^3\left(\frac{\pi}{4}+\frac{au}{2}\right)$

368. $\displaystyle\int \frac{du}{(1+\sin au)^2} = \frac{1}{2a}\tan\left(\frac{\pi}{4}-\frac{au}{2}\right) - \frac{1}{6a}\tan^3\left(\frac{\pi}{4}-\frac{au}{2}\right)$

369. $\displaystyle\int \frac{du}{p+q\sin au}$

$$= \begin{cases} \dfrac{2}{a\sqrt{p^2-q^2}}\tan^{-1}\dfrac{p\tan\frac{1}{2}au + q}{\sqrt{p^2-q^2}} \\[3ex] \dfrac{1}{a\sqrt{q^2-p^2}}\ln\left|\dfrac{p\tan\frac{1}{2}au + q - \sqrt{q^2-p^2}}{p\tan\frac{1}{2}au + q + \sqrt{q^2-p^2}}\right| \end{cases}$$

370. $\displaystyle\int \frac{du}{(p+q\sin au)^2} = \frac{q\cos au}{a(p^2-q^2)(p+q\sin au)}$

$$+ \frac{p}{p^2-q^2}\int \frac{du}{p+q\sin au}$$

371. $\displaystyle\int \frac{du}{p^2+q^2\sin^2 au} = \frac{1}{ap\sqrt{p^2+q^2}}\tan^{-1}\frac{\sqrt{p^2+q^2}\tan au}{p}$

372. $\displaystyle\int \frac{du}{p^2-q^2\sin^2 au}$

$$= \begin{cases} \dfrac{1}{ap\sqrt{p^2-q^2}}\tan^{-1}\dfrac{\sqrt{p^2-q^2}\tan au}{p} \\[3ex] \dfrac{1}{2ap\sqrt{q^2-p^2}}\ln\left|\dfrac{\sqrt{q^2-p^2}\tan au + p}{\sqrt{q^2-p^2}\tan au - p}\right| \end{cases}$$

INTEGRALS INVOLVING $\sin au$ AND $\cos au$

373. $\displaystyle\int \sin au \cos au \, du = \frac{\sin^2 au}{2a}$

374. $\displaystyle\int \sin pu \cos qu \, du = -\frac{\cos(p-q)u}{2(p-q)} - \frac{\cos(p+q)u}{2(p+q)}$

375. $\displaystyle\int \sin^n au \cos au \, du = \frac{\sin^{n+1} au}{(n+1)a}$

376. $\displaystyle\int \cos^n au \sin au \, du = -\frac{\cos^{n+1} au}{(n+1)a}$

377. $\displaystyle\int \sin^2 au \cos^2 au \, du = \frac{u}{8} - \frac{\sin 4au}{32a}$

378. $\displaystyle\int \frac{du}{\sin au \cos au} = \frac{1}{a} \ln |\tan au|$

379. $\displaystyle\int \frac{du}{\sin^2 au \cos au} = \frac{1}{a} \ln \left| \tan \left(\frac{\pi}{4} + \frac{au}{2} \right) \right| - \frac{1}{a \sin au}$

380. $\displaystyle\int \frac{du}{\sin au \cos^2 au} = \frac{1}{a} \ln \left| \tan \frac{au}{2} \right| + \frac{1}{a \cos au}$

381. $\displaystyle\int \frac{du}{\sin^2 au \cos^2 au} = -\frac{2 \cot 2au}{a}$

382. $\displaystyle\int \frac{\sin^2 au}{\cos au} \, du = -\frac{\sin au}{a} + \frac{1}{a} \ln \left| \tan \left(\frac{au}{2} + \frac{\pi}{4} \right) \right|$

383. $\displaystyle\int \frac{\cos^2 au}{\sin au} \, du = \frac{\cos au}{a} + \frac{1}{a} \ln \left| \tan \frac{au}{2} \right|$

384. $\displaystyle\int \frac{du}{\cos au(1 \pm \sin au)} = \mp \frac{1}{2a(1 \pm \sin au)}$
$$+ \frac{1}{2a} \ln \left| \tan \left(\frac{au}{2} + \frac{\pi}{4} \right) \right|$$

385. $\displaystyle\int \frac{du}{\sin au(1 \pm \cos au)} = \pm \frac{1}{2a(1 \pm \cos au)} + \frac{1}{2a} \ln \left| \tan \frac{au}{2} \right|$

386. $\displaystyle\int \frac{du}{\sin au \pm \cos au} = \frac{1}{a\sqrt{2}} \ln \left| \tan \left(\frac{au}{2} \pm \frac{\pi}{8} \right) \right|$

387. $\displaystyle\int \frac{\sin au \, du}{\sin au \pm \cos au} = \frac{u}{2} \mp \frac{1}{2a} \ln |\sin au \pm \cos au|$

388. $\displaystyle\int \frac{\cos au\,du}{\sin au \pm \cos au} = \mp\frac{u}{2} + \frac{1}{2a}\ln|\sin au \pm \cos au|$

389. $\displaystyle\int \frac{\sin au\,du}{p + q\cos au} = -\frac{1}{aq}\ln|p + q\cos au|$

390. $\displaystyle\int \frac{\cos au\,du}{p + q\sin au} = \frac{1}{aq}\ln|p + q\sin au|$

391. $\displaystyle\int \frac{\sin au\,du}{(p + q\cos au)^n} = \frac{1}{aq(n-1)(p+q\cos au)^{n-1}}$

392. $\displaystyle\int \frac{\cos au\,du}{(p + q\sin au)^n} = \frac{-1}{aq(n-1)(p+q\sin au)^{n-1}}$

393. $\displaystyle\int \frac{du}{p\sin au + q\cos au}$

$$= \frac{1}{a\sqrt{p^2 + q^2}}\ln\left|\tan\left(\frac{au + \tan^{-1}(q/p)}{2}\right)\right|$$

394. $\displaystyle\int \frac{du}{p\sin au + q\cos au + r} =$

$$\begin{cases} \dfrac{2}{a\sqrt{r^2 - p^2 - q^2}}\tan^{-1}\left(\dfrac{p + (r-q)\tan(au/2)}{\sqrt{r^2 - p^2 - q^2}}\right) \\[2em] \dfrac{1}{a\sqrt{p^2 + q^2 - r^2}}\ln\left|\dfrac{p - \sqrt{p^2 + q^2 - r^2} + (r-q)\tan(au/2)}{p + \sqrt{p^2 + q^2 - r^2} + (r-q)\tan(au/2)}\right| \end{cases}$$

395. $\displaystyle\int \frac{du}{p\sin au + q(1 + \cos au)} = \frac{1}{ap}\ln\left|q + p\tan\frac{au}{2}\right|$

396. $\displaystyle\int \frac{du}{p\sin au + q\cos au \pm \sqrt{p^2 + q^2}} =$

$$\frac{-1}{a\sqrt{p^2 + q^2}}\tan\left(\frac{\pi}{4} \mp \frac{au + \tan^{-1}(q/p)}{2}\right)$$

397. $\displaystyle\int \frac{du}{p^2\sin^2 au + q^2\cos^2 au} = \frac{1}{apq}\tan^{-1}\left(\frac{p\tan au}{q}\right)$

398. $\displaystyle\int \frac{du}{p^2\sin^2 au - q^2\cos^2 au} = \frac{1}{2apq}\tan\left(\frac{p\tan au - q}{p\tan au + q}\right)$

399. $\displaystyle\int \sin^m au \cos^n au \, du$

$$= \begin{cases} -\dfrac{\sin^{m-1} au \cos^{n+1} au}{a(m+n)} + \dfrac{m-1}{m+n} \displaystyle\int \sin^{m-2} au \cos^n au \, du \\[4mm] \dfrac{\sin^{m+1} au \cos^{n-1} au}{a(m+n)} + \dfrac{n-1}{m+n} \displaystyle\int \sin^m au \cos^{n-2} au \, du \end{cases}$$

400. $\displaystyle\int \dfrac{\sin^m au}{\cos^n au} \, du$

$$= \begin{cases} \dfrac{\sin^{m-1} au}{a(n-1)\cos^{n-1} au} - \dfrac{m-1}{n-1} \displaystyle\int \dfrac{\sin^{m-2} au}{\cos^{n-2} au} \, du \\[4mm] \dfrac{\sin^{m+1} au}{a(n-1)\cos^{n-1} au} - \dfrac{m-n+2}{n-1} \displaystyle\int \dfrac{\sin^m au}{\cos^{n-2} au} \, du \\[4mm] \dfrac{-\sin^{m-1} au}{a(m-n)\cos^{n-1} au} + \dfrac{m-1}{n-1} \displaystyle\int \dfrac{\sin^{m-2} au}{\cos^n au} \, du \end{cases}$$

401. $\displaystyle\int \dfrac{\cos^m au}{\sin^n au} \, du$

$$= \begin{cases} \dfrac{-\cos^{m-1} au}{a(n-1)\sin^{n-1} au} - \dfrac{m-1}{n-1} \displaystyle\int \dfrac{\cos^{m-2} au}{\sin^{n-2} au} \, du \\[4mm] \dfrac{-\cos^{m+1} au}{a(n-1)\sin^{n-1} au} - \dfrac{m-n+2}{n-1} \displaystyle\int \dfrac{\cos^m au}{\sin^{n-2} au} \, du \\[4mm] \dfrac{\cos^{m-1} au}{a(m-n)\sin^{n-1} au} + \dfrac{m-1}{n-1} \displaystyle\int \dfrac{\cos^{m-2} au}{\sin^n au} \, du \end{cases}$$

402. $\displaystyle\int \dfrac{du}{\sin^m au \cos^n au} =$

$$\begin{cases} \dfrac{1}{a(n-1)\sin^{m-1} au \cos^{n-1} au} - \dfrac{m+n-2}{n-1} \displaystyle\int \dfrac{du}{\sin^m au \cos^{n-2} au} \\[4mm] \dfrac{1}{a(m-1)\sin^{m-1} au \cos^{n-1} au} + \dfrac{m+n-2}{m-1} \displaystyle\int \dfrac{du}{\sin^{m-2} au \cos^n au} \end{cases}$$

INTEGRALS INVOLVING cot au

414. $\displaystyle\int \cot au\, du = \frac{1}{a}\ln|\sin au|$

415. $\displaystyle\int \cot^2 au\, du = -\frac{\cot au}{a} - u$

416. $\displaystyle\int \cot^3 au\, du = -\frac{\cot^2 au}{2a} - \frac{1}{a}\ln|\sin au|$

417. $\displaystyle\int \cot^n au\, du = -\frac{\cot^{n-1} au}{(n-1)a} - \int \cot^{n-2} au\, du$

418. $\displaystyle\int \cot^n au\, \csc^2 au\, du = -\frac{\cot^{n+1} au}{(n+1)a}$

419. $\displaystyle\int \frac{\csc^2 au}{\cot au}\, du = -\frac{1}{a}\ln|\cot au|$

420. $\displaystyle\int \frac{du}{\cot au} = -\frac{1}{a}\ln|\cos au|$

421. $\displaystyle\int u\cot au\, du = \frac{1}{a^2}\left\{ au - \frac{(au)^3}{9} - \frac{(au)^5}{225} - \cdots \right.$
$$\left. -\frac{2^{2n}B_n(au)^{2n+1}}{(2n+1)!} - \cdots \right\}$$

422. $\displaystyle\int \frac{\cot au}{u}\, du = -\frac{1}{au} - \frac{au}{3} - \frac{(au)^3}{135} - \cdots$
$$-\frac{2^{2n}B_n(au)^{2n-1}}{(2n-1)(2n)!} - \cdots$$

423. $\displaystyle\int u\cot^2 au\, du = \frac{u\cot au}{a} + \frac{1}{a^2}\ln|\sin au| - \frac{u^2}{2}$

424. $\displaystyle\int \frac{du}{p + q\cot au} = \frac{pu}{p^2 + q^2}$
$$-\frac{q}{a(p^2 + q^2)}\ln|p\sin au + q\cos au|$$

236 Chapter 12

INTEGRALS INVOLVING sec au

425. $\int \sec\, au\, du = \frac{1}{a}\ln|\sec\, au + \tan au| = \frac{1}{a}\ln\left|\tan\left(\frac{au}{2}+\frac{\pi}{4}\right)\right|$

426. $\int \sec^2 au\, du = \frac{\tan au}{a}$

427. $\int \sec^3 au\, du = \frac{\sec\, au\tan au}{2a} + \frac{1}{2a}\ln|\sec\, au + \tan au|$

428. $\int \sec^n au\, du = \frac{\sec^{n-2} au\tan au}{a(n-1)} + \frac{n-2}{n-1}\int \sec^{n-2} au\, du$

429. $\int \sec^n au\tan\, au\, du = \frac{\sec^n au}{na}$

430. $\int \frac{du}{\sec\, au} = \frac{\sin au}{a}$

431. $\int u\sec\, au\, du = \frac{1}{a^2}\left\{\frac{(au)^2}{2} + \frac{(au)^4}{8} + \frac{5(au)^6}{144} + \cdots\right.$

$$\left. + \frac{E_n(au)^{2n+2}}{(2n+2)(2n)!} + \cdots\right\}$$

432. $\int \frac{\sec\, au}{u}du = \ln|u| + \frac{(au)^2}{4} + \frac{5(au)^4}{96} + \frac{61(au)^6}{4320} + \cdots$

$$+ \frac{E_n(au)^{2n}}{2n(2n)!} + \cdots$$

433. $\int u\sec^2 au\, du = \frac{u}{a}\tan au + \frac{1}{a^2}\ln|\cos au|$

434. $\int \frac{du}{q+p\sec\, au} = \frac{u}{q} - \frac{p}{q}\int \frac{du}{p+q\cos au}$

INTEGRALS INVOLVING csc au

435. $\int \csc\, au\, du = \frac{1}{a}\ln|\csc\, au - \cot au| = \frac{1}{a}\ln\left|\tan\frac{au}{2}\right|$

436. $\int \csc^2 au\, du = -\frac{\cot au}{a}$

437. $\displaystyle\int \csc^3 au\, du = -\frac{\csc au \cot au}{2a} + \frac{1}{2a} \ln\left|\tan\frac{au}{2}\right|$

438. $\displaystyle\int \csc^n au\, du = -\frac{\csc^{n-2} au \cot au}{a(n-1)} + \frac{n-2}{n-1}\int \csc^{n-2} au\, du$

439. $\displaystyle\int \csc^n au \cot u\, du = -\frac{\csc^n au}{na}$

440. $\displaystyle\int \frac{du}{\csc au} = -\frac{\cos au}{a}$

441. $\displaystyle\int u \csc au\, du = \frac{1}{a^2}\left\{ au + \frac{(au)^3}{18} + \frac{7(au)^5}{1800} + \cdots\right.$

$$+\frac{2(2^{2n-1}-1)B_n(au)^{2n+1}}{(2n+1)!} + \cdots\left.\right\}$$

442. $\displaystyle\int \frac{\csc au}{u}\, du = -\frac{1}{au} + \frac{au}{6} + \frac{7(au)^3}{1080} + \cdots$

$$+\frac{2(2^{2n-1}-1)B_n(au)^{2n-1}}{(2n-1)(2n)!} + \cdots$$

443. $\displaystyle\int u \csc^2 au\, du = -\frac{u \cot au}{a} + \frac{1}{a^2}\ln|\sin au|$

444. $\displaystyle\int \frac{du}{q + p\csc au} = \frac{u}{q} - \frac{p}{q}\int \frac{du}{p + q\sin au}$

INTEGRALS INVOLVING INVERSE TRIGONOMETRIC FUNCTIONS

445. $\displaystyle\int \cos^{-1}\frac{u}{a}\, du = u\cos^{-1}\frac{u}{a} - \sqrt{a^2 - u^2}$

446. $\displaystyle\int u\cos^{-1}\frac{u}{a}\, du = \left(\frac{u^2}{2} - \frac{a^2}{4}\right)\cos^{-1}\frac{u}{a} - \frac{u\sqrt{a^2 - u^2}}{4}$

447. $\displaystyle\int u^2 \cos^{-1}\frac{u}{a}\, du = \frac{u^3}{3}\cos^{-1}\frac{u}{a} - \frac{(u^2 + 2a^2)\sqrt{a^2 - u^2}}{9}$

448. $\displaystyle\int \frac{\cos^{-1}(u/a)}{u}\, du = \frac{\pi}{2}\ln|u| - \int \frac{\sin^{-1}(u/a)}{u}\, du$

449. $\displaystyle\int \frac{\cos^{-1}(u/a)}{u^2}\, du = -\frac{\cos^{-1}(u/a)}{u} + \frac{1}{a}\ln\left|\frac{a + \sqrt{a^2 - u^2}}{u}\right|$

450. $\displaystyle\int \left(\cos^{-1}\frac{u}{a}\right)^2 du = u\left(\cos^{-1}\frac{u}{a}\right)^2 - 2u - 2\sqrt{a^2 - u^2}\cos^{-1}\frac{u}{a}$

451. $\displaystyle\int \sin^{-1}\frac{u}{a}\,du = u\sin^{-1}\frac{u}{a} + \sqrt{a^2 - u^2}$

452. $\displaystyle\int u\sin^{-1}\frac{u}{a}\,du = \left(\frac{u^2}{2} - \frac{a^2}{4}\right)\sin^{-1}\frac{u}{a} + \frac{u\sqrt{a^2 - u^2}}{4}$

453. $\displaystyle\int u^2\sin^{-1}\frac{u}{a}\,du = \frac{u^3}{3}\sin^{-1}\frac{u}{a} + \frac{(u^2 + 2a^2)\sqrt{a^2 - u^2}}{9}$

454. $\displaystyle\int \frac{\sin^{-1}(u/a)}{u}\,du = \frac{u}{a} + \frac{(u/a)^3}{2\cdot 3\cdot 3} + \frac{1\cdot 3(u/a)^5}{2\cdot 4\cdot 5\cdot 5}$
$$+ \frac{1\cdot 3\cdot 5(u/a)^7}{2\cdot 4\cdot 6\cdot 7\cdot 7} + \cdots$$

455. $\displaystyle\int \frac{\sin^{-1}(u/a)}{u^2}\,du = -\frac{\sin^{-1}(u/a)}{u} - \frac{1}{a}\ln\left|\frac{a + \sqrt{a^2 - u^2}}{u}\right|$

456. $\displaystyle\int \left(\sin^{-1}\frac{u}{a}\right)^2 du = u\left(\sin^{-1}\frac{u}{a}\right)^2 - 2u + 2\sqrt{a^2 - u^2}\sin^{-1}\frac{u}{a}$

457. $\displaystyle\int \tan^{-1}\frac{u}{a}\,du = u\tan^{-1}\frac{u}{a} - \frac{a}{2}\ln(u^2 + a^2)$

458. $\displaystyle\int u\tan^{-1}\frac{u}{a}\,du = \frac{1}{2}(u^2 + a^2)\tan^{-1}\frac{u}{a} - \frac{au}{2}$

459. $\displaystyle\int u^2\tan^{-1}\frac{u}{a}\,du = \frac{u^3}{3}\tan^{-1}\frac{u}{a} - \frac{au^2}{6} + \frac{a^3}{6}\ln(u^2 + a^2)$

460. $\displaystyle\int \frac{\tan^{-1}(u/a)}{u}\,du = \frac{u}{a} - \frac{(u/a)^3}{3^2} + \frac{(u/a)^5}{5^2} - \frac{(u/a)^7}{7^2} + \cdots$

461. $\displaystyle\int \frac{\tan^{-1}(u/a)}{u}\,du = -\frac{1}{u}\tan^{-1}\frac{u}{a} - \frac{1}{2a}\ln\left(\frac{u^2 + a^2}{u^2}\right)$

462. $\displaystyle\int \cot^{-1}\frac{u}{a}\,du = u\cot^{-1}\frac{u}{a} + \frac{a}{2}\ln(u^2 + a^2)$

463. $\displaystyle\int u\cot^{-1}\frac{u}{a}\,du = \frac{1}{2}(u^2 + a^2)\cot^{-1}\frac{u}{a} + \frac{au}{2}$

464. $\displaystyle\int u^2\cot^{-1}\frac{u}{a}\,du = \frac{u^3}{3}\cot^{-1}\frac{u}{a} - \frac{au^2}{6} + \frac{a^3}{6}\ln(u^2 + a^2)$

465. $\displaystyle\int \frac{\cot^{-1}(u/a)}{u}\,du = \frac{\pi}{2}\ln|u| - \int \frac{\tan^{-1}(u/a)}{u}\,du$

466. $\displaystyle\int \frac{\cot^{-1}(u/a)}{u^2}\,du = -\frac{\cot^{-1}(u/a)}{u} + \frac{1}{2a}\ln\left(\frac{u^2 + a^2}{u^2}\right)$

467. $\displaystyle\int \sec^{-1}\frac{u}{a}\,du =$

$$
\begin{cases}
u\sec^{-1}\dfrac{u}{a} - a\ln|u+\sqrt{u^2-a^2}|, \\[2mm]
\qquad\qquad 0 < \sec^{-1}\dfrac{u}{a} < \dfrac{\pi}{2} \\[4mm]
u\sec^{-1}\dfrac{u}{a} + a\ln|u+\sqrt{u^2-a^2}|, \\[2mm]
\qquad\qquad \dfrac{\pi}{2} < \sec^{-1}\dfrac{u}{a} < \pi
\end{cases}
$$

468. $\displaystyle\int u\sec^{-1}\frac{u}{a}\,du =$

$$
\begin{cases}
\dfrac{u^2}{2}\sec^{-1}\dfrac{u}{a} - \dfrac{a\sqrt{u^2-a^2}}{2}, \\[2mm]
\qquad\qquad 0 < \sec^{-1}\dfrac{u}{a} < \dfrac{\pi}{2} \\[4mm]
\dfrac{u^2}{2}\sec^{-1}\dfrac{u}{a} + \dfrac{a\sqrt{u^2-a^2}}{2}, \\[2mm]
\qquad\qquad \dfrac{\pi}{2} < \sec^{-1}\dfrac{u}{a} < \pi
\end{cases}
$$

469. $\displaystyle\int u^2\sec^{-1}\frac{u}{a}\,du =$

$$
\begin{cases}
\dfrac{u^3}{3}\sec^{-1}\dfrac{u}{a} - \dfrac{au\sqrt{u^2-a^2}}{6} - \dfrac{a^3}{6}\ln|u+\sqrt{u^2-a^2}|, \\[2mm]
\qquad\qquad 0 < \sec^{-1}\dfrac{u}{a} < \dfrac{\pi}{2} \\[4mm]
\dfrac{u^3}{3}\sec^{-1}\dfrac{u}{a} + \dfrac{au\sqrt{u^2-a^2}}{6} + \dfrac{a^3}{6}\ln|u+\sqrt{u^2-a^2}|, \\[2mm]
\qquad\qquad \dfrac{\pi}{2} < \sec^{-1}\dfrac{u}{a} < \pi
\end{cases}
$$

470. $\displaystyle\int \frac{\sec^{-1}(u/a)}{u}\,du = \frac{\pi}{a}\ln|u| + \frac{a}{u} + \frac{(u/a)^3}{2\cdot 3\cdot 3} + \frac{1\cdot 3(u/a)^5}{2\cdot 4\cdot 5\cdot 5}$

$$
+ \frac{1\cdot 3\cdot 5(u/a)^7}{2\cdot 4\cdot 6\cdot 7\cdot 7} + \cdots
$$

471. $\displaystyle\int \frac{\sec^{-1}(u/a)}{u}\,du =$

$$
\begin{cases}
-\dfrac{\sec^{-1}(u/a)}{u} + \dfrac{\sqrt{u^2-a^2}}{au}, \\[2mm]
\qquad\qquad 0 < \sec^{-1}\dfrac{u}{a} < \dfrac{\pi}{2} \\[4mm]
-\dfrac{\sec^{-1}(u/a)}{u} - \dfrac{\sqrt{u^2-a^2}}{au}, \\[2mm]
\qquad\qquad \dfrac{\pi}{2} < \sec^{-1}\dfrac{u}{a} < \pi
\end{cases}
$$

472. $\displaystyle\int \csc^{-1}\frac{u}{a}\,du = \begin{cases} u\csc^{-1}\dfrac{u}{a} + a\ln|u + \sqrt{u^2 - a^2}|, \\[2mm] \qquad\qquad 0 < \csc^{-1}\dfrac{u}{a} < \dfrac{\pi}{2} \\[4mm] u\csc^{-1}\dfrac{u}{a} + a\ln|u + \sqrt{u^2 - a^2}|, \\[2mm] \qquad\qquad \dfrac{\pi}{2} < \csc^{-1}\dfrac{u}{a} < 0 \end{cases}$

473. $\displaystyle\int u\csc^{-1}\frac{u}{a}\,du = \begin{cases} \dfrac{u^2}{2}\csc^{-1}\dfrac{u}{a} + \dfrac{a\sqrt{u^2 - a^2}}{2}, \\[2mm] \qquad\qquad 0 < \csc^{-1}\dfrac{u}{a} < \dfrac{\pi}{2} \\[4mm] \dfrac{u^2}{2}\csc^{-1}\dfrac{u}{a} - \dfrac{a\sqrt{u^2 - a^2}}{2}, \\[2mm] \qquad\qquad \dfrac{\pi}{2} < \csc^{-1}\dfrac{u}{a} < 0 \end{cases}$

474. $\displaystyle\int u^2 \csc^{-1}\frac{u}{a}\,du =$

$\begin{cases} \dfrac{u^3}{3}\csc^{-1}\dfrac{u}{a} - \dfrac{au\sqrt{u^2 - a^2}}{6} - \dfrac{a^3}{6}\ln|u + \sqrt{u^2 - a^2}|, \\[2mm] \qquad\qquad 0 < \csc^{-1}\dfrac{u}{a} < \dfrac{\pi}{2} \\[4mm] \dfrac{u^3}{3}\csc^{-1}\dfrac{u}{a} + \dfrac{au\sqrt{u^2 - a^2}}{6} + \dfrac{a^3}{6}\ln|u + \sqrt{u^2 - a^2}|, \\[2mm] \qquad\qquad \dfrac{\pi}{2} < \csc^{-1}\dfrac{u}{a} < 0 \end{cases}$

475. $\displaystyle\int \frac{\csc^{-1}(u/a)}{u}\,du = -\left(\frac{a}{u} + \frac{(a/u)^3}{2\cdot 3\cdot 3} + \frac{1\cdot 3(a/u)^5}{2\cdot 4\cdot 5\cdot 5}\right.$

$\left. + \frac{1\cdot 3\cdot 5(a/u)^7}{2\cdot 4\cdot 6\cdot 7\cdot 7} + \cdots\right)$

476. $\displaystyle\int \frac{\csc^{-1}\frac{u}{a}}{u^2}\,du = \begin{cases} -\dfrac{\csc^{-1}\dfrac{u}{a}}{u} - \dfrac{\sqrt{u^2 - a^2}}{au}, \\[2mm] \qquad\qquad 0 < \csc^{-1}\dfrac{u}{a} < \dfrac{\pi}{2} \\[4mm] -\dfrac{\csc^{-1}\dfrac{u}{a}}{u} + \dfrac{\sqrt{u^2 - a^2}}{au}, \\[2mm] \qquad\qquad -\dfrac{\pi}{2} < \csc^{-1}\dfrac{u}{a} < 0 \end{cases}$

477. $\int u^n \sin^{-1} \frac{u}{a} \, du = \frac{u^{n+1}}{n+1} \sin^{-1} \frac{u}{a} - \frac{1}{n+1} \int \frac{u^{n+1}}{\sqrt{a^2 - u^2}} \, du$

478. $\int u^n \cos^{-1} \frac{u}{a} \, du = \frac{u^{n+1}}{n+1} \cos^{-1} \frac{u}{a} + \frac{1}{n+1} \int \frac{u^{n+1}}{\sqrt{a^2 - u^2}} \, du$

479. $\int u^n \tan^{-1} \frac{u}{a} \, du = \frac{u^{n+1}}{n+1} \tan^{-1} \frac{u}{a} - \frac{a}{n+1} \int \frac{u^{n+1}}{u^2 + a^2} \, du$

480. $\int u^n \cot^{-1} \frac{u}{a} \, du = \frac{u^{n+1}}{n+1} \cot^{-1} \frac{u}{a} - \frac{a}{n+1} \int \frac{u^{n+1}}{u^2 + a^2} \, du$

481. $\int u^n \sec^{-1} \frac{u}{a} \, du = \begin{cases} \dfrac{u^{n+1} \sec^{-1}(u/a)}{n+1} - \dfrac{a}{n+1} \displaystyle\int \dfrac{u^n \, du}{\sqrt{u^2 - a^2}}, \\ \qquad\qquad\qquad 0 < \sec^{-1} \dfrac{u}{a} < \dfrac{\pi}{2} \\[2mm] \dfrac{u^{n+1} \sec^{-1}(u/a)}{n+1} + \dfrac{a}{n+1} \displaystyle\int \dfrac{u^n \, du}{\sqrt{u^2 - a^2}}, \\ \qquad\qquad\qquad \dfrac{\pi}{2} < \sec^{-1} \dfrac{u}{a} < \pi \end{cases}$

482. $\int u^n \csc^{-1} \frac{u}{a} \, du = \begin{cases} \dfrac{u^{n+1} \csc^{-1}(u/a)}{n+1} - \dfrac{a}{n+1} \displaystyle\int \dfrac{u^n \, du}{\sqrt{u^2 - a^2}} \\ \qquad\qquad\qquad 0 < \csc^{-1} \dfrac{u}{a} < \dfrac{\pi}{2} \\[2mm] \dfrac{u^{n+1} \csc^{-1}(u/a)}{n+1} - \dfrac{a}{n+1} \displaystyle\int \dfrac{u^n \, du}{\sqrt{u^2 - a^2}} \\ \qquad\qquad\qquad -\dfrac{\pi}{2} < \csc^{-1} \dfrac{u}{a} < 0 \end{cases}$

INTEGRALS INVOLVING e^{au}

483. $\int e^{au} \, du = \frac{e^{au}}{a}$

484. $\int u e^{au} \, du = \frac{e^{au}}{a} \left(u - \frac{1}{a} \right)$

485. $\int u^2 e^{au} \, du = \frac{e^{au}}{a} \left(u^2 - \frac{2u}{a} + \frac{2}{a^2} \right)$

486. $\int u^n e^{au} \, du = \frac{u^n e^{au}}{a} - \frac{n}{a} \int u^{n-1} e^{au} \, du$

$$= \frac{e^{au}}{a} \left(u^n - \frac{nu^{n-1}}{a} + \frac{n(n-1)u^{n-2}}{a^2} - \cdots \right.$$

$$\left. + \frac{(-1)^n n!}{a^n} \right), \text{ if } n = \text{positive integer}$$

487. $\displaystyle\int \frac{e^{au}}{u} \, du = \ln|u| + \frac{au}{1 \cdot 1!} + \frac{(au)^2}{2 \cdot 2!} + \frac{(au)^3}{3 \cdot 3!} + \cdots$

488. $\displaystyle\int \frac{e^{au}}{u^n} \, du = \frac{-e^{au}}{(n-1)u^{n-1}} + \frac{a}{n-1} \int \frac{e^{au}}{u^{n-1}} \, du$

489. $\displaystyle\int \frac{du}{p + qe^{au}} = \frac{u}{p} - \frac{1}{ap} \ln|p + qe^{au}|$

490. $\displaystyle\int \frac{du}{(p + qe^{au})^2} = \frac{u}{p^2} + \frac{1}{ap(p + qe^{au})} - \frac{1}{ap^2} \ln|p + qe^{au}|$

491. $\displaystyle\int \frac{du}{pe^{au} + qe^{-au}} = \begin{cases} \dfrac{1}{a\sqrt{pq}} \tan^{-1}\left(\sqrt{\dfrac{p}{q}} \, e^{au} \right) \\[3mm] \dfrac{1}{2a\sqrt{-pq}} \ln\left| \dfrac{e^{au} - \sqrt{-q/p}}{e^{au} + \sqrt{-q/p}} \right| \end{cases}$

492. $\displaystyle\int e^{au} \sin bu \, du = \frac{e^{au}(a \sin bu - b \cos bu)}{a^2 + b^2}$

493. $\displaystyle\int e^{au} \cos bu \, du = \frac{e^{au}(a \cos bu + b \sin bu)}{a^2 + b^2}$

494. $\displaystyle\int ue^{au} \sin bu \, du = \frac{ue^{au}(a \sin bu - b \cos bu)}{a^2 + b^2}$

$$- \frac{e^{au}\{(a^2 - b^2) \sin bu - 2ab \cos bu\}}{(a^2 + b^2)^2}$$

495. $\displaystyle\int ue^{au} \cos bu \, du = \frac{ue^{au}(a \cos bu + b \sin bu)}{a^2 + b^2}$

$$- \frac{e^{au}\{(a^2 - b^2) \cos bu + 2ab \sin bu\}}{(a^2 + b^2)^2}$$

496. $\displaystyle\int e^{au} \ln|u| \, du = \frac{e^{au} \ln|u|}{a} - \frac{1}{a} \int \frac{e^{au}}{u} \, du$

497. $\displaystyle\int e^{au} \sin^n bu \, du = \frac{e^{au} \sin^{n-1} bu}{a^2 + n^2b^2} (a \sin bu - nb \cos bu)$

$$+ \frac{n(n-1)b^2}{a^2 + n^2b^2} \int e^{au} \sin^{n-2} bu \, du$$

498. $\displaystyle \int e^{au} \cos^n bu \, du = \frac{e^{au} \cos^{n-1} bu}{a^2 + n^2 b^2} (a \cos bu + nb \sin bu)$

$$+ \frac{n(n-1)b^2}{a^2 + n^2 b^2} \int e^{au} \cos^{n-2} bu \, du$$

INTEGRALS INVOLVING $\ln |u|$

499. $\displaystyle \int \ln |u| du = u \ln |u| - u$

500. $\displaystyle \int (\ln |u|)^2 du = u(\ln |u|)^2 - 2u \ln |u| + 2u$

501. $\displaystyle \int (\ln |u|)^n \, du = u(\ln |u|)^n - n \int (\ln |u|)^{n-1} \, du$

502. $\displaystyle \int u \ln |u| \, du = \frac{u^2}{2} \left(\ln |u| - \frac{1}{2} \right)$

503. $\displaystyle \int u^m \ln |u| \, du = \frac{u^{m+1}}{m+1} \left(\ln |u| - \frac{1}{m+1} \right)$

504. $\displaystyle \int \frac{\ln |u|}{u} \, du = \frac{1}{2} \ln^2 |u|$

505. $\displaystyle \int \frac{\ln |u|}{u^2} \, du = -\frac{\ln |u|}{u} - \frac{1}{u}$

506. $\displaystyle \int \frac{(\ln |u|)^n \, du}{u} = \frac{(\ln |u|)^{n+1}}{n+1}$

507. $\displaystyle \int \frac{du}{u \ln |u|} = \ln |\ln |u||$

508. $\displaystyle \int \frac{du}{\ln |u|} = \ln |\ln |u|| + \ln |u| + \frac{(\ln |u|)^2}{2 \cdot 2!} + \frac{(\ln |u|)^3}{3 \cdot 3!} + \cdots$

509. $\displaystyle \int \frac{u^m \, du}{\ln |u|} \ln |\ln |u|| + (m+1) \ln |u| + \frac{(m+1)^2 (\ln |u|)^2}{2 \cdot 2!}$

$$+ \frac{(m+1)^3 (\ln |u|)^3}{3 \cdot 3!} + \cdots$$

510. $\displaystyle \int u^m (\ln |u|)^n du = \frac{u^{m+1}(\ln |u|)^n}{m+1} - \frac{n}{m+1} \int u^m (\ln |u|)^{n-1} du$

511. $\displaystyle \int \ln(u^2 + a^2) \, du = u \ln(u^2 + a^2) - 2u + 2a \tan^{-1} \frac{u}{a}$

512. $\displaystyle\int \ln\left|u^2 - a^2\right| du = u \ln\left|u^2 - a^2\right| - 2u + a \ln\left|\dfrac{u+a}{u-a}\right|$

513. $\displaystyle\int u^m \ln\left|u^2 \pm a^2\right| du = \dfrac{u^{m+1} \ln\left|u^2 \pm a^2\right|}{m+1} - \dfrac{2}{m+1}$

$$\int \dfrac{u^{m+2}}{u^2 \pm a^2}\, du$$

INTEGRALS INVOLVING cosh *au*

514. $\displaystyle\int \cosh au\, du = \dfrac{\sinh au}{a}$

515. $\displaystyle\int u \cosh au\, du = \dfrac{u \sinh au}{a} - \dfrac{\cosh au}{a^2}$

516. $\displaystyle\int u^2 \cosh au\, du = -\dfrac{2u \cosh au}{a^2} + \left(\dfrac{u^2}{a} + \dfrac{2}{a^3}\right)\sinh au$

517. $\displaystyle\int \dfrac{\cosh au}{u}\, du = \ln|u| + \dfrac{(ax)^2}{2 \cdot 2!} + \dfrac{(au)^4}{4 \cdot 4!} + \dfrac{(au)^6}{6 \cdot 6!} + \cdots$

518. $\displaystyle\int \dfrac{\cosh au}{u^2}\, du = -\dfrac{\cosh au}{u} + a \int \dfrac{\sinh au}{u}\, du$

519. $\displaystyle\int \dfrac{du}{\cosh au} = \dfrac{2}{a} \tan^{-1} e^{au}$

520. $\displaystyle\int \dfrac{u\, du}{\cosh au} = \dfrac{1}{a^2}\left\{\dfrac{(au)^2}{2} - \dfrac{(au)^4}{8} + \dfrac{5(au)^6}{144} + \cdots\right.$

$$\left. + \dfrac{(-1)^n E_n (au)^{2n+2}}{(2n+2)(2n)!} + \cdots\right\}$$

521. $\displaystyle\int \cosh^2 au\, du = \dfrac{u}{2} + \dfrac{\sinh au \cosh au}{2a}$

522. $\displaystyle\int u \cosh^2 au\, du = \dfrac{u^2}{4} + \dfrac{u \sinh 2au}{4a} - \dfrac{\cosh 2au}{8a^2}$

523. $\displaystyle\int \dfrac{du}{\cosh^2 au} = \dfrac{\tanh au}{a}$

524. $\displaystyle\int \cosh au \cosh pu\, du = \dfrac{\sinh(a-p)u}{2(a-p)} + \dfrac{\sinh(a+p)u}{2(a+p)}$

525. $\displaystyle\int \cosh au \sin pu\, du = \dfrac{a \sinh au \sin pu - p \cosh au \cos pu}{a^2 + p^2}$

526. $\displaystyle\int \cosh au \cos pu\, du = \frac{a \sinh au \cos pu + p \cosh au \sin pu}{a^2 + p^2}$

527. $\displaystyle\int \frac{du}{\cosh au + 1} = \frac{1}{a} \tanh \frac{au}{2}$

528. $\displaystyle\int \frac{du}{\cosh au - 1} = -\frac{1}{a} \coth \frac{au}{2}$

529. $\displaystyle\int \frac{u\, du}{\cosh au + 1} = \frac{u}{a} \tanh \frac{au}{2} - \frac{2}{a^2} \ln \cosh \frac{au}{2}$

530. $\displaystyle\int \frac{u\, du}{\cosh au - 1} = -\frac{u}{a} \coth \frac{au}{2} + \frac{2}{a^2} \ln \left| \sinh \frac{au}{2} \right|$

531. $\displaystyle\int \frac{du}{(\cosh au + 1)^2} = -\frac{1}{2a} \tanh \frac{au}{2} - \frac{1}{6a} \tanh^3 \frac{au}{2}$

532. $\displaystyle\int \frac{du}{(\cosh au - 1)^2} = \frac{1}{2a} \coth \frac{au}{2} - \frac{1}{6a} \coth^3 \frac{au}{2}$

533. $\displaystyle\int \frac{du}{p + q \cosh au} = \begin{cases} \dfrac{2}{a\sqrt{q^2 - p^2}} \tan^{-1} \dfrac{qe^{au} + p}{\sqrt{q^2 - p^2}} \\[3ex] \dfrac{1}{a\sqrt{p^2 - q^2}} \ln \left| \dfrac{qe^{au} + p - \sqrt{p^2 - q^2}}{qe^{au} + p + \sqrt{p^2 - q^2}} \right| \end{cases}$

534. $\displaystyle\int \frac{du}{(p + q \cosh au)^2} = \frac{q \sinh au}{a(q^2 - p^2)(p + q \cosh au)} - \frac{p}{q^2 - p^2}$

$$\int \frac{du}{p + q \cosh au}$$

535. $\displaystyle\int \frac{du}{p^2 - q^2 \cosh^2 au} =$

$$\begin{cases} \dfrac{1}{2ap\sqrt{p^2 - q^2}} \ln \left| \dfrac{p \tanh au + \sqrt{p^2 - q^2}}{p \tanh au - \sqrt{p^2 - q^2}} \right| \\[3ex] \dfrac{1}{ap\sqrt{q^2 - p^2}} \tan^{-1} \dfrac{p \tanh au}{\sqrt{q^2 - p^2}} \end{cases}$$

536. $\displaystyle\int \frac{du}{p^2 + q^2 \cosh^2 au} =$

$$\begin{cases} \dfrac{1}{2ap\sqrt{p^2 + q^2}} \ln \left| \dfrac{p \tanh au + \sqrt{p^2 + q^2}}{p \tan au + \sqrt{q^2 - p^2}} \right| \\[3ex] \dfrac{1}{ap\sqrt{p^2 + q^2}} \tan^{-1} \dfrac{p \tanh au}{\sqrt{p^2 + q^2}} \end{cases}$$

537. $\displaystyle\int u^m \cosh au\,du = \frac{u^m \sinh au}{a} - \frac{m}{a}\int u^{m-1}\sinh au\,du$

538. $\displaystyle\int \cosh^n au\,du = \frac{\cosh^{n-1} au \sinh au}{an}$

$$+ \frac{n-1}{n}\int \cosh^{n-2} au\,du$$

539. $\displaystyle\int \frac{\cosh au}{u^n}\,du = \frac{-\cosh au}{(n-1)u^{n-1}} + \frac{a}{n-1}\int \frac{\sinh au}{u^{n-1}}\,du$

540. $\displaystyle\int \frac{du}{\cosh^n au} = \frac{\sinh au}{a(n-1)\cosh^{n-1} au} + \frac{n-2}{n-1}\int \frac{du}{\cosh^{n-2} au}$

541. $\displaystyle\int \frac{u\,du}{\cosh^n au}$

$$= \frac{u\sinh au}{a(n-1)\cosh^{n-1} au} + \frac{1}{(n-1)(n-2)a^2 \cosh^{n-2} au}$$

$$+ \frac{n-2}{n-1}\int \frac{u\,du}{\cosh^{n-2} au}$$

INTEGRALS INVOLVING sinh au

542. $\displaystyle\int \sinh au\,du = \frac{\cosh au}{a}$

543. $\displaystyle\int u\sinh au\,du = \frac{u\cosh au}{a} - \frac{\sinh au}{a^2}$

544. $\displaystyle\int u^2\sinh au\,du = \left(\frac{u^2}{a} + \frac{2}{a^3}\right)\cosh au - \frac{2u}{a^2}\sinh au$

545. $\displaystyle\int \frac{\sinh au}{u}\,du = au + \frac{(au)^3}{3\cdot 3!} + \frac{(au)^5}{5\cdot 5!} + \cdots$

546. $\displaystyle\int \frac{\sinh au}{u^2}\,du = -\frac{\sinh au}{u} + a\int \frac{\cosh au}{u}\,du$

547. $\displaystyle\int \frac{du}{\sinh au} = \frac{1}{a}\ln\left|\tanh \frac{au}{2}\right|$

548. $\displaystyle\int \frac{u\,du}{\sinh au} = \frac{1}{a^2}\left\{ au - \frac{(au)^3}{18} + \frac{7(au)^5}{1800} - \cdots \right.$

$$\left. + \frac{2(-1)^n(2^{2n}-1)B_n(au)^{2n+1}}{(2n+1)!} + \cdots \right\}$$

549. $\displaystyle\int \sinh^2 au\,du = \frac{\sinh au \cosh au}{2a} - \frac{u}{2}$

550. $\displaystyle\int u \sinh^2 au\,du = \frac{u \sinh 2au}{4a} - \frac{\cosh 2au}{8a^2} - \frac{u^2}{4}$

551. $\displaystyle\int \frac{du}{\sinh^2 au} = -\frac{\coth au}{a}$

552. $\displaystyle\int \sinh au \sinh pu\,du = \frac{\sinh(a+p)u}{2(a+p)} - \frac{\sinh(a-p)u}{2(a-p)}$

553. $\displaystyle\int \sinh au \sin pu\,du = \frac{a \cosh au \sin pu - p \sinh au \cos pu}{a^2+p^2}$

554. $\displaystyle\int \sinh au \cos pu\,du = \frac{a \cosh au \cos pu + p \sinh au \sin pu}{a^2+p^2}$

555. $\displaystyle\int \frac{du}{p + q \sinh au} = \frac{1}{a\sqrt{p^2+q^2}} \ln\left|\frac{qe^{au}+p-\sqrt{p^2+q^2}}{qe^{au}+p+\sqrt{p^2+q^2}}\right|$

556. $\displaystyle\int \frac{du}{(p + q \sinh au)^2} = \frac{-q \cosh au}{a(p^2+q^2)(p+q\sinh au)}$
$$+ \frac{p}{p^2+q^2}\int \frac{du}{p+q\sinh au}$$

557. $\displaystyle\int \frac{du}{p^2 + q^2 \sinh^2 au} =$

$$\begin{cases} \dfrac{1}{ap\sqrt{q^2-p^2}} \tan^{-1} \dfrac{\sqrt{q^2-p^2}\,\tanh au}{p} \\[4mm] \dfrac{1}{2ap\sqrt{p^2-q^2}} \ln\left|\dfrac{p+\sqrt{p^2-q^2}\,\tanh au}{p-\sqrt{p^2-q^2}\,\tanh au}\right| \end{cases}$$

558. $\displaystyle\int \frac{du}{p^2 - q^2 \sinh^2 au} =$

$$\frac{1}{2ap\sqrt{p^2+q^2}} \ln\left|\frac{p+\sqrt{p^2+q^2}\,\tanh au}{p-\sqrt{p^2+q^2}\,\tanh au}\right|$$

559. $\displaystyle\int u^m \sinh au\,du = \frac{u^m \cosh au}{a} - \frac{m}{a}\int u^{m-1}\cosh au\,du$

560. $\displaystyle\int \sinh^n au\,du = \frac{\sinh^{n-1} au \cosh au}{an} - \frac{n-1}{n}\int \sinh^{n-2} au\,du$

561. $\displaystyle\int \frac{\sinh au}{u^n}\,du = \frac{-\sinh au}{(n-1)u^{n-1}} + \frac{a}{n-1}\int \frac{\cosh au}{u^{n-1}}\,du$

562. $\displaystyle\int \frac{du}{\sinh^n au} = \frac{-\cosh au}{a(n-1)\sinh^{n-1} au} - \frac{n-2}{n-1}\int \frac{du}{\sinh^{n-2} au}$

563. $\displaystyle\int \frac{u\,du}{\sinh^n au}$

$$= \frac{-u\cosh au}{a(n-1)\sinh^{n-1}au} - \frac{1}{a^2(n-1)(n-2)\sinh^{n-2}au}$$

$$-\frac{n-2}{n-1}\int \frac{u\,du}{\sinh^{n-2}au}$$

INTEGRALS INVOLVING $\sinh au$ AND $\cosh au$

564. $\displaystyle\int \sinh au\cosh au\,du = \frac{\sinh^2 au}{2a}$

565. $\displaystyle\int \sinh pu\cosh qu\,du = \frac{\cosh(p+q)u}{2(p+q)} + \frac{\cosh(p-q)u}{2(p-q)}$

566. $\displaystyle\int \sinh^n au\cosh au\,du = \frac{\sinh^{n+1}au}{(n+1)a}$

567. $\displaystyle\int \cosh^n au\sinh au\,du = \frac{\cosh^{n+1}au}{(n+1)a}$

568. $\displaystyle\int \sinh^2 au\cosh^2 au\,du = \frac{\sinh 4au}{32a} - \frac{u}{8}$

569. $\displaystyle\int \frac{du}{\sinh au\cosh au} = \frac{1}{a}\ln|\tanh au|$

570. $\displaystyle\int \frac{du}{\sinh^2 au\cosh au} = -\frac{1}{a}\tan^{-1}\sinh au - \frac{\cosh au}{a}$

571. $\displaystyle\int \frac{du}{\sinh au\cosh^2 au} = \frac{\text{sech}}{a} + \frac{1}{a}\ln\left|\tanh\frac{au}{2}\right|$

572. $\displaystyle\int \frac{du}{\sinh^2 au\cosh^2 au} = -\frac{2\coth 2au}{a}$

573. $\displaystyle\int \frac{\sinh^2 au}{\cosh au}\,du = \frac{\sinh au}{a} - \frac{1}{a}\tan^{-1}\sinh au$

574. $\displaystyle\int \frac{\cosh^2 au}{\sinh au}\,du = \frac{\cosh au}{a} + \frac{1}{a}\ln\left|\tanh\frac{au}{2}\right|$

575. $\displaystyle\int \frac{du}{\cosh au(1+\sinh au)} = \frac{1}{2a}\ln\left|\frac{1+\sinh au}{\cosh au}\right| + \frac{1}{a}\tan^{-1}e^{au}$

576. $\displaystyle\int \frac{du}{\sinh au(\cosh au + 1)} = \frac{1}{2a}\ln\left|\tanh\frac{au}{2}\right| + \frac{1}{2a(\cosh au + 1)}$

577. $\displaystyle\int \frac{du}{\cosh au(1 + \sinh au)} = \frac{1}{2a}\ln\left|\tanh\frac{au}{2}\right| - \frac{1}{2a(\cosh au - 1)}$

INTEGRALS INVOLVING tanh au

578. $\displaystyle\int \tanh au\, du = \frac{1}{a}\ln\cosh au$

579. $\displaystyle\int \tanh^2 au\, du = u - \frac{\tanh au}{a}$

580. $\displaystyle\int \tanh^3 au\, du = \frac{1}{a}\ln\cosh au - \frac{\tanh^2 au}{2a}$

581. $\displaystyle\int \tanh^n au\,\operatorname{sech}^2 au\, du = \frac{\tanh^{n+1} au}{(n+1)a}$

582. $\displaystyle\int \frac{\operatorname{sech}^2 au}{\tanh au}\, du = \frac{1}{a}\ln|\tanh au|$

583. $\displaystyle\int \frac{du}{\tanh au} = \frac{1}{a}\ln|\sinh au|$

584. $\displaystyle\int u\tanh au\, du$

$$= \frac{1}{a^2}\left\{ \frac{(au)^3}{3} - \frac{(au)^5}{15} + \frac{2(au)^7}{105} - \cdots \right.$$

$$\left. + \frac{(-1)^{n-1}2^{2n}(2^{2n}-1)B_n(au)^{2n+1}}{(2n+1)!} + \cdots \right\}$$

585. $\displaystyle\int u\tanh^2 au\, du = \frac{u^2}{2} - \frac{u\tanh au}{a} + \frac{1}{a^2}\ln\cosh au$

586. $\displaystyle\int \frac{\tanh au}{u}\, du = au - \frac{(au)^3}{9} + \frac{2(au)^5}{75} - \cdots$

$$+ \frac{(-1)^{n-1}2^{2n}(2^{2n}-1)B_n(au)^{2n+1}}{(2n-1)!(2n)!} + \cdots$$

587. $\displaystyle\int \frac{du}{p + q\tanh au} = \frac{pu}{p^2 - q^2}$

$$- \frac{q}{a(p^2 - q^2)}\ln|p\sinh au + q\cosh au|$$

588. $\displaystyle\int \tanh^n au\,du = \frac{-\tanh^{n-1} au}{a(n-1)} + \int \tanh^{n-2} au\,du$

INTEGRALS INVOLVING coth au

589. $\displaystyle\int \coth au\,du = \frac{1}{a}\ln|\sinh au|$

590. $\displaystyle\int \coth^2 au\,du = u - \frac{\coth au}{a}$

591. $\displaystyle\int \coth^3 au\,du = \frac{1}{a}\ln|\sinh au| - \frac{\coth^2 au}{2a}$

592. $\displaystyle\int \coth^n au\,\mathrm{csch}^2 au\,du = \frac{\coth^{n+1} au}{(n+1)a}$

593. $\displaystyle\int \frac{\mathrm{csch}^2 au}{\coth au}\,du = -\frac{1}{a}\ln|\cosh au|$

594. $\displaystyle\int \frac{du}{\coth au} = \frac{1}{a}\ln(\cosh au)$

595. $\displaystyle\int u\coth au\,du = \frac{1}{a^2}\left\{ au + \frac{(au)^3}{9} - \frac{(au)^5}{225} + \cdots \right.$

$$\left. + \frac{(-1)^{n-1} 2^{2n} B_n (au)^{2n+1}}{(2n+1)!} + \cdots \right\}$$

596. $\displaystyle\int u\coth^2 au\,du = \frac{u^2}{2} - \frac{u\coth au}{a} + \frac{1}{a^2}\ln|\sinh au|$

597. $\displaystyle\int \frac{\coth au}{u}\,du = -\frac{1}{au} + \frac{au}{3} - \frac{(au)^3}{135} + \cdots$

$$+ \frac{(-1)^n 2^{2n} B_n (au)^{2n-1}}{(2n-1)(2n)!} + \cdots$$

598. $\displaystyle\int \frac{du}{p + q\coth au}$

$$= \frac{pu}{p^2 - q^2} - \frac{q}{a(p^2 - q^2)}\ln|p\sinh au + q\cosh au|$$

599. $\displaystyle\int \coth^n au\,du = -\frac{\coth^{n-1} au}{a(n-1)} + \int \coth^{n-2} au\,du$

INTEGRALS INVOLVING sech au

600. $\displaystyle\int \mathrm{sech}\,au\,du = \frac{2}{a}\ln|\tan^{-1} e^{au}|$

601. $\displaystyle\int \mathrm{sech}^2 au\,du = \frac{\tanh au}{a}$

602. $\displaystyle\int \operatorname{sech}^3 au \, du = \frac{\operatorname{sech} au \tanh au}{2a} + \frac{1}{2a} \tan^{-1} \sinh au$

603. $\displaystyle\int \operatorname{sech}^n au \tanh au \, du = -\frac{\operatorname{sech}^n au}{na}$

604. $\displaystyle\int \frac{du}{\operatorname{sech} au} = \frac{\sinh au}{a}$

605. $\displaystyle\int u \operatorname{sech} au \, du = \frac{1}{a^2} \left\{ \frac{(au)^2}{2} - \frac{(au)^4}{8} + \frac{5(au)^6}{144} + \cdots \right.$

$$+ \left. \frac{(-1)^n E_n (au)^{2n+2}}{(2n+2)(2n)!} + \cdots \right\}$$

606. $\displaystyle\int u \operatorname{sech}^2 au \, du = -\frac{u \tanh au}{a} - \frac{1}{a^2} \ln \cosh au$

607. $\displaystyle\int \frac{\operatorname{sech} au}{u} \, du = \ln |u| - \frac{(au)^2}{4} + \frac{5(au)^4}{96} - \frac{61(au)^6}{4320}$

$$+ \cdots + \frac{(-1)^n E_n (au)^{2n}}{2n(2n)!} + \cdots$$

608. $\displaystyle\int \frac{du}{q + p \operatorname{sech} au} = \frac{u}{q} - \frac{p}{q} \int \frac{du}{p + q \cosh au}$

609. $\displaystyle\int \operatorname{sech}^n au \, du = \frac{\operatorname{sech}^{n-2} au \tanh au}{a(n-1)} + \frac{n-2}{n-1} \int \operatorname{sech}^{n-2} au \, du$

INTEGRALS INVOLVING csch au

610. $\displaystyle\int \operatorname{csch} au \, du = \frac{1}{a} \ln \left| \tanh \frac{au}{2} \right|$

611. $\displaystyle\int \operatorname{csch}^2 au \, du = -\frac{\coth au}{a}$

612. $\displaystyle\int \operatorname{csch}^3 au \, du = -\frac{\operatorname{csch} au \coth au}{2a} - \frac{1}{2a} \ln \left| \tanh \frac{au}{2} \right|$

613. $\displaystyle\int \operatorname{csch}^n au \coth au \, du = -\frac{\operatorname{csch}^n au}{na}$

614. $\displaystyle\int \frac{du}{\operatorname{csch} au} = \frac{1}{a} \cosh au$

615. $\displaystyle\int u \operatorname{csch} au \, du = \frac{1}{a^2} \left\{ au - \frac{(au)^3}{18} + \frac{7(au)^5}{1800} + \cdots \right.$

$$+ \left. \frac{2(-1)^n (2^{2n-1} - 1) B_n (au)^{2n+1}}{(2n+1)!} + \cdots \right\}$$

616. $\displaystyle\int u\operatorname{csch}^2 au\,du = -\frac{u\operatorname{csch}au}{a} + \frac{1}{a^2}\ln|\sinh au|$

617. $\displaystyle\int \frac{\operatorname{csch}au}{u}\,du = -\frac{1}{au} - \frac{au}{6} + \frac{7(au)^3}{1080} + \cdots$

$$+ \frac{(-1)^n 2(2^{2n}-1)B_n(au)^{2n-1}}{(2n-1)(2n)!} + \cdots$$

618. $\displaystyle\int \frac{du}{q + p\operatorname{csch}au} = \frac{u}{q} - \frac{p}{q}\int \frac{du}{p + q\sinh au}$

619. $\displaystyle\int \operatorname{csch}^n au\,du = \frac{-\operatorname{csch}^{n-2}au\coth au}{a(n-1)}$

$$-\frac{n-2}{n-1}\int \operatorname{csch}^{n-2}au\,du$$

INTEGRALS INVOLVING INVERSE HYPERBOLIC FUNCTIONS

620. $\displaystyle\int \sinh^{-1}\frac{u}{a}\,du = u\sinh^{-1}\frac{u}{a} - \sqrt{u^2 + a^2}$

621. $\displaystyle\int u\sinh^{-1}\frac{u}{a}\,du = \left(\frac{u^2}{2} + \frac{a^2}{4}\right)\sinh^{-1}\frac{u}{a} - \frac{u\sqrt{u^2+a^2}}{4}$

622. $\displaystyle\int u^2\sinh^{-1}\frac{u}{a}\,du = \frac{u^3}{3}\sinh^{-1}\frac{u}{a} + \frac{(2a^2 - u^2)\sqrt{u^2+a^2}}{9}$

623. $\displaystyle\int \frac{\sinh^{-1}(u/a)}{u}\,du$

$$= \begin{cases} \dfrac{u}{a} - \dfrac{(u/a)^3}{2\cdot 3\cdot 3} + \dfrac{1\cdot 3(u/a)^5}{2\cdot 4\cdot 5\cdot 5} \\ \qquad\qquad - \dfrac{1\cdot 3\cdot 5(u/a)^7}{2\cdot 4\cdot 6\cdot 7\cdot 7} + \cdots, & |u| < a \\[2mm] \dfrac{\ln^2|2u/a|}{2} - \dfrac{(a/u)^{2_3}}{2\cdot 2\cdot 2} - \dfrac{1\cdot 3(a/u)^4}{2\cdot 4\cdot 4\cdot 4} \\ \qquad\qquad - \dfrac{1\cdot 3\cdot 5(a/u)^6}{2\cdot 4\cdot 6\cdot 6\cdot 6} + \cdots, & u > a \\[2mm] -\dfrac{\ln^2|-2u/a|}{2} + \dfrac{(a/u)^2}{2\cdot 2\cdot 2} - \dfrac{1\cdot 3(a/u)^4}{2\cdot 4\cdot 4\cdot 4} \\ \qquad\qquad + \dfrac{1\cdot 3\cdot 5(a/u)^6}{2\cdot 4\cdot 6\cdot 6\cdot 6} - \cdots, & u > -a \end{cases}$$

624. $\displaystyle\int \frac{\sin^{-1}(u/a)}{u^2}\,du = -\frac{\sinh^{-1}(u/a)}{u} - \frac{1}{a}\ln\left|\frac{a + \sqrt{u^2 + a^2}}{u}\right|$

625. $\displaystyle\int \cosh^{-1}\frac{u}{a}\,du = \begin{cases} u\cosh^{-1}(u/a) - \sqrt{u^2 - a^2}, \\[2pt] \qquad\qquad\qquad \cosh^{-1}(u/a) > 0 \\[4pt] u\cosh^{-1}(u/a) + \sqrt{u^2 - a^2}, \\[2pt] \qquad\qquad\qquad \cosh^{-1}(u/a) < 0 \end{cases}$

626. $\displaystyle\int u\cosh^{-1}\frac{u}{a}\,du$

$= \begin{cases} \frac{1}{4}(2u^2 - a^2)\cosh^{-1}(u/a) - \frac{1}{4}u\sqrt{u^2 - a^2}, \\[2pt] \qquad\qquad\qquad\qquad\qquad \cosh^{-1}(u/a) > 0 \\[4pt] \frac{1}{4}(2u^2 - a^2)\cosh^{-1}(u/a) + \frac{1}{4}u\sqrt{u^2 - a^2}, \\[2pt] \qquad\qquad\qquad\qquad\qquad \cosh^{-1}(u/a) < 0 \end{cases}$

627. $\displaystyle\int u^2\cosh^{-1}\frac{u}{a}\,du$

$= \begin{cases} \frac{1}{3}u^3\cosh^{-1}(u/a) - \frac{1}{9}(u^2 + 2a^2)\sqrt{u^2 - a^2}, \\[2pt] \qquad\qquad\qquad\qquad\qquad \cosh^{-1}(u/a) > 0 \\[4pt] \frac{1}{3}u^3\cosh^{-1}(u/a) + \frac{1}{9}(u^2 + 2a^2)\sqrt{u^2 - a^2}, \\[2pt] \qquad\qquad\qquad\qquad\qquad \cosh^{-1}(u/a) < 0 \end{cases}$

628. $\displaystyle\int \frac{\cosh^{-1}(u/a)}{u}\,du$

$= \pm\left[\frac{1}{2}\ln^2 |2u/a| + \frac{(a/u)^2}{2\cdot 2\cdot 2} + \frac{1\cdot 3(a/u)^4}{2\cdot 4\cdot 4\cdot 4}\right.$

$\left. + \frac{1\cdot 3\cdot 5(a/u)^6}{2\cdot 4\cdot 6\cdot 6\cdot 6} + \cdots\right]$

$\quad +$ if $\cosh^{-1}(u/a) > 0$, $-$ if $\cosh^{-1}(u/a) < 0$

629. $\displaystyle\int \frac{\cosh^{-1}(u/a)}{u^2}\,du$

$= -\frac{\cosh^{-1}(u/a)}{u} \mp \frac{1}{a}\ln\left|\frac{a + \sqrt{u^2 + a^2}}{u}\right|$

$\quad -$ if $\cosh^{-1}(u/a) > 0$, $+$ if $\cosh^{-1}(u/a) < 0$

630. $\displaystyle\int \tanh^{-1}\frac{u}{a}\,du = u\tanh^{-1}\frac{u}{a} + \frac{a}{2}\ln|a^2 - u^2|$

631. $\displaystyle\int u\tanh^{-1}\frac{u}{a}\,du = \frac{au}{2} + \frac{1}{2}(u^2 - a^2)\tanh^{-1}\frac{u}{a}$

632. $\displaystyle\int u^2\tanh^{-1}\frac{u}{a}\,du = \frac{au^2}{6} + \frac{u^3}{3}\tanh^{-1}\frac{u}{a} + \frac{a^3}{6}\ln|a^2 - u^2|$

633. $\displaystyle\int \frac{\tanh^{-1}(u/a)}{u}\,du = \frac{u}{a} + \frac{(u/a)^3}{3^2} + \frac{(u/a)^5}{5^2} + \cdots$

634. $\displaystyle\int \frac{\tanh^{-1}(u/a)}{u^2}\,du = -\frac{\tanh^{-1}}{u} + \frac{1}{2a}\ln\left|\frac{u^2}{a^2 - u^2}\right|$

635. $\displaystyle\int \coth^{-1}\frac{u}{a}\,du = u\coth^{-1}\frac{u}{a} + \frac{a}{2}\ln|u^2 - a^2|$

636. $\displaystyle\int u\coth^{-1}\frac{u}{a}\,du = \frac{au}{2} + \frac{1}{2}(u^2 - a^2)\coth^{-1}\frac{u}{a}$

637. $\displaystyle\int u^2\coth^{-1}\frac{u}{a}\,du = \frac{au^2}{6} + \frac{u^3}{3}\coth^{-1}\frac{u}{a} + \frac{a^3}{6}\ln|u^2 - a^2|$

638. $\displaystyle\int \frac{\coth^{-1}(u/a)}{u}\,du = -\left(\frac{a}{u} + \frac{(a/u)^3}{3^2} + \frac{(a/u)^5}{5^2} + \cdots\right)$

639. $\displaystyle\int \frac{\coth^{-1}(u/a)}{u^2}\,du = -\frac{\coth^{-1}(u/a)}{u} + \frac{1}{2a}\ln\left|\frac{u^2}{u^2 - a^2}\right|$

640. $\displaystyle\int \text{sech}^{-1}\frac{u}{a}\,du = \begin{cases} u\,\text{sech}^{-1}(u/a) + a\sin^{-1}(u/a), \\ \qquad\qquad \text{sech}^{-1}(u/a) > 0 \\ u\,\text{sech}^{-1}(u/a) - a\sin^{-1}(u/a), \\ \qquad\qquad \text{sech}^{-1}(u/a) < 0 \end{cases}$

641. $\displaystyle\int u\,\text{sech}^{-1}\frac{u}{a}\,du = \begin{cases} \frac{1}{2}u^2\,\text{sech}^{-1}(u/a) - \frac{1}{2}a\sqrt{a^2 - u^2}, \\ \qquad\qquad \text{sech}^{-1}(u/a) > 0 \\ \frac{1}{2}u^2\,\text{sech}^{-1}(u/a) + \frac{1}{2}a\sqrt{a^2 - u^2}, \\ \qquad\qquad \text{sech}^{-1}(u/a) < 0 \end{cases}$

642. $\displaystyle\int \frac{\text{sech}^{-1}}{u}\,du$

$$= \begin{cases} -\frac{1}{2}\ln\left|\frac{a}{u}\right|\ln\left|\frac{4a}{u}\right| - \frac{(u/a)^2}{2\cdot2\cdot2} - \frac{1\cdot3(u/a)^4}{2\cdot4\cdot4\cdot4} - \cdots, \\ \qquad\qquad\qquad\qquad \text{sech}^{-1}(u/a) > 0 \\ \frac{1}{2}\ln\left|\frac{a}{u}\right|\ln\left|\frac{4a}{u}\right| + \frac{(u/a)^2}{2\cdot2\cdot2} - \frac{1\cdot3(u/a)^4}{2\cdot4\cdot4\cdot4} + \cdots, \\ \qquad\qquad\qquad\qquad \text{sech}^{-1}(u/a) < 0 \end{cases}$$

643. $\displaystyle\int \operatorname{csch}^{-1}\frac{u}{a}\,du = u\operatorname{csch}^{-1}\frac{u}{a} \pm a\sinh^{-1}\frac{u}{a}$

$$[\text{`` + '' if } u > 0, \text{`` − '' if } u < 0]$$

644. $\displaystyle\int u\operatorname{csch}^{-1}\frac{u}{a}\,du = \frac{u^2}{2}\operatorname{csch}^{-1}\frac{u}{a} \pm \frac{a\sqrt{u^2+a^2}}{2}$

$$[\text{`` + '' if } u > 0, \text{`` − '' if } u < 0]$$

645. $\displaystyle\int \frac{\operatorname{csch}^{-1}(u/a)}{u}\,du$

$$= \begin{cases} \frac{1}{2}\ln\left|\frac{a}{u}\right|\ln\left|\frac{4a}{u}\right| + \frac{1(u/a)^2}{2\cdot2\cdot2} - \frac{1\cdot3(u/a)^4}{2\cdot4\cdot4\cdot4} + \cdots, \\ \qquad\qquad\qquad\qquad\qquad\qquad 0 < u < a \\[2mm] \frac{1}{2}\ln\left|-\frac{u}{a}\right|\ln\left|-\frac{u}{4a}\right| - \frac{(u/a)^2}{2\cdot2\cdot2} + \frac{1\cdot3(u/a)^4}{2\cdot4\cdot4\cdot4} - \cdots, \\ \qquad\qquad\qquad\qquad\qquad\qquad -a < u < 0 \\[2mm] -\frac{a}{u} + \frac{(a/u)^3}{2\cdot3\cdot3} - \frac{1\cdot3(a/u)^5}{2\cdot4\cdot5\cdot5} + \cdots, \\ \qquad\qquad\qquad\qquad\qquad\qquad |u| > a \end{cases}$$

646. $\displaystyle\int u^m \sinh^{-1}\frac{u}{a}\,du = \frac{u^{m+1}}{m+1}\sinh^{-1}\frac{u}{a} - \frac{1}{m+1}\int \frac{u^{m+1}}{\sqrt{u^2+a^2}}\,du$

647. $\displaystyle\int u^m \cosh^{-1}\frac{u}{a}\,du$

$$= \begin{cases} \frac{u^{m+1}}{m+1}\cosh^{-1}\frac{u}{a} - \frac{1}{m+1}\int \frac{u^{m+1}}{\sqrt{u^2-a^2}}\,du, \\ \qquad\qquad\qquad\qquad\qquad \cosh^{-1}(u/a) > 0 \\[2mm] \frac{u^{m+1}}{m+1}\cosh^{-1}\frac{u}{a} + \frac{1}{m+1}\int \frac{u^{m+1}}{\sqrt{u^2-a^2}}\,du, \\ \qquad\qquad\qquad\qquad\qquad \cosh^{-1}(u/a) < 0 \end{cases}$$

648. $\displaystyle\int u^m \tanh^{-1}\frac{u}{a}\,du = \frac{u^{m+1}}{m+1}\tanh^{-1}\frac{u}{a} - \frac{a}{m+1}\int \frac{u^{m+1}}{a^2-u^2}\,du$

649. $\displaystyle\int u^m \coth^{-1}\frac{u}{a}\,du = \frac{u^{m+1}}{m+1}\coth^{-1}\frac{u}{a} - \frac{a}{m+1}\int \frac{u^{m+1}}{a^2-u^2}\,du$

650. $\displaystyle\int u^m \operatorname{sech}^{-1}\frac{u}{a}\,du$

$$= \begin{cases} \frac{u^{m+1}}{m+1}\operatorname{sech}^{-1}\frac{u}{a} + \frac{a}{m+1}\int \frac{u^m\,du}{\sqrt{a^2-u^2}}, \\ \qquad\qquad\qquad\qquad\qquad \operatorname{sech}^{-1}(u/a) > 0 \\[2mm] \frac{u^{m+1}}{m+1}\operatorname{sech}^{-1}\frac{u}{a} - \frac{a}{m+1}\int \frac{u^m\,du}{\sqrt{a^2-u^2}}, \\ \qquad\qquad\qquad\qquad\qquad \operatorname{sech}^{-1}(u/a) < 0 \end{cases}$$

651. $\displaystyle\int u^m \operatorname{csch}^{-1}\frac{u}{a}\,du = \frac{u^{m+1}}{m+1}\operatorname{csch}^{-1}\frac{u}{a} \pm \frac{a}{m+1}\int \frac{u^m\,du}{\sqrt{u^2+a^2}},$

$$[\text{``}+\text{''} \text{ if } u>0,\ \text{``}-\text{''} \text{ if } u<0]$$

12.5 Bernoulli and Euler Numbers; Gamma and Beta Functions

Bernoulli and Euler Numbers

The *Bernoulli numbers* $B_1, B_2, B_3, \ldots$ are defined by the series

$$\frac{x}{e^x-1} = 1 - \frac{x}{2} + \frac{B_1x^2}{2!} - \frac{B_2x^4}{4!} + \frac{B_3x^6}{6!} - \cdots \quad |x|<2\pi$$

The *Euler numbers* $E_1, E_2, E_3, \ldots$ are defined by the series

$$\sec x = 1 + \frac{E_1x^2}{2!} + \frac{E_2x^4}{4!} + \frac{E_3x^6}{6!} + \cdots \quad |x| < \frac{\pi}{2}$$

TABLE OF FIRST FEW BERNOULLI AND EULER NUMBERS

Bernoulli numbers	Euler numbers
$B_1 = 1/6$	$E_1 = 1$
$B_2 = 1/30$	$E_2 = 5$
$B_3 = 1/42$	$E_3 = 61$
$B_4 = 1/30$	$E_4 = 1,385$
$B_5 = 5/66$	$E_5 = 50,521$
$B_6 = 691/2730$	$E_6 = 2,702,765$
$B_7 = 7/6$	$E_7 = 199,360,981$
$B_8 = 3617/510$	$E_8 = 19,391,512,145$
$B_9 = 43,867/798$	$E_9 = 2,404,879,675,441$
$B_{10} = 174,611/330$	$E_{10} = 370,371,188,237,525$
$B_{11} = 854,513/138$	$E_{11} = 69,348,874,393,137,901$
$B_{12} = 236,364,091/2730$	$E_{12} = 15,514,534,163,557,086,905$

GAMMA FUNCTION

For $n>0$, $\quad \Gamma(n) = \displaystyle\int_0^\infty t^{n-1}e^{-t}\,dt; \Gamma(n+1) = n\Gamma(n)$

For $n = 0, 1, 2, \ldots$ $\quad \Gamma(n+1) = n!$

For $n<0$ $\quad \Gamma(n) = \dfrac{\Gamma(n+1)}{n}$

BETA FUNCTION

$$B(m, n) = \int_0^1 t^{m-1}(1-t)^{n-1} dt \; m > 0, n > 0$$

$$B(m, n) = \frac{\Gamma(m)\Gamma(n)}{\Gamma(m+n)}$$

12.6 Definite Integral Formulas

DEFINITE INTEGRAL AT A POINT or EQUAL LIMITS

1. $\displaystyle\int_a^a f(x)\,dx = 0$

OPPOSITE OF A DEFINITE INTEGRAL or LIMIT REVERSAL

2. $\displaystyle\int_a^b f(x)\,dx = -\int_b^a f(x)\,dx$

SUM/DIFFERENCE

3. $\displaystyle\int_a^b \{f(x) \pm g(x)\}\,dx = \int_a^b f(x)\,dx \pm \int_a^b g(x)\,dx$

CONSTANT

4. $\displaystyle\int_a^b c f(x)\,dx = c\int_a^b f(x)\,dx$ where c is any constant

INTERIOR POINT (subdivision rule)

5. $\displaystyle\int_a^b f(x)\,dx = \int_a^c f(x)\,dx + \int_c^b f(x)\,dx$

MEAN-VALUE THEOREM

6. $\displaystyle\int_a^b f(x)\,dx = (b-a)f(c)$ where c is between a and b

IMPROPER INTEGRALS

7. $\displaystyle\int_a^\infty f(x)\,dx = \lim_{b\to\infty}\int_a^b f(x)\,dx$

8. $\displaystyle\int_{-\infty}^\infty f(x)\,dx = \lim_{a\to-\infty}\int_a^c f(x)\,dx + \lim_{b\to\infty}\int_c^b f(x)\,dx$

9. $\displaystyle\int_a^b f(x)\,dx = \lim_{\epsilon\to 0}\int_a^{b-\epsilon} f(x)\,dx$ if b is a singular point

10. $\displaystyle\int_a^b f(x)\,dx = \lim_{\epsilon\to 0}\int_{a+\epsilon}^b f(x)\,dx$ if a is a singular point

11. $\displaystyle\int_a^b f(x)g(x)\,dx = f(c)\int_a^b g(x)\,dx$ where c is between a and b

This is a generalization of formula 6 and is valid if $f(x)$ and $g(x)$ are continuous in $a \le x \le b$ and $g(x) \ge 0$.

APPROXIMATION FORMULAS FOR DEFINITE INTEGRALS

In the following formulas, the interval from $x = a$ to $x = b$ is subdivided into n equal parts by the points $a = x_0, x_1, x_2, \cdots, x_{n-1}, x_n = b$, and we let $y_0 = f(x_0)$, $y_1 = f(x_1)$, $y_2 = f(x_2)$, $\cdots$, $y_n = f(x_n)$, $h = (b-a)/n$.

Rectangular formula

12. $\displaystyle\int_a^b f(x)\,dx \approx h(y_0 + y_1 + y_2 + \cdots + y_{n-1})$

Trapezoidal formula

13. $\displaystyle\int_a^b f(x)\,dx \approx \frac{h}{2}(y_0 + 2y_1 + 2y_2 + \cdots + 2y_{n-1} + y_n)$

Simpson's formula (or parabolic formula) for n even

14. $\displaystyle\int_a^b f(x)\,dx \approx \frac{h}{3}(y_0 + 4y_1 + 2y_2 + 4y_3 + \cdots$

$$+ 2y_{n-2} + 4y_{n-1} + y_n)$$

DEFINITE INTEGRALS INVOLVING RATIONAL OR IRRATIONAL EXPRESSIONS

15. $\displaystyle\int_0^\infty \frac{dx}{x^2 + a^2} = \frac{\pi}{2a}$

16. $\displaystyle\int_0^\infty \frac{x^{p-1}\,dx}{1+x} = \frac{\pi}{\sin p\pi}, \quad 0 < p < 1$

17. $\displaystyle\int_0^\infty \frac{x^m\,dx}{x^n + a^n} = \frac{\pi a^{m+1-n}}{n\sin[(m+1)\pi/n]}, \quad 0 < m+1 < n$

18. $\displaystyle\int_0^\infty \frac{x^m\,dx}{1 + 2x\cos\beta + x^2} = \frac{\pi}{\sin m\pi}\frac{\sin m\beta}{\sin\beta}$

19. $\displaystyle\int_0^a \frac{dx}{\sqrt{a^2 - x^2}} = \frac{\pi}{2}$

20. $\displaystyle\int_0^a \sqrt{a^2 - x^2}\, dx = \frac{\pi a^2}{4}$

21. $\displaystyle\int_0^a x^m (a^n - x^n)^p\, dx = \frac{a^{m+1+np}\Gamma[(m+1)/n]\Gamma(p+1)}{n\Gamma[(m+1)/n + p + 1]}$

22. $\displaystyle\int_0^\infty \frac{x^m\, dx}{(x^n + a^n)^r}$

$$= \frac{(-1)^{r-1}\pi a^{m+1-nr}\Gamma[(m+1)/n]}{n\sin[(m+1)\pi/n](r-1)!\,\Gamma[(m+1)/n - r + 1]},$$
$$0 < m + 1 < nr$$

DEFINITE INTEGRALS INVOLVING TRIGONOMETRIC FUNCTIONS

All variables are considered positive unless otherwise indicated.

23. $\displaystyle\int_0^\pi \sin mx \sin nx\, dx = \begin{cases} 0, & m, n \text{ integers and } m \neq n \\ \pi/2, & m, n \text{ integers and } m = n \end{cases}$

24. $\displaystyle\int_0^\pi \cos mx \cos nx\, dx = \begin{cases} 0, & m, n \text{ integers and } m \neq n \\ \pi/2, & m, n \text{ integers and } m = n \end{cases}$

25. $\displaystyle\int_0^\pi \sin mx \cos nx\, dx$

$$= \begin{cases} 0, & m, n \text{ integers and } m + n \text{ even} \\ 2m/(m^2 - n^2), & m, n \text{ integers and } m + n \text{ odd} \end{cases}$$

26. $\displaystyle\int_0^{\pi/2} \sin^2 x\, dx = \int_0^{\pi/2} \cos^2 x\, dx = \frac{\pi}{4}$

27. $\displaystyle\int_0^{\pi/2} \sin^{2m} x\, dx = \int_0^{\pi/2} \cos^{2m} x\, dx = \frac{1 \cdot 3 \cdot 5 \cdots 2m - 1}{2 \cdot 4 \cdot 6 \cdots 2m} \frac{\pi}{2},$
$$m = 1, 2, \cdots$$

28. $\displaystyle\int_0^{\pi/2} \sin^{2m+1} x\, dx = \int_0^{\pi/2} \cos^{2m+1} x\, dx = \frac{2 \cdot 4 \cdot 6 \cdots 2m}{1 \cdot 3 \cdot 5 \cdots 2m + 1},$
$$m = 1, 2, \cdots$$

29. $\displaystyle\int_0^{\pi/2} \sin^{2p-1} x \cos^{2q-1} x\, dx = \frac{\Gamma(p)\Gamma(q)}{2\Gamma(p+q)}$

30. $\displaystyle\int_0^\infty \frac{\sin px}{x}\, dx = \begin{cases} \pi/2, & p > 0 \\ 0, & p = 0 \\ -\pi/2, & p < 0 \end{cases}$

31. $\displaystyle\int_0^\infty \frac{\sin px \cos qx}{x}\, dx = \begin{cases} 0, & q > p > 0 \\ \pi/2, & 0 < q < p \\ \pi/4, & p = q > 0 \end{cases}$

32. $\displaystyle\int_0^\infty \frac{\sin px \sin qx}{x^2}\, dx = \begin{cases} \pi p/2, & 0 < p \leq q \\ \pi q/2, & p \geq q > 0 \end{cases}$

33. $\displaystyle\int_0^\infty \frac{\sin^2 px}{x^2}\,dx = \frac{\pi p}{2}$

34. $\displaystyle\int_0^\infty \frac{x \sin mx}{x^2 + a^2}\,dx = \frac{\pi}{2}e^{-ma}$

35. $\displaystyle\int_0^\infty \frac{1 - \cos px}{x^2}\,dx = \frac{\pi p}{2}$

36. $\displaystyle\int_0^\infty \frac{\sin mx}{x(x^2 + a^2)}\,dx = \frac{\pi}{2a^2}(1 - e^{-ma})$

37. $\displaystyle\int_0^\infty \frac{\cos px - \cos qx}{x}\,dx = \ln\left|\frac{q}{p}\right|$

38. $\displaystyle\int_0^{2\pi} \frac{dx}{a + b\sin x} = \frac{2\pi}{\sqrt{a^2 - b^2}}$

39. $\displaystyle\int_0^\infty \frac{\cos px - \cos qx}{x^2}\,dx = \frac{\pi(q - p)}{2}$

40. $\displaystyle\int_0^{2\pi} \frac{dx}{a + b\cos x} = \frac{2\pi}{\sqrt{a^2 - b^2}}$

41. $\displaystyle\int_0^\infty \frac{\cos mx}{x^2 + a^2}\,dx = \frac{\pi}{2a}e^{-ma}$

42. $\displaystyle\int_0^{\pi/2} \frac{dx}{a + b\cos x} = \frac{\cos^{-1}(b/a)}{\sqrt{a^2 - b^2}}$

43. $\displaystyle\int_0^{2\pi} \frac{dx}{(a + b\sin x)^2} = \int_0^{2\pi} \frac{dx}{(a + b\cos x)^2} = \frac{2\pi a}{(a^2 - b^2)^{3/2}}$

44. $\displaystyle\int_0^{2\pi} \frac{dx}{1 - 2a\cos x + a^2} = \frac{2\pi}{1 - a^2}, 0 < a < 1$

45. $\displaystyle\int_0^\pi \frac{x \sin x\,dx}{1 - 2a\cos x + a^2} = \begin{cases} (\pi/a)\ln|1 + a|, & |a| < 1 \\ \pi\ln|1 + 1/a|, & |a| > 1 \end{cases}$

46. $\displaystyle\int_0^\pi \frac{\cos mx\,dx}{1 - 2a\cos x + a^2} = \frac{\pi a^m}{1 - a^2}, a^2 < 1, m = 0, 1, 2, \cdots$

47. $\displaystyle\int_0^\infty \sin ax^2\,dx = \int_0^\infty \cos ax^2\,dx = \frac{1}{2}\sqrt{\frac{\pi}{2a}}$

48. $\displaystyle\int_0^\infty \sin ax^n\,dx = \frac{1}{na^{1/n}}\Gamma(1/n)\sin\frac{\pi}{2n}, n > 1$

49. $\displaystyle\int_0^\infty \cos ax^n\,dx = \frac{1}{na^{1/n}}\Gamma(1/n)\cos\frac{\pi}{2n}, n > 1$

50. $\displaystyle\int_0^\infty \frac{\sin x}{\sqrt{x}}\,dx = \int_0^\infty \frac{\cos x}{\sqrt{x}}\,dx = \sqrt{\frac{\pi}{2}}$

51. $\displaystyle\int_0^\infty \frac{\sin x}{x^p}\,dx = \frac{\pi}{2\Gamma(p)\sin(p\pi/2)}, 0 < p < 1$

52. $\displaystyle\int_0^\infty \frac{\cos x}{x^p}\,dx = \frac{\pi}{2\Gamma(p)\cos(p\pi/2)}, 0 < p < 1$

53. $\displaystyle\int_0^\infty \sin ax^2 \cos 2bx\,dx = \frac{1}{2}\sqrt{\frac{\pi}{2a}}\left(\cos\frac{b^2}{a} - \sin\frac{b^2}{a}\right)$

54. $\displaystyle\int_0^\infty \cos ax^2 \cos 2bx\,dx = \frac{1}{2}\sqrt{\frac{\pi}{2a}}\left(\cos\frac{b^2}{a} + \sin\frac{b^2}{a}\right)$

55. $\displaystyle\int_0^\infty \frac{\sin^3 x}{x^3}\,dx = \frac{3\pi}{8}$

56. $\displaystyle\int_0^\infty \frac{\sin^4 x}{x^4}\,dx = \frac{\pi}{3}$

57. $\displaystyle\int_0^\infty \frac{\tan x}{x}\,dx = \frac{\pi}{2}$

58. $\displaystyle\int_0^{\pi/2} \frac{dx}{1 + \tan^m x} = \frac{\pi}{4}$

59. $\displaystyle\int_0^{\pi/2} \frac{x}{\sin x}\,dx = 2\left\{\frac{1}{1^2} - \frac{1}{3^2} + \frac{1}{5^2} - \frac{1}{7^2} + \cdots\right\}$

60. $\displaystyle\int_0^1 \frac{\tan^{-1} x}{x}\,dx = \frac{1}{1^2} - \frac{1}{3^2} + \frac{1}{5^2} - \frac{1}{7^2} + \cdots$

61. $\displaystyle\int_0^1 \frac{\sin^{-1} x}{x}\,dx = \frac{\pi}{2}\ln 2$

62. $\displaystyle\int_0^1 \frac{1 - \cos x}{x}\,dx - \int_1^\infty \frac{\cos x}{x}\,dx = \gamma$

63. $\displaystyle\int_0^\infty \left(\frac{1}{1 + x^2} - \cos x\right)\frac{dx}{x} = \gamma$

64. $\displaystyle\int_0^\infty \frac{\tan^{-1} px - \tan^{-1} qx}{x}\,dx = \frac{\pi}{2}\ln\left|\frac{p}{q}\right|$

DEFINITE INTEGRALS INVOLVING EXPONENTIAL FUNCTIONS

65. $\displaystyle\int_0^\infty e^{-ax}\cos bx\,dx = \frac{a}{a^2 + b^2}$

66. $\displaystyle\int_0^\infty e^{-ax}\sin bx\,dx = \frac{b}{a^2 + b^2}$

67. $\displaystyle\int_0^\infty \frac{e^{-ax}\sin bx}{x}\,dx = \tan^{-1}\frac{b}{a}$

68. $\displaystyle\int_0^\infty \frac{e^{-ax} - e^{-bx}}{x}\,dx = \ln\left|\frac{b}{a}\right|$

69. $\displaystyle\int_0^\infty e^{-ax^2}\,dx = \frac{1}{2}\sqrt{\frac{\pi}{a}}$

70. $\displaystyle\int_0^\infty e^{-ax^2}\cos bx\,dx = \frac{1}{2}\sqrt{\frac{\pi}{a}}\,e^{-b^2/4a}$

71. $\displaystyle\int_0^\infty e^{-(ax^2+bx+c)}\,dx = \frac{1}{2}\sqrt{\frac{\pi}{a}}\,e^{(b^2-4ac)/4a}\operatorname{erfc}\left(\frac{b}{2\sqrt{a}}\right)$

where $\operatorname{erfc}(p) = \dfrac{2}{\sqrt{\pi}}\displaystyle\int_p^\infty e^{-x^2}\,dx$

72. $\displaystyle\int_0^\infty e^{-(ax^2+bx+c)}\,dx = \sqrt{\frac{\pi}{a}}\,e^{(b^2-4ac)/4a}$

73. $\displaystyle\int_0^\infty x^n e^{-ax}\,dx = \frac{\Gamma(n+1)}{a^{n+1}}$

74. $\displaystyle\int_0^\infty x^m e^{-ax^2}\,dx = \frac{\Gamma[(m+1)/2]}{2a^{(m+1)/2}}$

75. $\displaystyle\int_0^\infty e^{-(ax^2+b/x^2)}\,dx = \frac{1}{2}\sqrt{\frac{\pi}{a}}\,e^{-2\sqrt{ab}}$

76. $\displaystyle\int_0^\infty \frac{x\,dx}{e^x - 1} = \frac{1}{1^2}\cdot\frac{1}{2^2}\cdot\frac{1}{3^2}\cdot\frac{1}{4^2} + \cdots = \frac{\pi^2}{6}$

77. $\displaystyle\int_0^\infty \frac{x^{n-1}}{e^x - 1}\,dx = \Gamma(n)\left(\frac{1}{1^n} + \frac{1}{2^n} + \frac{1}{3^n} + \cdots\right)$

78. $\displaystyle\int_0^\infty \frac{x\,dx}{e^x + 1} = \frac{1}{1^2} - \frac{1}{2^2} + \frac{1}{3^2} - \frac{1}{4^2} + \cdots = \frac{\pi^2}{12}$

79. $\displaystyle\int_0^\infty \frac{x^{n-1}}{e^x + 1}\,dx = \Gamma(n)\left(\frac{1}{1^n} - \frac{1}{2^n} + \frac{1}{3^n} - \cdots\right)$

80. $\displaystyle\int_0^\infty \frac{\sin mx}{e^{2\pi x} - 1}\,dx = \frac{1}{4}\coth\frac{m}{2} - \frac{1}{2m}$

81. $\displaystyle\int_0^\infty \left(\frac{1}{1+x} - e^{-x}\right)\frac{dx}{x} = \gamma$

82. $\displaystyle\int_0^\infty \frac{e^{-x^2} - e^{-x}}{x}\,dx = \frac{1}{2}\gamma$

83. $\displaystyle\int_0^\infty \left(\frac{1}{e^x - 1} - \frac{e^{-x}}{x}\right)\,dx = \gamma$

84. $\displaystyle\int_0^\infty \frac{e^{-ax} - e^{-bx}}{x \sec px} \, dx = \frac{1}{2} \ln \left(\frac{b^2 + p^2}{a^2 + p^2} \right)$

85. $\displaystyle\int_0^\infty \frac{e^{-ax} - e^{-bx}}{x \csc px} \, dx = \tan^{-1} \frac{b}{p} - \tan^{-1} \frac{a}{p}$

86. $\displaystyle\int_0^\infty \frac{e^{-ax}(1 - \cos x)}{x^2} \, dx = \cot^{-1} a - \frac{a}{2} \ln(a^2 + 1)$

DEFINITE INTEGRALS INVOLVING LOGARITHMIC FUNCTIONS

87. $\displaystyle\int_0^1 x^m (\ln |x|)^n \, dx = \frac{(-1)^n n!}{(m+1)^{n+1}} \quad m > -1, n = 0, 1, 2, \cdots$

If $n \neq 0, 1, 2, \ldots$ replace $n!$ by $\Gamma(n+1)$

88. $\displaystyle\int_0^1 \frac{\ln |x|}{1 + x} \, dx = -\frac{\pi^2}{12}$

89. $\displaystyle\int_0^1 \frac{\ln |x|}{1 - x} \, dx = -\frac{\pi^2}{6}$

90. $\displaystyle\int_0^1 \frac{\ln |1 + x|}{x} \, dx = \frac{\pi^2}{12}$

91. $\displaystyle\int_0^1 \frac{\ln |1 - x|}{x} \, dx = -\frac{\pi^2}{6}$

92. $\displaystyle\int_0^1 \ln |x| \ln |1 + x| \, dx = 2 - 2 \ln 2 - \frac{\pi^2}{12}$

93. $\displaystyle\int_0^1 \ln |x| \ln |1 - x| \, dx = 2 - \frac{\pi^2}{6}$

94. $\displaystyle\int_0^\infty \frac{x^{p-1} \ln |x|}{1 + x} \, dx = -\pi^2 \csc p\pi \cot p\pi \quad 0 < p < 1$

95. $\displaystyle\int_0^1 \frac{x^m - x^n}{\ln |x|} \, dx = \ln \left| \frac{m+1}{n+1} \right|$

96. $\displaystyle\int_0^\infty e^{-x} \ln |x| \, dx = -\gamma$

97. $\displaystyle\int_0^\infty e^{-x^2} \ln |x| \, dx = -\frac{\sqrt{\pi}}{4}(\gamma + 2 \ln 2)$

98. $\displaystyle\int_0^\infty \ln \left| \frac{e^x + 1}{e^x - 1} \right| \, dx = \frac{\pi^2}{4}$

99. $\displaystyle\int_0^{\pi/2} \ln|\sin x|\,dx = \int_0^{\pi/2} \ln|\cos x|\,dx = -\frac{\pi}{2}\ln 2$

100. $\displaystyle\int_0^{\pi/2} (\ln|\sin x|)^2\,dx = \int_0^{\pi/2} (\ln|\cos x|)^2\,dx = \frac{\pi}{2}(\ln 2)^2 + \frac{\pi^3}{24}$

101. $\displaystyle\int_0^{\pi} x\ln|\sin x|\,dx = -\frac{\pi^2}{2}\ln 2$

102. $\displaystyle\int_0^{\pi/2} \sin x\ln|\sin x|\,dx = \ln 2 - 1$

103. $\displaystyle\int_0^{2\pi} \ln|a + b\sin x|\,dx = \int_0^{2\pi} \ln|a + b\cos x|\,dx$

$$= 2\pi\ln|a + \sqrt{a^2 - b^2}|$$

104. $\displaystyle\int_0^{\pi} \ln|a + b\cos x|\,dx = \pi\ln\left|\frac{a + \sqrt{a^2 - b^2}}{2}\right|$

105. $\displaystyle\int_0^{\pi} \ln|a^2 - 2ab\cos x + b^2|\,dx = \begin{cases} 2\pi\ln|a|, & a \geq b > 0 \\ 2\pi\ln|b|, & b \geq a > 0 \end{cases}$

106. $\displaystyle\int_0^{\pi/4} \ln|1 + \tan x|\,dx = \frac{\pi}{8}\ln 2$

107. $\displaystyle\int_0^{\pi/2} \sec x\ln\left|\frac{1 + b\cos x}{1 + a\cos x}\right|\,dx = \frac{1}{2}\{(\cos^{-1} b)^2\}$

108. $\displaystyle\int_0^{a} \ln\left|2\sin\frac{x}{2}\right|\,dx = -\left(\frac{\sin a}{1^2} + \frac{\sin 2a}{2^2} + \frac{\sin 3a}{3^2} + \cdots\right)$

DEFINITE INTEGRALS INVOLVING HYPERBOLIC FUNCTIONS

109. $\displaystyle\int_0^{\infty} \frac{\sin ax}{\sinh bx}\,dx = \frac{\pi}{2b}\tanh\frac{a\pi}{2b}$

110. $\displaystyle\int_0^{\infty} \frac{\cos ax}{\cosh bx}\,dx = \frac{\pi}{2b}\operatorname{sech}\frac{a\pi}{2b}$

111. $\displaystyle\int_0^{\infty} \frac{x\,dx}{\sinh ax} = \frac{\pi^2}{4a^2}$

112. $\displaystyle\int_0^{\infty} \frac{x^n\,dx}{\sinh bx} = \frac{2^{n+1} - 1}{2^n a^{n+1}}\Gamma(n+1)\left\{\frac{1}{1^{n+1}} + \frac{1}{2^{n+1}} + \frac{1}{3^{n+1}} + \cdots\right\}$

113. $\displaystyle\int_0^\infty \frac{\sinh ax}{e^{bx}+1}\,dx = \frac{\pi}{2b}\csc\frac{a\pi}{b} - \frac{1}{2a}$

114. $\displaystyle\int_0^\infty \frac{\sinh ax}{e^{bx}-1}\,dx = \frac{1}{2a} - \frac{\pi}{2b}\cot\frac{a\pi}{b}$

MISCELLANEOUS DEFINITE INTEGRALS

115. $\displaystyle\int_0^\infty \frac{f(ax)-f(bx)}{x}\,dx = \{f(0)-f(\infty)\}\ln\left|\frac{b}{a}\right|$

This is called *Frullani's integral*. It holds if $f'(x)$ is continuous and $\displaystyle\int_0^\infty \frac{f(x)-f(\infty)}{x}\,dx$ converges.

116. $\displaystyle\int_0^1 \frac{dx}{x^x} = \frac{1}{1^1} + \frac{1}{2^2} + \frac{1}{3^3} + \cdots$

117. $\displaystyle\int_{-a}^a (a+x)^{m-1}(a-x)^{n-1}\,dx = (2a)^{m+n-1}\frac{\Gamma(m)\Gamma(n)}{\Gamma(m+n)}$

CHAPTER 13
Series

13.1 Series of Constants

1. $1 + 2 + 3 + \cdots + n = \frac{1}{2}n(n+1)$

2. $1 + 3 + 5 + \cdots + (2n-1) = n^2$

3. $1^2 + 2^2 + 3^2 + \cdots + n^2 = \dfrac{n(n+1)(2n+1)}{6}$

4. $1^3 + 2^3 + 3^3 + \cdots + n^3 = \dfrac{n^2(n+1)^2}{4}$
   $$= (1 + 2 + 3 + \cdots + n)^2$$

5. $1^4 + 2^4 + 3^4 + \cdots + n^4 = \dfrac{n(n+1)(2n+1)(3n^2+3n-1)}{30}$

6. $1^5 + 2^5 + 3^5 + \cdots + n^5 = \dfrac{n^6}{6} + \dfrac{n^5}{2} + \dfrac{5n^4}{12} - \dfrac{n^2}{12}$

7. $1^2 + 3^2 + 5^2 + \cdots + (2n-1)^2 = \frac{1}{3}n(4n^2-1)$

8. $1^3 + 3^3 + 5^3 + \cdots + (2n-1)^3 = n^2(2n^2-1)$

9. $2^2 + 4^2 + 6^2 + 8^2 + \cdots + (2n)^2 = \dfrac{2n(n+1)(2n+1)}{3}$

10. $1 \cdot 2 + 2 \cdot 3 + 3 \cdot 4 + \cdots + n(n+1) = \dfrac{n(n+1)(n+2)}{3}$

11. $1 \cdot 2 \cdot 3 + 2 \cdot 3 \cdot 4 + 3 \cdot 4 \cdot 5 + \cdots + n(n+1)(n+2)$
    $$= \frac{1}{4}n(n+1)(n+2)(n+3)$$

12. $1 - \dfrac{1}{2} + \dfrac{1}{3} - \dfrac{1}{4} + \dfrac{1}{5} - \cdots = \ln 2$

13. $1 - \dfrac{1}{3} + \dfrac{1}{5} - \dfrac{1}{7} + \dfrac{1}{9} - \cdots = \dfrac{\pi}{4}$

14. $\dfrac{1}{1 \cdot 3} + \dfrac{1}{3 \cdot 5} + \dfrac{1}{5 \cdot 7} + \dfrac{1}{7 \cdot 9} + \cdots = \dfrac{1}{2}$

15. $\dfrac{1}{1 \cdot 3} + \dfrac{1}{2 \cdot 4} + \dfrac{1}{3 \cdot 5} + \dfrac{1}{4 \cdot 6} + \cdots = \dfrac{3}{4}$

13.2   Taylor Series

TAYLOR SERIES FOR FUNCTIONS OF ONE VARIABLE

16. $f(x) = f(c) + f'(c)(x - c) + \dfrac{f''(c)(x - c)^2}{2!} + \cdots$

$\qquad + \dfrac{f^{(n-1)}(c)(x - c)^{n-1}}{(n-1)!} + R_n$

where R_n, the remainder after n terms, is given by either of the following forms:

Lagrange's form $R_n = \dfrac{f^{(n)}(z)(x - a)^n}{n!}$

Cauchy's form $R_n = \dfrac{f^{(n)}(z)(x - z)^{n-1}(x - a)}{(n-1)!}$

The value z, which may be different in the two forms, lies between c and x. The result holds if $f(x)$ has continuous derivatives of at least order n.

If $\lim\limits_{n \to \infty} R_n = 0$, the infinite series obtained is called the *Taylor Series* for $f(x)$ about $x = a$. If $c = 0$, the series is often called a *Maclaurin series*. Both series, often called power series, generally converge for all values of x in some interval called the *interval of convergence* and diverge for all x outside this interval.

BINOMIAL SERIES

17. $(a + x)^n = a^n + na^{n-1}x + \dfrac{n(n-1)}{2!}a^{n-2}x^2$

$\qquad + \dfrac{n(n-1)(n-2)}{3!}a^{n-3}x^3 + \cdots$

$\qquad = a^n + \dbinom{n}{1}a^{n-1}x + \dbinom{n}{2}a^{n-2}x^2 + \dbinom{n}{3}a^{n-3}x^3 + \cdots$

18. $(a + x)^2 = a^2 + 2ax + x^2$

19. $(a + x)^3 = a^3 + 3a^2x + 3ax^2 + x^3$

20. $(a + x)^4 = a^4 + 4a^3x + 6a^2x^2 + 4ax^3 + x^4$

21. $(1 + x)^{-1} = 1 - x + x^2 - x^3 + x^4 - \cdots \qquad -1 < x < 1$

22. $(1 + x)^{-2} = 1 - 2x + 3x^2 - 4x^3 + 5x^4 - \cdots \qquad -1 < x < 1$

23. $(1 + x)^{-3} = 1 - 3x + 6x^2 - 10x^3 + 15x^4 - \cdots \qquad -1 < x < 1$

24. $(1 + x)^{-1/2} = 1 - \dfrac{1}{2}x + \dfrac{1 \cdot 3}{2 \cdot 4}x^2 - \dfrac{1 \cdot 3 \cdot 5}{2 \cdot 4 \cdot 6}x^3 + \cdots$

$\qquad\qquad\qquad\qquad\qquad\qquad -1 < x \le 1$

25. $(1+x)^{1/2} = 1 + \dfrac{1}{2}x - \dfrac{1}{2 \cdot 4}x^2 + \dfrac{1 \cdot 3}{2 \cdot 4 \cdot 6}x^3 - \cdots$

$$-1 < x \leq 1$$

26. $(1+x)^{-1/3} = 1 - \dfrac{1}{3}x - \dfrac{1 \cdot 4}{3 \cdot 6}x^2 - \dfrac{1 \cdot 4 \cdot 7}{3 \cdot 6 \cdot 9}x^3 + \cdots$

$$-1 < x \leq 1$$

27. $(1+x)^{1/3} = 1 + \dfrac{1}{3}x - \dfrac{2}{3 \cdot 6}x^2 + \dfrac{2 \cdot 5}{3 \cdot 6 \cdot 9}x^3 - \cdots$

$$-1 < x \leq 1$$

SERIES FOR EXPONENTIAL AND LOGARITHMIC FUNCTIONS

28. $e^x = 1 + x + \dfrac{x^2}{2!} + \dfrac{x^3}{3!} + \cdots$ $\qquad -\infty < x < \infty$

29. $a^x = e^{x \ln |a|} = 1 + x \ln |a| + \dfrac{(x \ln |a|)^2}{2!} + \dfrac{(x \ln |a|)^3}{3!} + \cdots$

$$-\infty < x < \infty$$

30. $\ln |1 + x| = x - \dfrac{x^2}{2} + \dfrac{x^3}{3} - \dfrac{x^4}{4} + \cdots$ $\qquad -1 < x \leq 1$

31. $\dfrac{1}{2} \ln \left| \dfrac{1+x}{1-x} \right| = x + \dfrac{x^3}{3} + \dfrac{x^5}{5} + \dfrac{x^7}{7} + \cdots$ $\qquad -1 < x < 1$

32. $\ln |x| = 2 \left\{ \left(\dfrac{x-1}{x+1} \right) + \dfrac{1}{3} \left(\dfrac{x-1}{x+1} \right)^3 + \dfrac{1}{5} \left(\dfrac{x-1}{x+1} \right)^5 + \cdots \right\}$

$$x > 0$$

33. $\ln |x| = \left(\dfrac{x-1}{x} \right) + \dfrac{1}{2} \left(\dfrac{x-1}{x} \right)^2 + \dfrac{1}{3} \left(\dfrac{x-1}{x} \right)^3 + \cdots$

$$x \geq \dfrac{1}{2}$$

SERIES FOR TRIGONOMETRIC FUNCTIONS

34. $\sin x = x - \dfrac{x^3}{3!} + \dfrac{x^5}{5!} - \dfrac{x^7}{7!} + \cdots$ $\qquad -\infty < x < \infty$

35. $\cos x = 1 - \dfrac{x^2}{2!} + \dfrac{x^4}{4!} - \dfrac{x^6}{6!} + \cdots$ $\qquad -\infty < x < \infty$

36. $\tan x = x + \dfrac{x^3}{3} + \dfrac{2x^5}{15} + \dfrac{17x^7}{315} + \cdots$

$$+ \dfrac{2^{2n}(2^{2n} - 1)B_n x^{2n-1}}{(2n)!} + \cdots \qquad |x| < \dfrac{\pi}{2}$$

37. $\cot x = \dfrac{1}{x} - \dfrac{x}{3} - \dfrac{x^3}{45} - \cdots - \dfrac{2^{2n}B_n x^{2n-1}}{(2n)!} - \cdots \quad 0 < |x| < \pi$

38. $\sec x = 1 + \dfrac{x^2}{2} + \dfrac{5x^4}{24} + \dfrac{61x^6}{720} + \cdots + \dfrac{E_n x^{2n}}{(2n)!} + \cdots$ $|x| < \dfrac{\pi}{2}$

39. $\csc x = \dfrac{1}{x} + \dfrac{x}{6} + \dfrac{7x^3}{360} + \dfrac{31x^5}{15,\,120} + \cdots$

$\qquad\qquad + \dfrac{2(2^{2n-1} - 1)B_n x^{2n-1}}{(2n)!} + \cdots$ $0 < |x| < \pi$

40. $\sin^{-1} x = x + \dfrac{1}{2}\dfrac{x^3}{3} + \dfrac{1\cdot 3}{2\cdot 4}\dfrac{x^5}{5} + \dfrac{1\cdot 3\cdot 5}{2\cdot 4\cdot 6}\dfrac{x^7}{7} + \cdots$ $|x| < 1$

41. $\cos^{-1} x = \dfrac{\pi}{2} - \sin^{-1} x = \dfrac{\pi}{2} - \left(x + \dfrac{1}{2}\dfrac{x^3}{3} + \dfrac{1\cdot 3}{2\cdot 4}\dfrac{x^5}{5} + \cdots\right)$

$\qquad\qquad\qquad\qquad\qquad\qquad\qquad\qquad\qquad\qquad |x| < 1$

42. $\tan^{-1} x = \begin{cases} x - \dfrac{x^3}{3} + \dfrac{x^5}{5} - \dfrac{x^7}{7} + \cdots, & \text{if } x^2 < 1 \text{ or} \\[2mm] \dfrac{\pi}{2} - \dfrac{1}{x} + \dfrac{1}{3x^3} - \dfrac{1}{5x^5} + \cdots, & \text{if } x \geq 1 \\[2mm] -\dfrac{\pi}{2} - \dfrac{1}{x} + \dfrac{1}{3x^3} - \dfrac{1}{5x^5} + \cdots, & \text{if } x > 1 \end{cases}$

43. $\cot^{-1} x = \dfrac{\pi}{2} - \tan^{-1} x$

$\qquad = \begin{cases} \dfrac{\pi}{2} - \left(x - \dfrac{x^3}{3} + \dfrac{x^5}{5} - \cdots\right), \text{ if } x^2 < 1 \text{ or} \\[3mm] p\pi + \dfrac{1}{x} - \dfrac{1}{3x^3} + \dfrac{1}{5x^5} - \cdots, [p = 0 \text{ if } x > 1, \\[3mm] \qquad\qquad\qquad\qquad\qquad\quad p = 1 \text{ if } x < -1] \end{cases}$

44. $\sec^{-1} x = \cos^{-1}\dfrac{1}{x} = \dfrac{\pi}{2} - \left(\dfrac{1}{x} + \dfrac{1}{2\cdot 3x^3} + \dfrac{1\cdot 3}{2\cdot 4\cdot 5x^5} + \cdots\right)$

$\qquad\qquad\qquad\qquad\qquad\qquad\qquad\qquad\qquad\qquad |x| > 1$

45. $\csc^{-1} x = \sin^{-1}\dfrac{1}{x} = \dfrac{1}{x} + \dfrac{1}{2\cdot 3x^3} + \dfrac{1\cdot 3}{2\cdot 4\cdot 5x^5} + \cdots$ $|x| > 1$

SERIES FOR HYPERBOLIC FUNCTIONS

46. $\sinh x = x + \dfrac{x^3}{3!} + \dfrac{x^5}{5!} + \dfrac{x^7}{7!} + \cdots$ $-\infty < x < \infty$

47. $\cosh x = 1 + \dfrac{x^2}{2!} + \dfrac{x^4}{4!} + \dfrac{x^6}{6!} + \cdots$ $-\infty < x < \infty$

48. $\tanh x = x - \dfrac{x^3}{3} + \dfrac{2x^5}{15} - \dfrac{17x^7}{315} + \cdots$

$\qquad\qquad \times \dfrac{(-1)^{n-1}2^{2n}(2^{2n} - 1)B_n x^{2n-1}}{(2n)!} + \cdots$ $|x| < \dfrac{\pi}{2}$

49. $\coth x = \dfrac{1}{x} + \dfrac{x}{3} - \dfrac{x^3}{45} + \dfrac{2x^5}{945} + \cdots$

$$+ \dfrac{(-1)^{n-1}2^{2n}B_n x^{2n-1}}{(2n)!} + \cdots \qquad 0 < |x| < \pi$$

50. $\operatorname{sech} x = 1 - \dfrac{x^2}{2} + \dfrac{5x^4}{24} - \dfrac{61x^6}{720} + \cdots$

$$+ \dfrac{(-1)^n E_n x^{2n}}{(2n)!} + \cdots \qquad |x| < \dfrac{\pi}{2}$$

51. $\operatorname{csch} x = \dfrac{1}{x} - \dfrac{x}{6} + \dfrac{7x^3}{360} - \dfrac{31x^5}{15,120} + \cdots$

$$+ \dfrac{(-1)^n 2(2^{2n-1}-1)B_n x^{2n-1}}{(2n)!} + \cdots \qquad 0 < |x| < \pi$$

52. $\sinh^{-1} x$

$$= \begin{cases} x - \dfrac{x^3}{2\cdot 3} + \dfrac{1\cdot 3x^5}{2\cdot 4\cdot 5} - \dfrac{1\cdot 3\cdot 5x^7}{2\cdot 4\cdot 6\cdot 7} + \cdots, |x| < 1 \text{ or} \\[2mm] \pm\left(\ln|2x| + \dfrac{1}{2\cdot 2x^2} - \dfrac{1\cdot 3}{2\cdot 4\cdot 4x^4} + \dfrac{1\cdot 3\cdot 5}{2\cdot 4\cdot 6\cdot 6x^6} - \cdots\right) \end{cases}$$

$$\begin{bmatrix} \text{``}+\text{''} \text{ if } x \geq 1 \\ \text{``}-\text{''} \text{ if } x \leq -1 \end{bmatrix}$$

53. $\cosh^{-1} x$

$$= \pm\left\{\ln|2x| - \left(\dfrac{1}{2\cdot 2x^2} + \dfrac{1\cdot 3}{2\cdot 4\cdot 4x^4} + \dfrac{1\cdot 3\cdot 5}{2\cdot 4\cdot 6\cdot 6x^6} + \cdots\right)\right\}$$

$$\begin{bmatrix} \text{``}+\text{''} \text{ if } \cosh^{-1} x > 0, x \geq 1 \\ \text{``}-\text{''} \text{ if } \cosh^{-1} x < 0, x \geq 1 \end{bmatrix}$$

54. $\tanh^{-1} x = x + \dfrac{x^3}{3} + \dfrac{x^5}{5} + \dfrac{x^7}{7} + \cdots \qquad |x| < 1$

55. $\coth^{-1} x = \dfrac{1}{x} + \dfrac{1}{3x^3} + \dfrac{1}{5x^5} + \dfrac{1}{7x^7} + \cdots \qquad |x| > 1$

MISCELLANEOUS SERIES

56. $e^{\sin x} = 1 + x + \dfrac{x^2}{2} - \dfrac{x^4}{8} - \dfrac{x^5}{15} + \cdots \qquad -\infty < x < \infty$

57. $e^{\cos x} = e\left(1 - \dfrac{x^2}{2} + \dfrac{x^4}{6} - \dfrac{31x^6}{720} + \cdots\right) \qquad -\infty < x < \infty$

58. $e^{\tan x} = 1 + x + \dfrac{x^2}{2} + \dfrac{x^3}{2} + \dfrac{3x^4}{8} + \cdots \qquad |x| < \dfrac{\pi}{2}$

59. $e^x \sin x = x + x^2 + \dfrac{2x^3}{3} - \dfrac{x^5}{30} - \dfrac{x^6}{90} + \cdots$

$$+ \dfrac{2^{n/2}\sin(n\pi/4)x^n}{n!} + \cdots \qquad -\infty < x < \infty$$

60. $e^x \cos x = 1 + x - \dfrac{x^3}{3} - \dfrac{x^4}{6} + \cdots + \dfrac{2^{n/2}\cos(n\pi/4)x^n}{n!} + \cdots$

$$-\infty < x < \infty$$

61. $\ln|\sin x| = \ln|x| - \dfrac{x^2}{6} - \dfrac{x^4}{180} - \dfrac{x^6}{2835} - \cdots$

$$- \dfrac{2^{2n-1}B_n x^{2n}}{n(2n)!} + \cdots \qquad 0 < |x| < \pi$$

62. $\ln|\cos x| = -\dfrac{x^2}{2} - \dfrac{x^4}{12} - \dfrac{x^6}{45} - \dfrac{17x^8}{2520} - \cdots$

$$- \dfrac{2^{2n-1}(2^{2n}-1)B_n x^{2n}}{n(2n)!} + \cdots \qquad |x| < \dfrac{\pi}{2}$$

63. $\ln|\tan x| = \ln|x| + \dfrac{x^2}{3} + \dfrac{7x^4}{90} + \dfrac{62x^6}{2835} + \cdots$

$$+ \dfrac{2^{2n}(2^{2n-1}-1)B_n x^{2n}}{n(2n)!} + \cdots \qquad 0 < |x| < \dfrac{\pi}{2}$$

64. $\dfrac{\ln|1+x|}{1+x} = x - \left(1 + \tfrac{1}{2}\right)x^2 + \left(1 + \tfrac{1}{2} + \tfrac{1}{3}\right)x^3 - \cdots \qquad |x| < 1$

APPENDICES

A. Mathematical Symbols

$\pm$	Plus or minus	$\mp$	Minus or plus
$=$	Equal to	$\neq$	Not equal to
$\equiv$	Identically equal to	$\not\equiv$	Not identically equal to
$\times$	Multiplication	$\div, /$	Division
$>$	Greater than	$<$	Less than
$\geq$	Greater than or equal to	$\leq$	Less than or equal to
$\simeq$	Congruent to	$\approx$	Approximately equal to
$\sim$	Similar to	$\rightarrow$	Approaches
$\propto$	Varies (proportional to)	ln	Natural logarithm
$\perp$	Perpendicular to	$\parallel$	Parallel to
$\sqrt{}$	Square root	$\sqrt[n]{}$	nth root
i	Imaginary unit $\sqrt{-1}$	∞	Infinity
$_nC_r$ or $\binom{n}{r} = \dfrac{n!}{r!(n-r)!}$		$_nP_r = n!/(n-r)!$	
$\lvert a \rvert$	Absolute value of a	$\cdots$	And so on

B. Greek Alphabet

A	α	Alpha		N	ν	Nu
B	β	Beta		Ξ	ξ	Xi
Γ	γ	Gamma		O	o	Omicron
Δ	δ	Delta		Π	π	Pi
E	ϵ	Epsilon		P	ρ	Rho
Z	ζ	Zeta		Σ	σ	Sigma
H	η	Eta		T	τ	Tau
Θ	θ	Theta		Υ	υ	Upsilon
I	ι	Iota		Φ	ϕ	Phi
K	κ	Kappa		X	χ	Chi
Λ	λ	Lambda		Ψ	ψ	Psi
M	μ	Mu		Ω	ω	Omega

C. Answers

Problem Set 1, Pages 11–15

1. a. $|\overline{TI}| = |\overline{AG}|, |\overline{RI}| = |\overline{NG}|$
   b. $|\overline{RI}| = |\overline{NG}|$
   c. $\angle T \simeq \angle A$
2. a. $|\overline{CB}| = |\overline{FE}|, |\overline{AB}| = |\overline{DE}|$
   b. $|\overline{AB}| = |\overline{DE}|$
   c. $\angle C \simeq \angle F$
3. $\overline{AB} \simeq \overline{ED}; \overline{AC} \simeq \overline{EF}; \overline{CB} \simeq \overline{FD}; \angle A \simeq \angle E; \angle B \simeq \angle D; \angle C \simeq \angle F$
4. $\overline{GH} \simeq \overline{G'H'}; \overline{GI} \simeq \overline{G'I'}; \overline{HI} \simeq \overline{H'I'}; \angle G \simeq \angle G'; \angle H \simeq \angle H'; \angle I \simeq \angle I'$
5. $\overline{RS} \simeq \overline{TU}; \overline{RT} \simeq \overline{RT}; \overline{ST} \simeq \overline{UR}; \angle SRT \simeq \angle UTR; \angle S \simeq \angle U; \angle STR \simeq \angle URT$
6. $\overline{WX} \simeq \overline{YZ}; \overline{WZ} \simeq \overline{YX}; \overline{XZ} \simeq \overline{XZ}; \angle W \simeq \angle Y; \angle WXZ \simeq \angle YZX; \angle WZX \simeq \angle YXZ$
7. congruent, ASA
8. congruent, SAS (or possibly SSS)
9. congruent, SAS
10. congruent, ASA
11. similar
12. not similar
13. not similar
14. similar
15. similar
16. similar
17. 4
18. 6
19. $\dfrac{16}{3}$
20. $\dfrac{40}{7}$
21. $\dfrac{8}{3}$
22. $\dfrac{10}{9}$
23. 24 ft
24. $\sqrt{640} \approx 25$ ft
25. 10 ft
26. $2\sqrt{2}$
27. $3\sqrt{2}$
28. 29 ft
29. $5\sqrt{13}$ ft; 18 ft; 55 ft
30. $\sqrt{3}$
31. $\dfrac{20}{3}$
32. 260 ft
33. 125
34. 24 ft
35. 29 ft
36. 9.19 cm^3
37. 4 ft
38. 3 ft
39. $\dfrac{32}{3}\pi$

Problem Set 2, Pages 42–45

1. 2^{12}
2. 5^{10}
3. 5^6
4. 2^{24}
5. 3^3
6. 3^{-3}
7. 2^3
8. 2^{-13}
9. 2
10. 2^3
11. 2^2
12. 2
13. $a^5 b^8 c^7$
14. $b^{-1} c^3$
15. $a^4 b^8 c^{12}$
16. $a^{10} b^{15} c^{-10}$
17. $a^2 b^{-2} c^2$
18. $a^2 b^2 c^2$
19. $a^4 b^4 c^{-4}$

20. $\dfrac{x^2 + y^2}{x^2 y^2}$

21. $\dfrac{x^4 y^4}{(x^2 + y^2)^2}$

22. $a^{15/2} b^{10} c^3$

23. $a^{-1/2} b^{-1/2}(2a + 3b)$

24. $a^{-1/2}(4a - 3b)$

25. $a^{-1/2} b(a + b)$

26. $a^{-1/2} b^{-1/3}(a + b^{2/3})$

27. $(x - 12)^3(x - 14)$

28. $6u(2u^2 - u - 4)$

29. $6x(2x + 3)(x + 1)$

30. $10x(4x + 5)^2(2x + 1)$

31. $(x + 1)^2(2x + 3)$
$(10x + 13)$

32. $2x(x^2 - 2)^4(2x^2 + 1)^3$
$(18x^2 - 11)$

33. $[7, \infty)$

34. $(-\infty, 36)$

35. $[\frac{1}{2}, \infty)$

36. $(-\infty, 2)$

37. $[-1, 5]$

38. $(-8, -3]$

39. $(-\frac{7}{3}, 1]$

40. $(-\dfrac{15}{2}, 4]$

41. $\{1, -6\}$

42. $\{-2, -3\}$

43. $\{0, \frac{7}{3}\}$

44. $\left\{ \pm\sqrt{\frac{2}{7}} \text{ or } \pm\dfrac{\sqrt{14}}{7} \right\}$

45. $\left\{ \dfrac{-5 \pm \sqrt{73}}{8} \right\}$

46. $\{\frac{3}{2}\}$

47. $\left\{ \dfrac{-1 \pm \sqrt{8w + 1}}{4} \right\}$

48. $\left\{ \dfrac{-w \pm \sqrt{w^2 - 40}}{4} \right\}$

49. $\left\{ \dfrac{1 \pm t}{2} \right\}$

50. $\left\{ \dfrac{-1 \pm \sqrt{8y - 47}}{4} \right\}$

51. $\left\{ 2, \dfrac{3t + 2}{4} \right\}$

52. $x = 3 \pm \sqrt{4 - (y - 2)^2}$

53. $(-\infty, -\frac{5}{2}) \cup (-1, \frac{7}{3})$

54. $(-\frac{2}{3}, \frac{3}{2}) \cup (2, \infty)$

55. $(-\infty, 0) \cup (\frac{1}{2}, 5)$

56. $(-\infty, -\frac{3}{2}) \cup (0, 2)$

57. $(-\infty, \infty)$

58. $[1 - \sqrt{7}, 1 + \sqrt{7}]$

59. -6

60. 1

61. -9

62. 7

63. 2

64. 1

65. -3

66. $-17\mathbf{i} + 8\mathbf{j} + 14\mathbf{k}$

67. -1

68. 2

69. 0

70. 0

71. $a^4 + 4a^3 b + 6a^2 b^2 + 4ab^3 + b^4$

72. $a^3 + 6a^2 b + 12ab^2 + 8b^3$

73. $27x^3 + 54x^2 y + 36xy^2 + 8y^3$

74. $-x^5 + 10x^4 y - 40x^3 y^2 + 80x^2 y^3 - 80xy^4 + 32y^5$

75. $\dfrac{1}{x^4} + \dfrac{4y}{x^3} + \dfrac{6y^2}{x^2} + \dfrac{4y^3}{x} + y^4$

76. $a^{5/2} + 10a^2 b + 40a^{3/2} b^2 + 80ab^3 + 80a^{1/2} b^4 + 32b^5$

77. $\{1, 2, -2\}$

78. $\{3, -3, \frac{1}{2}\}$

79. $\{2, 3, -3\}$

80. $\{-1, 2, -3\}$

81. $\{2, -2, -3\}$

82. $\{2, -3, \frac{1}{2}\}$

83. $\{-3, 5, -\frac{1}{2}\}$

84. $\{3\}$

85. $\{1, -1, 3, -6\}$

86. $\{2, -2, 3, -3\}$

87. $\{-3, -5, -7\}$
88. $\{-1, -2, 3, -4\}$
89. $\{1, -1\}$
90. $\{0, -1, -3, 1 - \sqrt{2}, 1 + \sqrt{2}\}$
91. $-\rho^2 \sin \phi$

Problem Set 3, Pages 61–63

1. $(3, 4)$
2. $(5, -3)$
3. $(4, 3)$
4. $(3, 1)$
5. $(-2, -5)$
6. $(3, 1)$
7. $(3, 1)$
8. $(4, -1)$
9. $(\frac{3}{2}, -3)$
10. $(\frac{1}{3}, -\frac{2}{3})$
11. $(3, 8)$
12. $(1, 1)$
13. $(2, 200)$
14. inconsistent
15. $(d, q) = (63, 84)$
16. $(8, 2)$
17. $(3, 15)$
18. $\left(-\dfrac{8}{5}, -\dfrac{21}{5}\right)$

19. $(\frac{3}{2}, \frac{1}{2}, -\frac{1}{2})$
20. $(2, 0, 1)$
21. $(-1, -2, 2)$
22. $(3, 2, 5)$
23. $(-1, 2, -3)$
24. $(2, -3, -1)$
25. $(1, -3, 5)$
26. $(2, -3, 2)$
27. $(5, 3, 2)$
28. $(1, 2, -\frac{1}{2})$
29. $(\frac{1}{5}, \frac{2}{5}, \frac{2}{5})$
30. $(A_1, A_2, A_3) = (-1, 1, -\frac{1}{2})$
31. a. $(3, 2)$
 b. $(-4, 7)$
 c. $(5, -4)$
 d. $(25, 14)$

32. a. $(3, -2)$
 b. $(-1, 4)$
 c. $(3, -5)$
 d. $(-5, 2)$
33. a. $(3, 1)$
 b. $(4, -2)$
 c. $(-2, 2)$
 d. $(12, -5)$
34. a. $(5, 6, 1)$
 b. $(-2, 4, 3)$
 c. $(-26, 52, 15)$
 d. $(3, -5, 2)$
35. a. $(1, 1, 1)$
 b. $(5, 4, -1)$
 c. $(2, -4, -1)$
 d. $(54, 53, -16)$

36. mix three containers of Spray I with four containers of Spray II
37. four units of Candy I, five units of Candy II, and six units of Candy III
38. three units of Candy I, seven units of Candy II, and five units of Candy III

Problem Set 4, Pages 75–76

1. $\dfrac{\pi}{30}$
2. $\dfrac{3\pi}{2}$
3. $\dfrac{5\pi}{9}$
4. $\dfrac{\pi^2}{90}$
5. $120°$
6. $45n°$
7. $\left(\dfrac{756}{\pi}\right)^{\circ} \approx 240.64°$
8. $\left(\dfrac{21,600}{\pi}\right)^{\circ} \approx 6{,}875.49°$ (This is about 19 revolutions.)

9. **a.** -1
    b. 0
    c. 1
    d. 0
    e. -1

10. **a.** $\dfrac{\sqrt{2}}{2}$

    b. $-\dfrac{\sqrt{2}}{2}$

    c. $-\dfrac{\sqrt{2}}{2}$

    d. $-\dfrac{\sqrt{2}}{2}$

    e. 0

11. 1

12.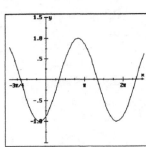

13.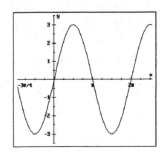

14.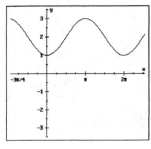

15.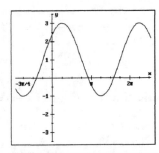

16.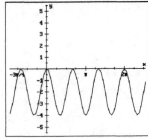

17.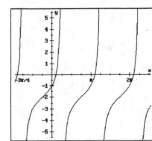

18.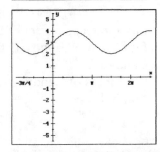

19.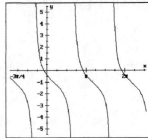

20.

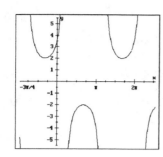

21.

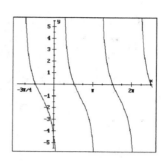

22. $\dfrac{\sqrt{6}-\sqrt{2}}{4}$

23. $\dfrac{\sqrt{6}-\sqrt{2}}{4}$

24. $\dfrac{\sqrt{2}+\sqrt{6}}{4}$

25. $\dfrac{\sqrt{2}-\sqrt{6}}{4}$

26. $\sin 2x = \sin(x+x)$

$$= \sin x \cos x + \cos x \sin x$$

$$= 2\sin x \cos x$$

27. $\sin(x+n\pi) = \sin x \cos n\pi + \cos x \sin n\pi$

$$= (-1)^n \sin x$$

since $\sin n\pi = 0$ and $\cos n\pi = (-1)^n$

28. $\cos(x+n\pi) = \cos x \cos n\pi - \sin x \sin n\pi$

$$= (-1)^n \cos x$$

since $\sin n\pi = 0$ and $\cos n\pi = (-1)^n$

29. $\sin(x+y) = \sin x \cos y + \cos x \sin y$

$\sin(x-y) = \sin x \cos y - \cos x \sin y$

Thus, $\sin(x+y) + \sin(x-y) = 2\sin x \cos y$

30. From the work in Problem 29,
$\sin(x+y) - \sin(x-y) = 2\cos x \sin y$

31. Let $A = x+y$ and $B = x-y$; then $x = \dfrac{A+B}{2}$ and $y = \dfrac{A-B}{2}$
By substitution into Problem 29, we have $\sin A + \sin B = $
$2\sin\left(\dfrac{A+B}{2}\right)\cos\left(\dfrac{A-B}{2}\right)$

32. Let $\alpha = \sin^{-1} \frac{1}{5}$, so $\sin\alpha = \frac{1}{5}$; and $\beta = \cos^{-1} \frac{1}{5}$, so $\cos\beta = \frac{1}{5}$.
Then $\cos\alpha = \sqrt{1 - \left(\frac{1}{5}\right)^2} = \frac{2}{5}\sqrt{6}$ and $\sin\beta = \frac{2}{5}\sqrt{6}$.

$$\cos(\alpha + 2\beta) = \cos\alpha \cos 2\beta - \sin\alpha \sin 2\beta$$
$$= \cos\alpha(\cos^2\beta - \sin^2\beta) - \sin\alpha(2\sin\beta\cos\beta)$$
$$= -\frac{2}{5}\sqrt{6}$$

33. Let $\alpha = \sin^{-1} \frac{1}{5}$, so $\sin\alpha = \frac{1}{5}$; and $\beta = \cos^{-1} \frac{1}{4}$, so $\cos\beta = \frac{1}{4}$.
Then $\cos\alpha = \frac{2}{5}\sqrt{6}$ and

$$\sin\beta = \sqrt{1 - \left(\frac{1}{4}\right)^2} = \frac{1}{4}\sqrt{15}.$$

$$\sin(\alpha + \beta) = \sin\alpha \cos\beta + \cos\alpha \sin\beta$$
$$= \frac{1}{5} \cdot \frac{1}{4} + \frac{2}{5}\sqrt{6} \cdot \frac{1}{4}\sqrt{15} = \frac{1 + 6\sqrt{10}}{20}$$

34. $\dfrac{\pi}{6}, \dfrac{5\pi}{6}$

35. $\dfrac{7\pi}{6}, \dfrac{11\pi}{6}$

36. $0, \dfrac{\pi}{2}, \pi, \dfrac{3\pi}{2}$

37. $0, \pi$

38. $\dfrac{\pi}{3}, \dfrac{3\pi}{4}, \dfrac{5\pi}{4}, \dfrac{5\pi}{3}$

39. $\dfrac{\pi}{6}, \dfrac{5\pi}{6}, \dfrac{7\pi}{6}, \dfrac{11\pi}{6}$

40. $0, \dfrac{\pi}{4}, \pi, \dfrac{5\pi}{4}$

41. $0, \dfrac{\pi}{3}, \pi, \dfrac{4\pi}{3}$

42. 2.24, 4.05

43. 4.71

44. 0.36, 1.21, 3.51, 4.35

45. 0.67, 2.48

46. 0.52, 1.57, 1.83, 2.62, 2.88, 3.67, 4.71, 4.97, 5.76, 6.02

47. 0.00, 1.57, 2.09, 3.14, 4.19, 4.71

48. 0.68, 2.08, 2.78, 4.17, 4.87, 6.27

49. 0.02, 1.59, 3.17, 4.74

50. 0.41, 1.16, 3.55, 4.30

51. 0.00, 1.05, 1.22, 1.92, 2.09, 3.14, 3.32, 4.01, 4.19, 5.24, 5.41, 6.11

52. 0.00, 1.05, 1.22, 1.92, 2.09, 3.14, 3.32, 4.01, 4.19, 5.24, 5.41, 6.11

Problem Set 5, Pages 90–91

1. **a.** $(2\sqrt{2}, 2\sqrt{2})$
   b. $(3, 3\sqrt{3})$
   c. $\left(-\frac{5}{2}, \frac{5}{2}\sqrt{3}\right)$

2. **a.** $\left(\frac{3}{2}\sqrt{3}, -\frac{3}{2}\right)$
   b. $\left(-\frac{3}{4}\sqrt{3}, -\frac{3}{4}\right)$
   c. $(2.61, 3.03)$

3. **a.** $(-1, 0)$
   b. $(0, -2)$
   c. $(0, 0)$

4. **a.** $\left(5\sqrt{2}, \dfrac{\pi}{4}\right)$
   b. $\left(2, \dfrac{2\pi}{3}\right)$
   c. $\left(4, \dfrac{5\pi}{3}\right)$

5. **a.** $\left(2\sqrt{2}, \dfrac{5\pi}{4}\right)$
   b. $\left(3\sqrt{2}, \dfrac{7\pi}{4}\right)$
   c. $\left(\sqrt{58}, \tan^{-1}\frac{7}{3}\right) \approx (7.6, 1.2)$

6. **a.** $\left(6, \dfrac{5\pi}{3}\right)$
   b. $\left(2, \dfrac{11\pi}{6}\right)$
   c. $(-3, 0)$

7. $x^2 + (y - 2)^2 = 4$ **8.** $x^2 + y^2 = 256$

9. $x^2 + y^2 = (x^2 + y^2 + y)^2$ **10.** $(x - 1)^2 + y^2 = 1$

11. $x = 1$ **12.** $x^2(x^2 + y^2) = 16y^2$

13. $x^2 + 2y^2 = 2$ **14.** $2x^2 - y^2 = 2$

15. yes   **16.** no

17. no   **18.** yes

19. yes   **20.** no

21. yes   **22.** yes

23. no   **24.** yes   **25.** no

26. yes   **27.** yes   **28.** yes

29.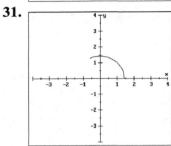

30.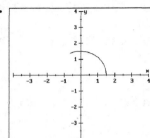

31.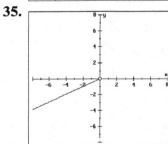

32.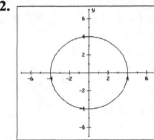

33.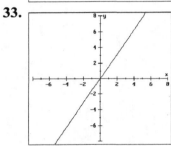

34.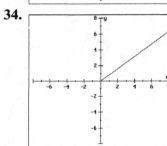

35.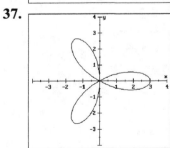

36.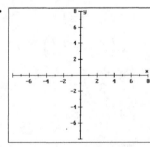

37.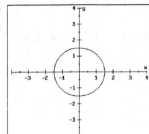

38.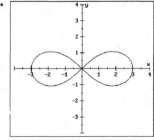

39.

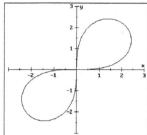

40.

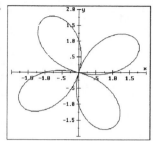

41.

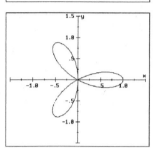

42.

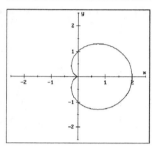

43.

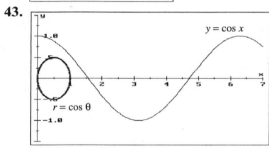

44.

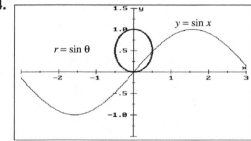

45.

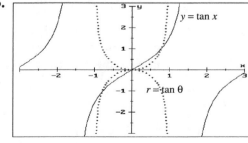

46.

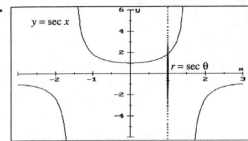

47.

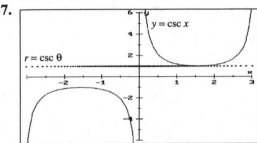

48.

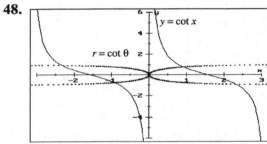

49.

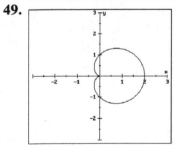

Let $P(r, \theta)$ be a point
on $r = \cos\theta + 1$.
Then $(-r, \theta + \pi)$ is
the same point:

$$-r = \cos(\theta + \pi) + 1$$

$$-r = \cos\theta\cos\pi$$

$$- \sin\pi + 1$$

So $r = \cos\theta - 1$. The
graph shows that both
graphs are the same.

50.

$$r = a\sin\theta + b\cos\theta$$

$$r^2 = ar\sin\theta + br\cos\theta$$

$$x^2 + y^2 = ay + bx$$

$$x^2 - bx + y^2 - ay = 0$$

$$x^2 - bx + \frac{b^2}{4} + y^2 - ay + \frac{a^2}{4} = \frac{a^2}{4} + \frac{b^2}{4}$$

$$\left(x - \frac{b}{2}\right)^2 + \left(y - \frac{a}{2}\right)^2 = \frac{a^2 + b^2}{4}$$

We recognize this as a circle with center

$\left(\dfrac{b}{2}, \dfrac{b}{2}\right)$ and radius $\dfrac{\sqrt{a^2 + b^2}}{2}$.

Problem Set 6, Pages 99–102

1. $V(0, 0); c = 2$ **2.** $V(0, 0); c = 3$

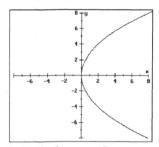   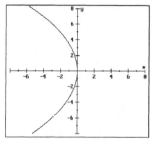

3. $V(0, 0); c = 5$ **4.** $V(0, 0); c = 5/8$

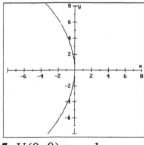   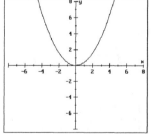

5. $V(0, 0); c = 1$ **6.** $V(0, 0); c = 1/2$

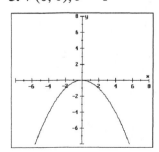   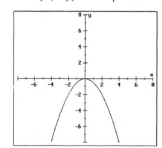

7. $V(0, 0); c = 5/8$ **8.** $V(0, 0); c = 3/4$

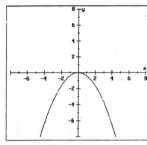 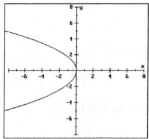

9. $V(0, 0); c = 5/4$ **10.** $V(4, 0); c = 3/16$

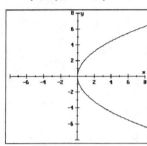 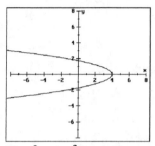

11. $x^2 = -\frac{4}{5}(y - 5)$ **12.** $x^2 = -\frac{3}{4}(y - 4)$
$V(0, 5); c = 1/5$ $V(0, 4); c = 3/16$

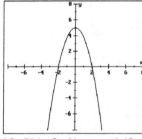 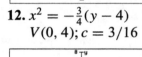

13. $V(-2, 1); c = 1/2$ **14.** $V(1, -3); c = 3/4$

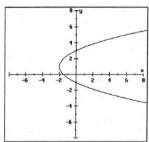 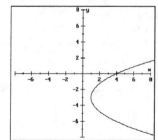

15. $V(-2, 1); c = 1/2$ **16.** $V(1, -3); c = 3/4$

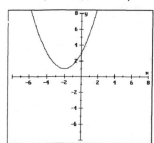

17. $\left(y - \frac{3}{2}\right)^2 = -4\left(x - \frac{5}{16}\right)$ **18.** $(y + 5)^2 = 4(x + 3)$
$V\left(\frac{5}{16}, \frac{3}{2}\right); c = 1$ $V(-3, -5); c = 1$

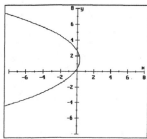
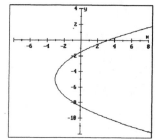

19. $(y + 2)^2 = 10(x - 7)$ **20.** $(x - 3)^2 = -9(y + 1)$
$V(7, -2); c = \frac{5}{2}$ $V(3, -1); c = \frac{9}{4}$

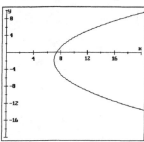
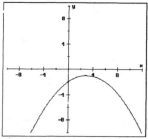

21. $\left(x + \frac{1}{3}\right)^2 = -2\left(y - \frac{4}{3}\right)$ **22.** $(x + 1)^2 = -\frac{2}{3}\left(y - \frac{16}{3}\right)$
$V\left(-\frac{1}{3}, \frac{4}{3}\right); c = \frac{1}{2}$ $V\left(-1, \frac{16}{3}\right); c = \frac{1}{6}$

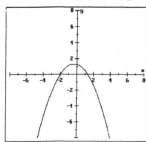
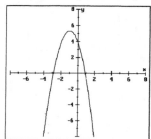

23.

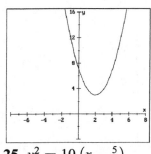

24.

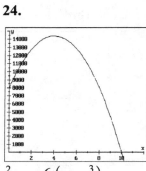

25. $y^2 = 10\left(x - \frac{5}{2}\right)$ **26.** $x^2 = -6\left(y - \frac{3}{2}\right)$

27. $(y-2)^2 = -16(x+1)$

28. $(x-4)^2 = 12(y+1)$

29. $(x+2)^2 = 24(y+3)$

30. $(y-4)^2 = 16(x+3)$

31. $(x+3)^2 = -\frac{1}{3}(y-2)$

32. $(y-2)^2 = -\frac{36}{7}(x-4)$

33. $y^2 = -12(x-3)$ **34.** $x^2 = 8(y+2)$

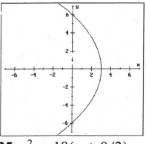
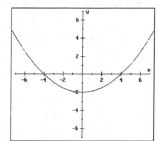
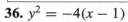

35. $x^2 = 18(y+9/2)$ **36.** $y^2 = -4(x-1)$

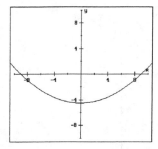
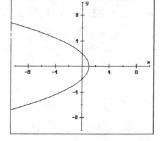

37. $y^2 = 8(x + 2)$ **38.** $y^2 = -6(x - 3/2)$

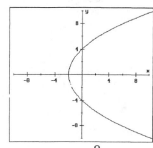   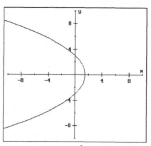

39. $r = \dfrac{8}{1 + \cos\theta}$ **40.** $r = \dfrac{4}{1 - \cos\theta}$

41. $r = \dfrac{4}{1 - \sin\theta}$ **42.** $r = \dfrac{3}{1 + \cos\theta}$

43. $r\sin^2\theta = 4\cos\theta$ **44.** $r\cos^2\theta = -2\sin\theta$

45. $4r^2\cos^2\theta = r\sin\theta - 3$

46. $r\cos\theta + 1 = 2(r\sin\theta - 3)^2$

47. $(0, 0)$ **48.** $(0, 0)$

49.   tangent line: $y + 2 = -(x - 1)$ or

$$x + y + 1 = 0$$

normal line: $y + 2 = x - 1$ or

$$x - y - 3 = 0$$

50. $x = 2$ **51.** $3x + y - 5 = 0$

52. $(y + 2)^2 = 6\left(x - \frac{5}{2}\right)$

53. $x^2 = -6(y + 3)$ **54.** $\frac{2}{3}$ ft or 8 in.

55. $F\left(\frac{9}{4}, 0\right)$ **56.** $x^2 = -4cy$

57. $y^2 = 4cx$ **58.** $y^2 = -4cx$

59. $V(0, 0); F(c, 0)$ or $y^2 = 4cx; P(c, y_0)$, so $y_0^2 = 4c^2$, which implies that $y_0 = \pm 2c$.

$$d = \sqrt{(c - c)^2 + (2c - 0)^2} = 2c$$

The focal chord has length $2d$ or $4c$.

60. Let $P(r, \theta)$ be a point on $r = \dfrac{p}{1 - \cos \theta}$. The alternate primary form is $P(-r, \theta + \pi)$. Thus,

$$-r = \frac{p}{1 - \cos(\theta + \pi)}$$

$$r = \frac{-p}{1 - \cos \theta \cos \pi + \sin \theta \sin \pi}$$

$$= \frac{-p}{1 + \cos \theta}$$

61. $y^2 = 4cx$, $x \geq 0$ and $c > 0$. The distance from the vertex to $P(x, y)$ is

$$(x - c)^2 + y^2 = d^2$$

$$(x - c)^2 + 4cx = d^2$$

62. $y^2 = 4cx$, $x \geq 0$ and $c > 0$. The derivative is $2yy' = 4c$; at $P_1(c, 2c)$, we have

$$m_1 = y' = 2c/y; \text{ at } (c, 2c), m_1 = 1$$

The tangent line is $T_1 : y - 2c = x - c$, or $y = x + c$. At $P_2(c, -2c)$,

$$m_2 = y' = 2c/y; \text{ at } (c, -2c), m_2 = -1$$

The tangent line is $T_2 : y + 2c = -x + c$, or $y = -x - c$. These tangents intersect when

$$x + c = -x - c$$

$$x = -c$$

If $x = -c$, then $y = 0$, and the ends of the focal chord intersect on the directrix.

63. $A = 4c^2$

64. Let $(x - h)^2 + (y - k)^2 = R^2$ be the equation of the circle and $x^2 = 4cy$ the equation of the parabola. The abscissas of the common points satisfy

$$(x - h)^2 + \left(\frac{x^2}{4c} - k\right)^2 = R^2$$

$$x^2 - 2hx + h^2 + \frac{x^4}{16c^2} - \frac{kx^2}{2c} + k^2 = R^2$$

Note that the coefficient of x^3 is 0. Suppose the polynomial in the left member has roots x_1, x_2, x_3, and x_4. Then

$$(x - x_1)(x - x_2)(x - x_3)(x - x_4) = 0$$

If we expand the left member, the coefficient of x^3 is $-(x_1 + x_2 + x_3 + x_4)$, which is 0, as previously found.

65.   **a.** $y - y_0 = \dfrac{x_0}{2c}(x - x_0)$

   b. $Q\left(0,\ y_0 - \dfrac{x_0{}^2}{2c}\right)$

   c.   For $|\overline{FP}|^2$, we have
$$x_0{}^2 + (y_0 - c)^2 = \left(\frac{x_0{}^2}{4c} + c\right)^2$$

For $|\overline{FQ}|^2$, we have

$$\left(y_0 - \frac{x_0{}^2}{2c} - c\right)^2 = \left(\frac{x_0{}^2}{4c} + c\right)^2$$

Thus, $|\overline{FP}| = |\overline{FQ}|$ so $\triangle QFP$ is isosceles.

   d. $\phi = \angle FQP = \theta = \angle FPQ$; since L is parallel to $\overline{FQ}$, $\angle LPT = \theta$ also.

Problem Set 7

1.

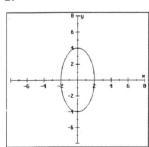

2.

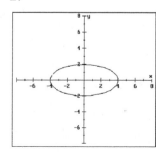

3.

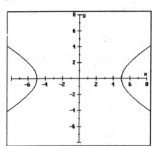

4.

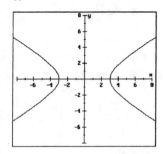

5.

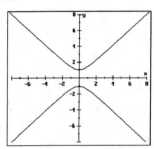

6.

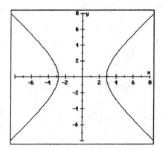

7.

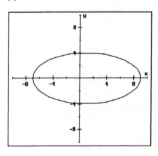

8.

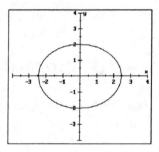

9.

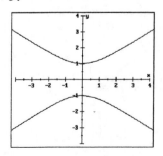

10.

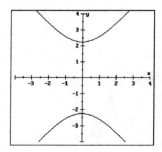

11.

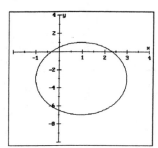

12.

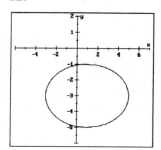

13.

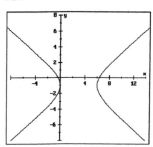

14.

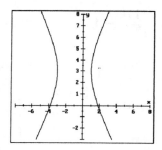

15. $\dfrac{(y-3)^2}{4} - \dfrac{(x-1)^2}{9} = 1$ **16.** $\dfrac{(x+1)^2}{4} - \dfrac{(y-1)^2}{1} = 1$

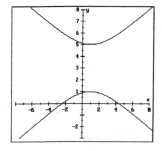

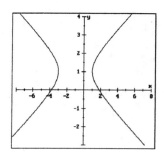

17. $\dfrac{(x+1)^2}{1/4} + \dfrac{(y-1)^2}{1} = 1$ **18.** $\dfrac{(x+1)^2}{1} + \dfrac{(y-1)^2}{1/4} = 1$

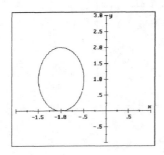   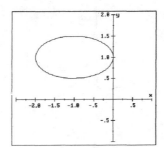

19. $\dfrac{x^2}{4} + \dfrac{(y-1)^2}{9} = 1$ **20.** $\dfrac{(x-1)^2}{9} + \dfrac{y^2}{4} = 1$

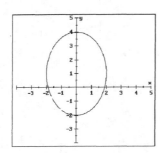   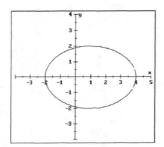

21. $\dfrac{x^2}{4} + \dfrac{(y-5)^2}{9} = 1$ **22.** $\dfrac{y^2}{16} + \dfrac{x^2}{7} = 1$

23. $\dfrac{x^2}{8} + \dfrac{y^2}{4} = 1$ **24.** $\dfrac{y^2}{4} - \dfrac{x^2}{5} = 1$

25. $x^2 - y^2 = 1$ **26.** $\dfrac{x^2}{25} - \dfrac{y^2}{24} = 1$

27. $\dfrac{x^2}{16} + \dfrac{y^2}{9} = 1$ **28.** $\dfrac{x^2}{9} - \dfrac{y^2}{16} = 1$

29. $\dfrac{(x-2)^2}{9} + \dfrac{(y-1)^2}{25} = 1$ **30.** $\dfrac{x^2}{36} + \dfrac{y^2}{35} = 1$

31. $\dfrac{y^2}{4} - \dfrac{x^2}{32} = 1$ **32.** $\dfrac{x^2}{36} + \dfrac{(y+3)^2}{20} = 1$

33. $\dfrac{x^2}{9} - \dfrac{(y+3)^2}{7} = 1$ **34.** $\dfrac{x^2}{9} - \dfrac{y^2}{81} = 1$

35.

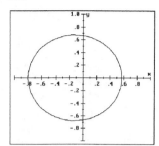

36.

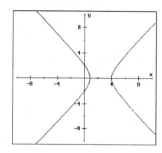

37.

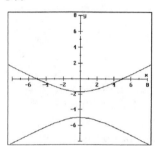

38.

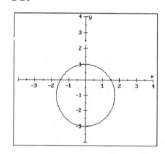

39. $y - 3 = \frac{5}{6}(x + 2)$ or $5x - 6y + 28 = 0$

40. There are two cases.

$$\frac{(x - b)^2}{9} + \frac{(y - 3)^2}{b^2} = 1$$

$$\frac{(x - a)^2}{a^2} + \frac{(y - 3)^2}{9} = 1$$

41. $P(\pm\sqrt{3}, -\frac{1}{2})$

42. $d = 3 - \sqrt{2}$

43. $\dfrac{(x - 1)^2}{4} - \dfrac{4(y + 1)^2}{81} = 1$

44. $\dfrac{x^2}{81} - \dfrac{y^2}{81} = 1$

45. $\dfrac{x^2}{4} - \dfrac{y^2}{1} = 1$

46. $\cosh t = \dfrac{x - x_0}{a}$ and $\sinh t = \dfrac{y - y_0}{b}$

Since $\cosh^2 t - \sinh^2 t = 1$, we have

$$\frac{(x - x_0)^2}{a^2} - \frac{(y - y_0)^2}{b^2} = 1$$

provided that $x \geq x_0 + a$, because $\cosh t \geq 1$.

47. $\sinh t = \dfrac{x - x_0}{a}$ and $\cosh t = \dfrac{y - y_0}{b}$

Since $\cosh^2 t - \sinh^2 t = 1$, we have

$$\frac{(y - y_0)^2}{b^2} - \frac{(x - x_0)^2}{a^2} = 1$$

provided that $y \geq y_0 + b$, because $\cosh t \geq 1$.

48. $y = \pm x$ are the asymptotes, which are perpendicular to each other. (Their slopes are negative reciprocals.) If the asymptotes are perpendicular to each other, their slopes are negative reciprocals and $m_1 = -1/m_2 = m$. Since the asymptotes make an angle of $\pm \pi/4$ with the positive x-axis, $m = 1$. The equations of the asymptotes, then, are $y = x + b$ and $y = -x + b$, with $b = 0$ because of standard position. Then $(y + x)(y - x) = K$ is the equation of the hyperbola $y^2 - x^2 = K$. The point $(a, 0)$ is a vertex, so $K = -a^2$ and $x^2 - y^2 = a^2$.

49. $\dfrac{x^2}{50^2} + \dfrac{y^2}{40.5^2} = 1$; The foci are $2c \approx 58.643$ million miles apart.

50. 9.2×10^7 mi and 9.5×10^7 mi.

51. Let d_1 be the distance that sound travels from the gun at A to the person at P. Let d_2 be the distance that sound travels from the gong at B to the person at P. Let x be the distance that it takes the bullet to reach the gong at B. Then $d_1 - d_2 = x$, and the person should stand on a branch of the hyperbola with foci at A and B.

52. The airplane is located at the point $(3.5387, \dfrac{\pi}{8})$.

53. Let d_1 be the distance from $P(x, y)$ to $F_1(-c, 0)$ and d_2 be the distance from $P(x, y)$ to $F_2(c, 0)$. By definition,

$$d_1 + d_2 = 2a$$

$$d_1 = 2a - d_2$$
$$d_1^2 = 4a^2 - 4ad_2 + d_2^2$$
$$(x+c)^2 + y^2 = 4a^2 - 4ad_2 + 4(x-c)^2 + y^2$$
$$2cx = 4a^2 - 4ad_2 - 2cx$$
$$cx = a^2 - ad_2$$
$$ad_2 = a^2 - cx$$
$$a^2[(x-c)^2 + y^2] = a^4 - 2a^2cx + c^2x^2$$
$$a^2x^2 - 2a^2cx + a^2c^2 + a^2y^2 = a^4 - 2a^2cx + c^2x^2$$
$$(a^2 - c^2)x^2 + a^2y^2 = a^2(a^2 - c^2)$$
$$b^2x^2 + a^2y^2 = a^2b^2$$
$$\frac{x^2}{a^2} + \frac{y^2}{b^2} = 1$$

54. Let d_1 be the distance from $P(x, y)$ to $F_1(-c, 0)$ and d_2 be the distance from $P(x, y)$ to $F_2(c, 0)$. By definition,

$$d_1 - d_2 = 2a$$
$$d_1 = 2a + d_2$$
$$d_1^2 = 4a^2 + 4ad_2 + d_2^2$$
$$(x+c)^2 + y^2 = (x-c)^2 + y^2 + 4a^2 + 4ad_2$$
$$2cx = 4a^2 + 4ad_2 - 2cx$$
$$cx = a^2 + ad_2$$
$$ad_2 = -a^2 + cx$$
$$a^2[(x-c)^2 + y^2] = a^4 - 2a^2cx + c^2x^2$$
$$a^2x^2 - 2a^2cx + a^2c^2 + a^2y^2 = a^4 - 2a^2cx + c^2x^2$$
$$(a^2 - c^2)x^2 + a^2y^2 = a^2(a^2 - c^2)$$
$$-b^2x^2 + a^2y^2 = -a^2b^2$$
$$\frac{x^2}{a^2} - \frac{y^2}{b^2} = 1$$

55. a. $A = C = 0$
     b. A and C have the same signs

c. $A = C$

d. A and C have opposite signs

e. $A > 0$ and

$$\frac{D^2}{4A} + \frac{E^2}{4C} < F$$

or

$A < 0$ and

$$\frac{D^2}{4A} + \frac{E^2}{4C} > F$$

56.   a.

$$\frac{x^2}{a^2} + \frac{y^2}{b^2} = 1$$

$$\frac{2x}{a^2} + \frac{2yy'}{b^2} = 0$$

$$y' = -\frac{b^2 x}{a^2 y}$$

The slope at $P_0(x_0, y_0)$ is

$$m = y' = -\frac{b^2 x_0}{a^2 y_0}$$

The equation of the tangent line is

$$y - y_0 = -\frac{b^2 x_0}{a^2 y_0}(x - x_0)$$

$$\frac{y_0 y}{b^2} - \frac{y_0^2}{b^2} + \frac{x_0 x}{a^2} - \frac{x_0^2}{a^2} = 0$$

$$\frac{x_0 x}{a^2} + \frac{y_0 y}{b^2} = \frac{x_0^2}{a^2} + \frac{y_0^2}{b^2}$$

$$\frac{x_0 x}{a^2} + \frac{y_0 y}{b^2} = 1$$

(since $P_0(x_0, y_0)$ lies on the ellipse).

b. At $P_0(\pm a, 0)$,

$$\frac{\pm ax}{a^2} = 1$$

or $x = \pm a$, a vertical tangent line.

At $P_0(0, \pm b)$

$$\frac{\pm by}{b^2} = 1$$

or $y = b$, a horizontal tangent line.

57.   From the hyperbola,

$$y = \pm \frac{b}{a} \sqrt{x^2 - a^2}$$

and from the asymptote $y = \pm \frac{b}{a}x$. Let d be the vertical distance between points on the hyperbola and points on the asymptote x. Then

$$\lim_{x \to \infty} \frac{b}{a}(\sqrt{x^2 - a^2} - x)$$

$$= \lim_{x \to \infty} \frac{b}{a} \left[\frac{(\sqrt{x^2 - a^2} - x)(\sqrt{x^2 - a^2} + x)}{\sqrt{x^2 - a^2} + x} \cdot x \right]$$

$$= \lim_{x \to \infty} \frac{b}{a} \left[\frac{x^2 - a^2 - x^2}{\sqrt{x^2 - a^2} + x} \right]$$

$$= -ab \lim_{x \to \infty} \frac{1}{\sqrt{x^2 - a^2} + x} = 0$$

Problem Set 8, Pages 129–130

1.

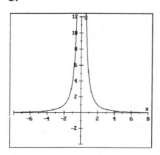

2.

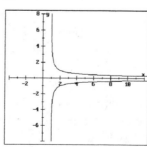

3.

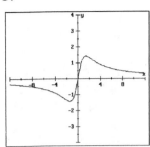

4.

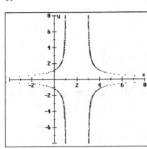

5. Symmetric with respect to the origin.
Extent: domain, all $x \neq 0$; range, all $y \neq 0$.
Asymptotes: $x = 0$, $y = 0$.
No intercepts.

6. Symmetric with respect to the origin.
Extent: domain, all $x \neq 0$; range, all $y \neq 0$.
Asymptotes: $x = 0$, $y = 0$.
No intercepts.

7. No symmetry with respect to the x-axis, y-axis, or origin.
Extent: domain, all $x \neq 0$; range, all $y \neq 1$.
Asymptotes: $x = 0$, $y = 1$.
Intercept: $(-1, 0)$.

8. No symmetry with respect to the x-axis, y-axis, or origin.
Extent: domain, all $x \neq -2$; range, $y \neq -1$.
Asymptotes: $x = -2$, $y = 1$
Intercepts: $\left(0, \frac{1}{2}\right)$, $(-1, 0)$.

9. No symmetry with respect to the x-axis, y-axis, or origin.
Extent: domain, all $x \neq -2$; range, all real numbers.
Asymptotes: $x = -2$, $y = 2x - 3$.
Intercepts: $(0, -5)$, $\left(-\frac{5}{2}, 0\right)$, $(2, 0)$.

10. No symmetry with respect to the x-axis, y-axis, or origin.
Extent: domain, all $x \neq -2$; range, all $y \neq -7$.
Intercepts: $(0, -1)$, $\left(\frac{1}{3}, 0\right)$.

11. No symmetry with respect to the x-axis, y-axis, or origin.
Extent: domain, all $x \neq -\frac{1}{2}$; range, $y \geq -1$, $y \neq \frac{5}{4}$.
Intercepts: $(0, 0)$, $(2, 0)$.

12. No symmetry with respect to the x-axis, y-axis, or origin.
Extent: domain, all $x \neq -2$; range, all $y \neq 3$.
Intercept: $(0, 7)$.

13. Symmetric with respect to the x-axis, y-axis, and origin.
Extent: domain, $-2 \leq x \leq 2$; range $-3 \leq y \leq 3$;
Intercepts: $(-2, 0)$, $(2, 0)$, $(0, 3)$, $(0, -3)$.

14. Symmetric with respect to the x-axis, y-axis, and origin.
Extent: domain, all real numbers; range,

$$y \geq \sqrt{5} \text{ or } y \leq -\sqrt{5}.$$

Asymptotes: $y = \pm\sqrt{3}x$
Intercepts: $(0, \sqrt{5})$, $(0, -\sqrt{5})$.

15. Symmetric with respect to the origin. Extent: domain, $-\dfrac{\sqrt{26}}{2} \leq x \leq \dfrac{\sqrt{26}}{2}$; range, $-\dfrac{\sqrt{26}}{2} \leq y \leq \dfrac{\sqrt{26}}{2}$.
Intercepts: $\left(0, \pm\dfrac{6}{13}\sqrt{26}\right)$, $\left(\pm\dfrac{6}{13}\sqrt{26}, 0\right)$.

16. Symmetric with respect to the x-axis.
Extent: domain, $x < 2$; range, all reals, $y \neq 0$.
Asymptotes: $x = 2$, $y = 0$.
Intercepts: $(0, 1)$, $(0, -1)$.

17. No symmetry with respect to the x-axis, y-axis, or origin.
Extent: domain, all reals $x \neq 3$, $x \neq 1$; range, $y < -4$ or $y > 0$.
Asymptotes: $x = 3$, $x = 1$, $y = 0$.
Intercept: $\left(0, \frac{4}{3}\right)$.

18. No symmetry with respect to the x-axis, y-axis, or origin.
Extent: domain, $x \geq -2^{2/3}$; range, all real numbers.
Asymptotes: no horizontal or vertical asymptotes.
Intercepts: $(0, 0)$, $(0, -4)$.

19. Symmetric with respect to the *x*-axis; *y*-axis, and origin.
Extent: domain, $x \le -2$ or $-1 < x < 1$ or $x \ge 2$; range, all real numbers.
Asymptotes: $x = 1, x = -1$.
Intercepts: $(0, 0), (2, 0), (-2, 0)$.

20. Symmetric with respect to the *x*-axis.
Extent: domain, $x \le 1$ or $x > 2$; range, all reals, $y \ne 1, y \ne -1$.
Asymptotes: $x = 2, y = 1, y = -1$.
Intercepts: $\left(0, \frac{1}{2}\sqrt{2}\right), \left(0, -\frac{1}{2}\sqrt{2}\right), (1, 0)$.

21. rotated hyperbola; $\theta = 45°$

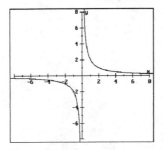

22. rotated hyperbola; $\theta = 45°$

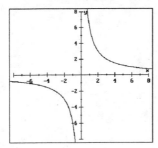

23. rational function $y = 1/x$, which has been translated to the point $(0, 1)$

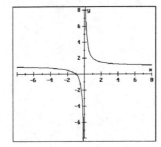

24. rational function $y = 1/x$, which has been translated to the point $(-2, 1)$

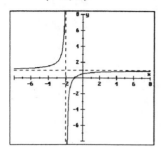

25. rational function

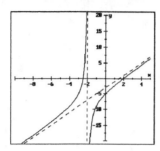

26. the line $y = 3x - 1$, with a deleted point at $x = -2$

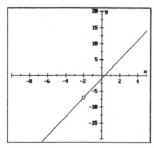

27. a parabola $y = x^2 - 2x$, with a deleted point at $x = -\frac{1}{2}$

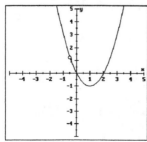

28.   a parabola $y = x^2 + 4x + 7$, with a deleted point at $x = -2$

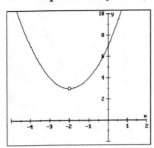

29.   Recognize as an ellipse: $\dfrac{x^2}{4} + \dfrac{y^2}{9} = 1$.

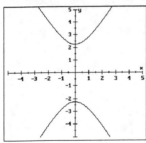

30.   Recognize as a hyperbola: $\dfrac{y^2}{5} - \dfrac{x^2}{\frac{5}{3}} = 1$.

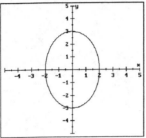

31.   vertical ellipse with 45° rotation; if you carry through the rotation, the equation is $\dfrac{x'^2}{9} + \dfrac{y'^2}{4} = 1$.

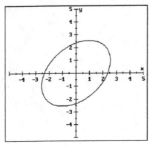

32.   See answer to Problem 16 for a description.

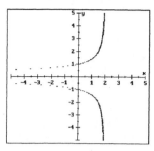

33.   See answer to Problem 17 for a description.

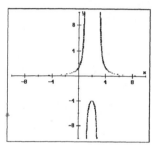

34.   See answer to Problem 18 for a description.

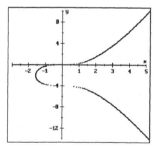

35.   See answer to Problem 19 for a description.

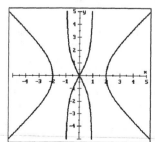

36.   See answer to Problem 20 for a description.

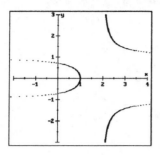

37.

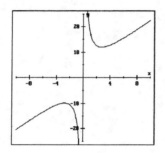

38.

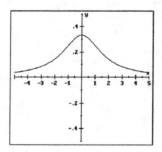

39.

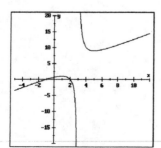

40.

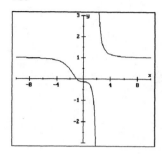

INDEX